Tony Rushmer has been a journalist for almost twenty-five years, covering a wide range of sports for national newspapers and magazines. Having established his own PR business in 2005, he has been directly involved in the racing industry, working for clients such as Newmarket Racecourses, York Racecourse, Sir Henry Cecil and Juddmonte Farms. He lives in Ely, a 25-minute minute drive from Newmarket – the historic home of horseracing.

The Triumph of Henry Cecil

The Authorised Biography

TONY RUSHMER

CONSTABLE

CONSTABLE

First published in Great Britain in 2019 by Constable
This paperback edition published in 2020 by Constable

3 5 7 9 10 8 6 4 2

A CIP catalogue record for this book
is available from the British Library.

ISBN: 978-1-47212-846-1

Typeset in Bembo by Hewer Text UK Ltd, Edinburgh
Printed and bound in Great Britain by Clays Ltd, Elcograf S.p.A.

Papers used by Constable are from well-managed
forests and other responsible sources.

Constable
An imprint of
Little, Brown Book Group
Carmelite House
50 Victoria Embankment
London EC4Y 0DZ

An Hachette UK Company
www.hachette.co.uk

www.littlebrown.co.uk

For Julie, Matthew and Ben

Contents

Foreword

Henry Cecil was a unique person and his is an extraordinary tale.

I first met Henry in the mid-1970s, when he was training in Newmarket from Marriott Stables on the Hamilton Road. At the time I was assistant to Sir Noel Murless, his father-in-law, at Warren Place on the other side of town.

Sir Noel retired in November 1976, and Henry came to Warren Place to train. He and his wife, Julie (née Murless), had already established a very successful team, including an excellent head man in Paddy Rudkin. The stable had recorded its first Classic victory in England in 1975 when Bolkonski – ridden by Frankie Dettori's father, Gianfranco – defeated Grundy in the 2,000 Guineas at Newmarket. A year later Marriott Stables won the race again, this time with Wollow, and Henry finished the 1976 season as champion trainer for the first time in his career.

Therefore, by the time that Henry and Julie arrived at Warren Place, they were already a powerful force in flat racing. But it was when they combined with Noel Murless's owners and staff that the framework for the great legend was created. The foundation stones of knowledge, experience and stability that Henry required to show his great flair as a trainer were securely in place.

In the late 1970s and the following decade, Warren Place proceeded to dominate English racing in a manner seldom seen through the ages. Perhaps the peak years were from 1984 to 1989, when Henry triumphed in nine Classics in England and was crowned champion trainer four times. The mid-to-late eighties brought him unrelenting success as he also won the Irish Derby and Irish Oaks (twice) and was victorious in the Prix de Diane and the Prix du Jockey Club, as well as many other top-class races.

However, life can never run completely smoothly for any of us and there came a time when Henry experienced more than his fair share of problems, some of which he would be the first to admit were self-inflicted. His career went into decline and he hit rock bottom.

Henry called me on a number of occasions when he was literally rattling around the house at Warren Place on his own – I was training at Manton at the time. The conversations, I will have to admit, were quite sad. I would listen to Henry and in response would say, 'Look, you're only one good horse away from getting rolling again. Hold steady; it will be alright.' And eventually it was.

But how did his business survive? Well, there are a number of vital issues here. First, although he did get very low, he never, ever, lost his love of being with the horses. He used to always say to me that they were his best friends. So that great passion endured. As did his competitive spirit. Never forget, Henry always loved to compete.

It's also important to mention that through his difficult period, two of the greatest owner-breeder operations in the history of racing stayed loyal to him – namely Prince Khalid Abdullah and the Niarchos family. They were a huge support, as was the late Lord Ashcombe, albeit in a slightly different way. Lord Ashcombe was a great friend to Henry and very understanding through the tough times.

Prince Khalid and the Niarchos family remained loyal because they understood that in Henry there was a rare genius. His style was completely instinctive; but a key element for him was that he required peace of mind and stability, which he lost in the difficult times.

Without that peace of mind, he was a rudderless ship in a storm and he was quite good at tormenting himself. But, fortunately, a few years into the new millennium his relationship with Jane McKeown blossomed and provided some very important security. They married in 2008 but, long before that, Jane had helped give Henry some much-needed direction. Without Jane's support, he was a man totally without a compass.

I returned to train in Newmarket from Clarehaven Stables for the 2006 season and found that Henry had become a very different man. He'd started to show one great quality that wasn't necessarily always apparent in the seventies and eighties – and that was humility. It was something he'd gained as a result of the difficult times and the public exposure that came with them. There, in the papers, every day, were comments such as 'you've hardly had a winner', 'hardly had a runner', 'your horses have been sick', 'you've lost it', 'you're past it'. And that is a very public humiliation.

Henry suffered that, but it's amazing how much more rounded a human being he became as a result. His humility became probably his most endearing characteristic. He was just a pleasure to be around. He was very different; he would just see things differently and talk with a lot of sensitivity.

He cared more about the people around him. Quite frankly, in his earlier days, he had been careless with a lot of people who loved him. Also, he wouldn't have been easy to be a close friend with during the eighties. But after the downturn – when he came back – he was just lovely. He became a good mate, who was a lot of fun to be around and would worry about other people, care about other people, which hadn't necessarily been his first thoughts in the early days.

He'd become a great giver – a giver of advice, a giver of fun, a giver of rose cuttings! He was always bringing me cuttings from his roses and telling me that our rose garden wasn't up to scratch!

I also fondly recall Henry giving a talk to the pupils at Radley School. Our son, Thady, who was a pupil at Radley, had asked him if he would go to the school and speak to the boys. By that stage Henry wasn't too well – it would probably have been the spring of Frankel's four-year-old career – but he was on marvellous form that evening.

We'd driven down together and I was his warm-up act, standing to say a few words. Then Henry spoke, and bear in mind a lot of the schoolmasters were there and GCSEs and A Levels were around the corner. 'I was just so hopeless at school and couldn't do anything,' he said. 'I didn't bother with the exams, so you know, don't worry about them, just follow your passion. If it doesn't work out with exams, don't worry too much about it.' I'm not sure that it was quite the address the schoolmasters had been hoping for, but that was Henry!

Then we sat there until about 11 o'clock at night as Henry signed numerous cards he'd brought along that were illustrated with photographs of Frankel and his other good horses. He was signing them for all these kids who were queued all the way around the lecture theatre. He truly was a very human human being.

Like all of us he had feet of clay, but his humanity came through. Underneath it all he was a charming, soft man. He had charm in spades. He could really win over anybody when he put his mind to it. It wasn't just the lovely ties and socks he wore. When Henry was talking to you and looking at you, anyone would drop their guard. He could disarm us all. He was very natural like that – it was one of his great gifts.

We'd often watch our horses at exercise on Warren Hill, and you could see with Henry that his training style wasn't technical, it was entirely feel. It was rather like a great concert pianist – something that can't be taught. It's intuitive. The greats of any sport possess that gift and, of course, they hone it but they have to stay on the straight and narrow in order to perform. When Henry was in the zone and concentrating on his horses, he had that incredible beyond-sixth-sense. He'd know what he was going to do. He couldn't explain why he was going to do it, but he simply felt it and saw it. And he had it in abundance. That was unique about Henry. It was a very delicate gift but, when he had that peace of mind, he could train like no one else.

Take his peerless handling of Frankel. He trained that horse to perfection. It was not that he just had the know-how; he also had the courage to train him. Henry made it very clear to the horse that he was the trainer and that the horse was not going to be allowed to train itself. Frankel was so exuberant; so loved galloping and using that magnificent stride of his that he might have over-trained himself and over-raced. However, Henry had that ability and courage to train him in a way where he wasn't playing second fiddle to Frankel, which can sometimes happen with a great horse. A trainer can lose their nerve, but Henry never did with Frankel.

He'd make me smile some mornings during the Frankel years. We'd stand together and watch the horse pass by and Henry would say, 'Wasn't he good? He didn't pull at all, did he? I can do this with him, do that with him now...'

I'd listen and then say, 'Hang on, here's mine coming up.' And over his shoulder he'd say, 'Oh, I haven't got time for them . . .' and he'd be gone!

He was a lot of fun to be with on the Heath, and it was there I'd often witness the huge courage he showed in fighting his illness. Sometimes, we would sit on the grass to watch the horses because it hurt him to stand. I also remember how it became really tough for him even just to get out of the car, but he never once complained. It was probably that passionate love of his horses that kept him going. When he was dying in Cambridge, the last thing he was working on was the next day's work-list for the string.

Professionally, he will be remembered as one of the all-time great trainers. In England, the ones that stand out are Henry, Alec Taylor Jr, Fred Darling and Noel Murless.

On a personal level, you don't forget someone like Henry and the very generous-spirited and thoughtful person that he became. I'll often think about him now when I stand on Warren Hill, recalling the times when he'd wander across to chat. He could shoot the breeze lightly or we could discuss serious subjects privately. There's no doubt he became a lovely man to be around.

Do I miss him? How could you not miss a man like Henry Cecil?

John Gosden
January 2019

John Gosden is one of the most successful trainers in the world, having saddled the winners of many prestigious races such as the Derby (twice), the Prix de l'Arc de Triomphe (three times) and the Breeders' Cup Classic. He was awarded an OBE in 2017 in recognition of his services to horse racing and training. Gosden became champion trainer in Britain for the third time in 2018.

It was just after six o'clock in the morning and Henry Cecil seemed cross with me. Not in a raised voice, beat-the-table kind of way – more exasperated than anything. My first day working at Warren Place had got off to a less-than-perfect start.

I had arrived trying to manage my own nervous anticipation, meandering around the drive that split the lawns from the area where rows and rows of his produce grew. Having got out of my car, it somehow didn't feel appropriate to wander in the main door of that imposing house; instead I chose to walk around the side of the building to the back.

Feeling a surge of butterflies in my stomach I climbed the four steps and knocked on an old-fashioned, heavy-looking wooden door. I waited and waited some more. After thirty seconds or so I knocked again, only this time opting to rap somewhat more firmly. A moment or two later, I heard the handle turn . . .

'What are you knocking at the door for?' muttered the master of the house. The irritation was clearly evident, not just from his clipped speech but also the frown on his face. 'There are people sleeping upstairs. You'll wake them up, you know? We don't knock. There's no need to.' He re-emphasised the point by repeating his terse address, using almost exactly the same words.

Not waiting for any excuse or apology, one of the greatest racehorse trainers of all time turned on his heels and headed off. The door was no longer closed but it was hardly like I'd been invited in.

For a moment or two, I mulled over my options. I could risk the possibility of more abrupt words by just tagging along in his slipstream. Or I could return to my car, beaten by my own apprehension. After a couple of seconds, curiosity forced me over the threshold. With the sound of his footfall becoming fainter, I nipped after him. I had become a Henry Cecil follower . . .

I'm a sports journalist. I started off in the mid-1990s freelancing for a local BBC radio station. I then became a football writer. I still am. I had always had an on and off interest in horseracing from the time I watched on television as Red Rum won the 1977 Grand National – his third and final victory in the famous steeplechase handicap. I was six years old.

It was twenty or so years later that I became addicted to the sport. That was when I was commissioned to write a magazine feature on the 1999 Dubai World Cup, racing's richest contest. It was quite an experience. The highlight was a media trip to Al Quoz, the private stable of Sheikh Mohammed bin Rashid Al Maktoum.

In 1992, the Sheikh, who would become the ruler of Dubai, established a string of thoroughbred horses to run under the name of Godolphin. Its royal blue silks were soon commonplace in the winner's enclosure at Europe's biggest meetings. The string was based in Newmarket for the turf season before many of the horses shipped to Dubai to winter at Al Quoz.

So it was that I was part of a press corps invited to watch their early morning exercise. Horse after horse stretched out immediately in front of where we all stood. I had never had a sensory experience like it; it certainly felt a lot more alluring than reporting on second-tier football at Ipswich Town or Norwich City.

The seemingly effortless dynamism of the animals was a sight to behold. The way those hind legs gathered underneath and, powered by bulging quarters, launched one impressive stride after another was mind-opening for me. The rhythmical sound of the horses' breathing as they advanced up the canter was almost as mesmerising. And, as the rising sun brought fresh warmth to the desert, the skyline of the emerging city of Dubai offered an extraordinary backdrop. How could I not be hooked?

I was lucky. On that trip I met a Newmarket-based racing writer called Sue Montgomery who said to stay in touch. She was happy to take me out on the gallops that spring. I lived a dozen miles away and didn't need a second invitation. Sue had a deep knowledge of the sport – I soon realised that I didn't. Over a series of early mornings that summer and the following one I started to recognise the faces and places in the town. Its rhythms and cyclical nature were a fascination. I had to find a way to work in this business.

Henry Cecil loved June. It was the month that brought the blossoming of the abundance of roses that surrounded his

Warren Place home, located a mile outside Newmarket. The rose garden of his 1920s Tudorbethan house could look spectacular at that time of the year.

Deeper into the spacious property, vegetables and fruit would also be ripening. Late morning, Cecil often wandered down to a greenhouse or his vegetable garden to pick something that would be eaten later on at supper. A small woodland area flanked the grounds on the east side and there were other imposing trees that grew closer to the house.

On a warm day Warren Place had a timeless charm of its own. Cecil was very attached to it. He was part of it. Having moved there in late 1976, he had helped to shape it into an early summer idyll.

But the reason why he looked forward so much to June had nothing to do with the gardens at Warren Place. Cecil was a dominant force in flat racing and, from 1970 to the end of the century, his year had the potential to be defined by the four days of Royal Ascot that took place in the second half of June.

Royal Ascot has always been the most prestigious turf meeting in the world. It appealed to Cecil on many levels. Ascot, a byword for style, gave him the opportunity to dress up. His shirts and ties for each day were invariably laid out a week or so before.

He was a handsome and charming man, and knew it. At six-feet two-inches or so tall and also broad-shouldered, Cecil stood out from the crowd. The effect was pronounced when he put on his black silk top-hat. You couldn't miss him in and around the paddock at Royal Ascot.

There were always picnic parties before and after racing in

the car parks. The sense of fun and *joie de vivre* appealed to Cecil. Possessing a naughty schoolboy streak, he could be the life and soul of any gathering if he chose. Ascot's social scene and fashion, however, weren't what really mattered to him. As a leading trainer he craved the competition offered by the Royal fixture. He was motivated by pitting his best horses up against those of his Newmarket rivals, as well as others from further afield, including Irish and French champions. Winning was all-important to Cecil. It was not good enough simply to be there. He never wanted to be an Ascot also-ran.

In 1970, aged twenty-seven, Cecil sent out Parthenon to triumph in the Queen Alexandra Stakes. It was his first victory at the meeting. Over the next thirty years he would regularly find himself in the Royal Ascot winner's enclosure, enjoying unparalleled success. In 1987 alone he saddled seven winners in four days.

Sprinters, milers, middle- and long-distance horses – Cecil trained them all. He proved it just about every June in front of royalty, lords and ladies and everyday racing fans who followed him with blind faith. Yes, June was *the* month.

In June 2006, Cecil was diagnosed with cancer. The trainer was sixty-three at the time. He had a sizeable mass in his abdomen. He had put up with a nagging discomfort deep in his stomach for a while. Now he knew why.

The timing of Cecil's cancer diagnosis couldn't have been worse. Things had just started to turn around following a low period, both personally and for his stable. He and his girlfriend Jane McKeown had got back together a year or so earlier. The size of the string of horses at Warren Place was slowly beginning to increase. Other measures were in place to help the business get back on a more solid footing. For the first time in a long time, Cecil was in a good place. And now this had come along. How's your luck?

That afternoon, he and Jane drove back from Cambridge after being told the upsetting news. The trainer seemed to have taken it well. He was calm and wanted to busy himself with evening stables at Warren Place. It seemed the right thing to do. Jane left him to it and returned for a couple of hours to her job in Newmarket at Godolphin.

When she came back to Warren Place, Cecil had obviously had a drink. Alcohol had been a contributory factor behind her decision to leave him a few years earlier. This time, circumstances were different. He would hardly be the first person to pour himself a glass or two after being told he had cancer.

But the fact that Cecil had become worse for wear so soon after his diagnosis brought into sharp focus something that had to be confronted. Without Jane needing to say the words, Cecil realised that similar incidents were not going to be tolerated. Repetitions simply weren't going to help. They would compromise all the hard work that Cecil and his small but not to be underestimated partner had done for the business over the past year. More importantly, on a personal level, it would jeopardise the future of their relationship.

From that episode some good emerged after a low twenty-four hours. Henry Cecil would never drink again. Not once. That decision epitomised the resolve with which he would face an uncertain future. 'There's no point in me lying down,' he would say in the days, weeks, months and years that followed his cancer diagnosis. 'If I lie down and rest, all I'll think about is how ill I am.'

Instead he consigned his illness to a very small compartment at the back of his mind. It was kept there under lock and key – the door only ever opened when it had to be.

I always found that if you did things for free you got a break. It happened with BBC radio work first. I did something similar to get a foothold in golf journalism. Doing things for nothing had always proved to be a way in. That was my thinking when I started writing a regular racing feature for the *Newmarket Weekly News* in 2002. It worked. By the end of the year I had my first racing client, trainer Jeremy Noseda.

I had been engaged to develop content for his website and used to visit him every week to write news stories. It was a game-changer. All of a sudden I was on the inside. It was access all areas.

A typical morning would see me riding shotgun in Noseda's Range Rover as we went onto Warren Hill to watch his horses canter not long after breakfast time. He never seemed to mind as I asked a ton of questions. Sometimes I consciously chose not to ask anything, preferring to watch and listen. 'He could just be a right horse,' Noseda would say, gazing after a fine-looking three-year-old heading away down the nearby walking ground. 'If I just had a little concern, it would be that he's slack in his pasterns there. It's probably not a case of "if" he goes wrong, but "when".' Drip, drip, drip, I was enjoying fascinating insight into the sport. Pedigrees, training programmes, feed, the nature and severity of injuries; the list was endless.

The dotcom era resulted in several trainers asking for my help. By the beginning of 2005 I had quit the golf magazine that had employed me for the previous four years. Racing had become my life. I began providing racecourse reporting copy for the Press Association from courses such as Newmarket and Yarmouth. I even got a picture byline in the *Racing Post*, the industry's daily title.

There were several perks to being a racing journalist. I would get invited on press trips to visit stables or watch horses gallop ahead of a big race. There was the odd supper or social engagement where I would enjoy the company of horsemen. At one of these held by Newmarket Racecourses, early in 2006, I was seated next to Jane McKeown. Her partner, Henry Cecil, sat on the other side of the table. The men were in lounge suits, or at least jacket and tie. All, that is, except Cecil. He wore an open-neck paisley shirt that had a light blue as its dominant colour.

I didn't know Cecil at all. We'd only spoken once before and that was after he'd had a winner at Yarmouth races the previous spring. I had tried to get a quote about his horse but Cecil, who was accompanied by Jane's younger daughter Carina, was keener on talking about what he had eaten for lunch. He had been to Yarmouth's noted fish restaurant. 'You must go there . . . try their crayfish tails with just a little black pepper,' he told me. 'They're delicious.'

I didn't speak a word to Cecil that night at the Newmarket supper, but Jane and I had a long conversation. She was friendly and funny. We spoke again on the phone a few days later and I ended up writing a magazine feature on Cecil. We all worked on it together, ensuring the content promoted the renewed drive and focus that had been lacking in the yard through several years.

In a classic case of one thing leading to another, it was agreed that I could take on the editorial element of his largely dormant website. We settled on a relatively small fee but money wasn't the main motivation. The deal, from my perspective, would allow me to learn more – hopefully much more – about life inside Warren Place. At the outset, I could hardly have imagined what would unfold.

The sport's greatest racehorse and arguably the greatest trainer combined to create racing's greatest comeback. It was a life and death story, and I saw it in close up.

Chapter One

'Why should I retire just because people think I should?'

Henry Richard Amherst Cecil was in his mid-twenties when he started training racehorses in Newmarket in 1969. Over the following thirty years he won just about every big prize that the sport offered. His success wasn't built on numbers or science; it was all about instinct and feel. He absorbed the rhythms of the stable as he wandered around in apparently aimless fashion. It turned out that the man who had a passion for beautiful gardens possessed green fingers when it came to nurturing racehorses. Champion jockey Richard Hughes rode plenty of Cecil-trained winners, and recognised the bond that existed between the trainer and his horses. 'He didn't just like them, he loved them,' says Hughes.

For most of his career Cecil lived and trained on the edge of Newmarket at Warren Place, a stable established in the 1920s. His great rival in the 1980s and 1990s was Sir Michael Stoute, who was also based in Newmarket. In fact, their respective stables were less than a mile apart. Both men possessed mighty firepower, backed by many of the leading owners of the era. They were racing's equivalent of Liverpool and Manchester

United, except that the two football clubs would usually only go head-to-head twice a season. Stoute and Cecil were forever taking one another on with their best horses at racing's major meetings. The pair, along with the rest of Newmarket's trainers, also used the same training grounds just about every working day. Imagine the managers at Anfield and Old Trafford having to prepare their respective teams alongside one another.

Cecil and Stoute were not friends but mutual respect ran deep. In 2017 when I interviewed Stoute for the Royal Ascot brochure, he offered a typically succinct but insightful appraisal of his long-time adversary. 'A formidable trainer; one of the greatest of all time. He had such a feel for horses; gifted, very gifted. Never mind the outward appearance: he was a fierce competitor, H. R. A. Cecil.'

Cecil became popular with the racing public and beyond – and not simply because he was an exceptional horseman. A slightly otherworldly aristocratic aura surrounded him, but he also had a lightness of touch when it came to meeting people. Owners, staff and the racing public fell under his spell. Being around Cecil was not an everyday experience.

Fellow trainer Ed Vaughan rented some boxes at Warren Place from late 2004 and the pair swiftly built a great friendship. Vaughan, a man of Cork, was in his first full year with a training licence back then. He took just seven horses to Warren Place ('and not very good ones at that,' adds the Irishman). Despite Cecil's own problems at the time, he couldn't do enough to make his new tenant feel welcome.

'I think he felt sorry for me,' Vaughan says, laughing. 'He had an instinct and could tell if you were maybe a bit down or having a bad day. He could always see it. He was one of those people that no matter how much time you spent with him or whatever kind of day it was, you always left feeling better.'

Gerhard Schoeningh, a London-based hedge-fund manager, found himself amused by Cecil's witty, often quirky, exchanges with the media. Not long into the current millennium, a seed was sown in his mind that he would like to have a horse in training at Warren Place. One day a mutual acquaintance introduced the two men, setting in motion a chain of events that led to Schoeningh becoming an owner with Cecil.

Schoeningh would venture up to Warren Place half a dozen or so times a year. Cecil told him at the outset that he wasn't the type of trainer who wanted to spend hours socialising at the racecourse, but that his new owner was always welcome to stay overnight and watch the horses exercise the following morning.

'When you drove to Warren Place you were slightly, I wouldn't say beaming with expectation, but you just knew that you'd have a very good time,' Schoeningh says. 'Then, leaving there, you'd still have a smile on your face. That is something Henry had. He instilled that feeling into probably hundreds of people.'

Cecil made sure his houseguest felt at home. He would pick flowers from the garden and put them in Schoeningh's bedroom, show him the drinks cabinet and offer the drawing room should he wish to watch television. 'I want you to be comfortable,' Cecil would say. 'You can do entirely as you please . . . I'm the only one here who can't!'

That wasn't quite true. In the yard there was never any doubt who was the boss. Cecil commanded the full respect of his staff. His leadership was instinctive, natural – similar to his approach to training racehorses. 'When you worked for Henry Cecil, you were incorporated into a very rare group,' says Dee Deacon, who rose to the role of head groom during fifteen years at Warren Place. 'We were so passionate about working for this man. He knew how to get the best out of his staff and could do that so easily just by smiling at them or giving them a "well done".'

Cecil forged a connection with the wider racing community beyond Warren Place. He offered acts of kindness, often to complete strangers, and his warmth extended to those in the media who covered the sport. When well-known racing broadcaster Derek Thompson was not long out of surgery for bowel cancer he bumped into Cecil on the gallops in Newmarket. Thompson was undergoing chemotherapy, a treatment that Cecil knew a lot about from his own cancer fight. They watched the Warren Place horses exercise before Cecil suggested they sit down. The two men chatted for an hour with the trainer offering endless encouragement and advice. 'You've got to be positive, you've got to keep fighting,' was the message that Cecil stressed.

'I'd lost about three stone and felt knackered,' says Thompson. 'But it was a beautiful morning and I'll never forget the guidance he gave me. I thought, "This guy is outstanding." It was one of the best hours of my life. I'll never forget it.'

Cecil was thoughtful when it came to written correspondence too. A Norwich-based nonagenarian used to send him homemade cards with a Warren Place theme. Cecil would always reply. In one response, the trainer expressed his thanks and then added, 'I have to meet you sometime . . . perhaps you will be able to come over and visit us at Warren Place in the not too distant future.' The nonagenarian was thrilled to receive hand-written responses from the trainer. I know because the recipient was my wife's grandfather Tom, not that Cecil was ever aware of that.

'Why should I retire just because people think I should?' Henry Cecil wasn't looking for a response to his question. It was asked purely in a rhetorical context and with more than a hint of defiance.

It was the spring of 2006 and I was interviewing Cecil for a racing industry publication for which I occasionally freelanced. It was my first visit to Warren Place and we were speaking in his study. The room was perhaps a little out of kilter with the times, but it was thick with atmosphere. The rag-roll style of decorating, in a rich burgundy, embellished with many greyish fleur de lys, gave it a decadent feel.

A decent-sized and sturdy wooden desk sat in front of rather grand windows. Cecil chose not to sit behind it for our meeting. Instead he opted for a single high-backed armchair, upholstered in a tartan comprised of mainly blues and green – a nod to his Scottish ancestry. He was born in Aberdeen in January 1943, just minutes before his twin brother David. Their father Henry Kerr Auchmuty Cecil was serving in the Parachute Regiment in Africa when he died shortly before their births. The military man's young widow Rohays relocated to a village near Newmarket and became acquainted with the champion trainer Captain Cecil Boyd-Rochfort. They married in July 1944; thus Henry Cecil grew up at Boyd-Rochfort's Freemason Lodge stables on Bury Road, surrounded by the racing world. In his early teens he rode out for the man he called 'Uncle Cecil', and several years later became Boyd-Rochfort's assistant.

Indeed, he would start his own career from Freemason Lodge after his stepfather's retirement.

I don't recall if there were any family photographs on show in Cecil's study but he had four brothers. Bow and Jamie were older than him, while Arthur Boyd-Rochfort was two and a half years younger than he and his twin David. By the time I met him Cecil had three children; Katie and Noel from his marriage to Julie (daughter of champion trainer Noel Murless) and Jake from his marriage to Natalie Payne.

To Cecil's right was a huge cabinet containing countless rows of lead soldiers and models of dozens of knights on horseback. There was a smaller cabinet on the other side of the room. In it, among other things, were a fossilised dinosaur's egg and a shark's tooth. A little to the left of the cabinet were the fireplace and hearth. In front of the fireplace were two sheepskin rugs, which had been stitched together.

With all its curios and rather old-fashioned qualities, the room wasn't dissimilar to how I imagined 221B Baker Street, the vibrant, albeit fictional, home of genius detective Sherlock Holmes. What was almost as intriguing was what the room didn't contain. If you dropped strangers into it, they would have puzzled over what the room's owner did for a living. The only clue was a small picture of a racehorse in full cry in front of a packed grandstand. The horse was Oh So Sharp, winner of three of British racing's five Classics and one of the greatest fillies of all time. Her photograph was tucked away, relatively low on the wall to the immediate right as you walked into the room.

Oh So Sharp's formidable season of achievements was 1985, the year in which Cecil would become champion trainer for the sixth time. He would claim the title on a further four occasions but by 2006 his career was in decline. The previous season Warren Place stables recorded just twelve victories at a 12 per cent strike-rate and accumulated £144,978 in prize money. Six years earlier, Cecil's racehorse string won £2,443,757 at a 24 per cent strike-rate. The numbers were no longer adding up in a sport renowned for its expense.

Cecil's old foe Stoute remained at the top of his profession in the early years of the new century. Indeed, he was champion once again in 2005. By that stage, the Barbadian's principal rival was Saeed bin Suroor, employed by Sheikh Mohammed at Godolphin. Meanwhile, in Tipperary, a young trainer called Aidan O'Brien was enjoying significant success at home and abroad with the horses bred by Irish bloodstock superpower Coolmore.

The racing landscape had changed immeasurably since Cecil's dominance. His time appeared to have long since been and gone. The trainer was also struggling with personal problems that gave further ammunition to those in and outside the sport who believed he was finished. It's only a matter of time, they said.

Cecil had agreed to see me for the magazine feature because, in his words, he was 'working on actually picking the whole thing up' – not packing it up. He was sixty-three, an age when many men are contemplating easier times ahead. The 'R' word was the last thing Cecil was planning. Clad in a pair of denim jeans and a navy Armani shirt, he looked half a dozen years younger than he was.

At my request he talked a little bit about a few of the stars he had developed, including Oh So Sharp. But Cecil wasn't one for nostalgia for the sake of it. If he had trained a horse's mother or an elder sibling and their characteristics might help with an existing member of the string, then that was different. That was handy information and could be put to use in the future. And the future, it quickly became apparent to me, was always what mattered most to Cecil. He didn't often reference the past and said he wasn't interested in writing an autobiography. 'There's plenty of time for that when I'm sitting on a beach in twenty years' time or whatever,' he said. His reluctance to reflect was largely due to the fact that there were horses in the yard that required all of his time and attention. Perhaps it was also because there were parts of his past that were painful and he preferred not to revisit them.

Either side of the turn of the twenty-first century Cecil went through profound personal and professional adversity. His second marriage fell apart in 1999. The following year his brother David died aged fifty-seven after battling pancreatic cancer. Those that were close to Cecil recall how he struggled to cope throughout his twin's illness. He was inconsolable on the November day that David passed away in 2000. Warren Place book-keeper Joan Plant extended a concerned hug when a grief-stricken Cecil came into the office. 'I'd never seen Henry emotional before,' says Plant. 'He was so, so distraught.'

The same month also saw Cecil convicted of a drink-driving offence. The trainer received a five-year ban and a £3000 fine after the car he was driving hit an elderly couple in a village near Newmarket. At the time, and for several years afterwards, there were some who felt he was lurching off the rails, never mind finding himself off the road long term.

On the face of it, Cecil's training business held up satisfactorily through 2000. In June he registered the twenty-third domestic Classic victory of his career thanks to Love Divine in the Oaks. The same month saw Subtle Power give him a sixty-eighth Royal Ascot winner, while Beat Hollow provided Warren Place with an overseas Group 1 success in Paris.

Appearances were deceptive; the horses were not as healthy as in previous years. Every yard expects a certain amount of coughs and sneezes through the season, especially among the youngest stock who have yet to build up immunity, but there was a feeling at Warren Place that a virus had set in.

Viruses are dreaded in racing stables as they invariably impact on the respiratory system. When a trainer mentions that a horse has had a 'dirty scope', it's a reference to how internal tests have revealed symptoms of infection that are likely to include traces of blood and mucus in the lungs.

Certainly, around that time, there were horses that were unwell at Warren Place. Cecil referenced a virus in 2001, explaining how the previous season it had weakened the lungs of some of the string, triggering bleeding. One of the main problems with respiratory viruses is that they have a nasty habit of lingering. Horses that seem unaffected in their training suddenly start to get found out in the closing stages of their races. Likewise those animals that have apparently recovered from illness can be exposed as still suffering from viral symptoms if they are returned to racing too soon.

Sickness hung over Warren Place for the next couple of seasons and results markedly slumped. David Lanigan, whose first full year as Cecil's assistant was 2003, remembers how the horses still weren't right in themselves. Some might run a promising race but would then regress. Sickness had left a mark that some individuals never fully shook off.

Lanigan highlights the case of a well-bred three-year-old called Tuning Fork, who was unraced the previous season during which he had been sick. The colt's eventual debut at Haydock in early May had been a resounding success as he won 'standing on his head', according to Lanigan. Less than a fortnight later Tuning Fork was considerably stepped up in class to contest the Group 2 Dante Stakes at York. He ran very creditably to finish second in a race considered to be the leading Derby trial but the horse never went on to Epsom. 'He lay flat out in his box for two days after the Dante,' says Lanigan.

Tuning Fork would run four more times in 2003, finishing stone-cold last twice and second last on the other two occasions. At the end of the season he left Warren Place but failed to add to his promising debut success in more than forty starts spanning until early February 2010.

The Irish Equine Centre was called into Warren Place to help with the string's health issues. Its testing identified the presence of *Aspergillus* fungus – a mould species. What percentage *Aspergillus* played in the string's decline is open to interpretation. Cecil's long-term trusted vet Charlie Smith believes there was more to it than just the presence of one particular form of contamination.

'From a veterinary point of view, if you go to any of the Newmarket yards, it's like boarding school for young horses,' says Smith, who is a partner at Newmarket Equine Hospital. 'There are always colds, always some level of bacterial and viral contamination.

'We certainly did have some that had repeated dirty scopes and it is always much easier, in my opinion, to blame it on a virus or a bacteria than the horses that you've got – that they're not good enough. Yes, the horses didn't have their best year health-wise for probably two or three years. But I also think, and I'm not sure why, it becomes a self-perpetuating problem that perhaps the horses aren't as good. You have a poor year; you don't get the same quality of horses the next year. It's quite easy in training to get on a downward spiral even if the horses' health improves. If you haven't got the quality of horses, they ain't going to win the races.'

Alan Cooper, the racing manager for the Niarchos family, offers an interesting take. In his role Cooper has had unique access to many of the top training establishments in France and England, including Warren Place. A thoughtful and observant man, Cooper feels a trainer's own condition has a bearing on the performance of his string.

'Over the years I've been privileged to work with many trainers,' he says. 'This is a generalisation and not referring to Henry in particular; I've found that if a trainer is really unhappy or not in form himself, somehow the horses are not in form. It's transmitted. If a trainer is in top form, the horses are in top form. You make that decision to run here, there and it flows.'

Cecil's string was down on numbers and quality as the noughties began to unfold. The strength in depth had started to wane in the mid-1990s after Sheikh Mohammed set up Godolphin. The Sheikh had enjoyed great success with horses trained at Warren Place in the 1980s. It was he who had owned Oh So Sharp and Cecil trained many other top-level winners for him. But the powerful alliance ended with the Sheikh's decision to have many of his horses trained under his own Godolphin banner. Other key owners at Warren Place died either side of the new century, while disappointing results and the general poor health of the string meant several more looked elsewhere. In Newmarket, there has always been plenty of choice.

Newmarket isn't somewhere a trainer can hide away when business is failing. The Suffolk town, some sixty-odd miles north-east of London, may only have a population of around twenty thousand but it is Britain's biggest racehorse training centre and the historic home of the sport, with the first recorded race staged in 1622. Almost three thousand horses exercise on the Newmarket Heath training grounds on a daily basis through the peak months (from March onwards) of the flat racing season and there are more than seventy trainers using the facilities. Two or three trainers will boast strings of 220-plus horses, while at the other end of the spectrum a handful have barely double figures in their yard.

More than fifty miles of turf gallops are laid out either side of Newmarket and are immaculately maintained by Jockey Club Estates. There is a large degree of artistry that goes into their preparation. Five of the gallops have had peat spread across them each autumn since 1900. Three are on Bury Side, two on Racecourse Side. Each of these gallops is renowned for its cushioning qualities that allow almost half a ton of horse to 'let down' safely and with confidence.

Anyone walking up Moulton Road on the east side of the town on a warm spring morning will witness the unique spectacle of hundreds of racehorses exercising across Long Hill to the left and up Warren Hill to the right. Horses seem to be everywhere. To the outsider, Newmarket can seem idyllic.

Scratch beneath the surface and there is another side to it. For a trainer whose business is struggling while rivals are thriving, 'the gallops', as they are known, can be a tough environment.

It is a town of the haves and the have-nots. There is a large degree of flux in that too. In racing you can be flying and your business booming but it doesn't always last. Just like football management, the sport is a results-driven business and some owners are impatient for success. A trainer might hope that a good season will buy them some loyalty if a couple of difficult ones follow, but that's not always the case. When a young gun down the road enjoys a breakthrough season, owners can be tempted to jump ship at the autumn yearling sales. Each year will see certain emerging trainers become all the rage, while others will drop out of fashion.

When things aren't going well, despite the vastness of the Heath, racehorse trainers can't easily cut themselves off in Newmarket. Just about all of them are visible from around 6.30 a.m. every day as the racing world stirs. Their horses step out onto Warren Hill – their sheer numbers making it the equine equivalent of London Bridge station at rush hour – and are scrutinised by other trainers, riders from rival strings and various folk associated with the industry: racing managers, bloodstock agents and the media. If a string has noticeably shrunk in size it will be noticed and discussed. Likewise, there will be comments if the horses under another's care look dull in their coats.

Trainers that are already considered on the wane may not be assessed in such a searching manner, but are likely to notice a difference on Newmarket Heath and at the races. Folk that gravitated towards them during heydays and high days may suddenly be latching onto others. The well-wishers that once used to want to shake hands now glance in another direction.

Visible evidence of others' achievements won't help lift the mood. That young gun from the nearby stable now has a string that almost stretches out of sight during morning exercise. At the bloodstock sales these younger men seem to be in demand. Owners view them as the future; new ideas, fresh faces and untold energy.

It's a different story for the fading trainer. The invites for lavish lunches in the right boxes at the principal meetings no longer drop through the letterbox. Media requests have dried up. No surprise there . . . there aren't any good ones in the yard to write about any more. And the office phone that once never stopped ringing has long since fallen silent.

In the first few years of the twenty-first century Cecil found himself increasingly on his own. During 2003 he separated from his girlfriend Jane McKeown, while the size of the string had begun to dwindle noticeably by the end of that year. There were around a hundred and fifty boxes across several different yards at Warren Place and in the good times all would have been full, with a list of horses waiting to come in. As Cecil's dip became a slump the majority of the stables became empty. It was a time of great financial uncertainty for Cecil's business. Privately, he feared that he might even have to sell Warren Place. The gossip about him around Newmarket was endless. Pretty much all of it focused around how he would be giving up in the not-too-distant future.

Unsurprisingly, the staff felt insecure. Dee Deacon, like many of her colleagues, had been there when Cecil had been mopping up Group 1 races for fun. An energetic and intelligent girl from Northampton, she had joined as a groom in the late 1990s. For her and those with whom she worked, the manner in which Warren Place fell away was completely unexpected and confusing.

'There were so many rumours going about that we were going to fold, we were going to pack up, Henry's retiring,' says Deacon. 'The lads were worried. This was their bread and butter so they were questioning it. The lads were getting all this stick as well. They'd go to the pubs on the night times – "where are you going to go next?"

'Henry wasn't stupid. He would pick up on this, so on a few occasions he'd call us in – there weren't many of us then – before first lot. "I've heard the rumours and I'll put you straight. Nothing is changing. I'm not going anywhere. I can't do anything else. This is my life, this is what I love. If we all stick together we will get through this. We'll progress and we'll go on. Let's prove them all wrong." Henry never wanted the lads ill at ease. He never wanted them to think they'd got to start looking elsewhere. So he would cover up so much of his own troubles and pain.'

Deacon is a chatty and engaging soul. She says she can be a worrier. The truth is, Deacon's a warrior too, certainly when it comes to the horses under her care. But just before one Christmas, during the downtimes, the groom was due to go away on holiday and was concerned about whether she would still have a job on her return. She plucked up the courage to broach the subject with her employer.

'Don't let me ever hear that you're worried about something like that,' said Cecil in response. 'You will always have a job with me. We'll go down to twenty horses, we'll go down to ten horses, but we will keep going. As long as I've got breath in my body, I will be training.' One day in the future they would prove to be poignant words.

If Deacon recognised that her boss was standing firm on the surface she could also sense his internal unhappiness. There had barely been a chink of light for Cecil through a series of seasons, which must have been as bewildering for him as they were depressing. How could it all have gone so wrong, so fast?

'He suffered blow after blow after blow,' says Deacon. 'Underlying, if you really knew the man, there were times when he did break and you'd see the odd crack here and there. I hate to see anybody upset like that anyway, so would ask, "Are you OK?" On the odd occasion he would confide in you. Not a lot, but I think if he knew you were genuine he would confide in you a little bit more.'

Cecil didn't always help himself. In particular, the drinking made things worse. For a tall and imposing man, he didn't need many drinks for its effects to take hold. If he was on his own within the corridors of Warren Place he would often pick up the phone. Long into the evening he would talk, mainly to those he trusted but occasionally there would be a business call after a bottle had been opened. Nick Gomersall was the racing manager for a handful of horses in training with Cecil and he remembers an episode from late 2003.

One horse had come second on its debut at Bath and was entered to run next at Lingfield Park. Gomersall had higher expectations after such a promising first start and mentioned to the Warren Place secretary about going to Newbury, where

Cecil would generally send better horses. That lunchtime the trainer called him back, outlining that the Gomersall-managed horses were only of average ability and that sights needed to be lowered. His message was clear: 'You don't tell me where to enter horses and where I don't.'

The call came to an abrupt end but that wasn't the last of the matter. 'At seven o'clock that night the phone rang and it was Henry,' recalls Gomersall. 'He'd had a couple between one o'clock and seven o'clock and completely forgot he gave me a bollocking and launched into me again!'

I knew enough to realise Cecil hadn't always been a saint but the man I sat down with for the first time that May afternoon was helpful and purposeful. He was slimmer than on past occasions, when I had seen him at the racecourse or on the Heath. It seemed that Cecil had emerged from all that time spent stuttering through the tunnel – but how?

In the two hours or so that we chatted he didn't try to dodge a single question. His love of training and the life around it seeped through. He even spoke of his pleasure at starting work by 5 a.m. And this from a man who had been beating the dawn chorus for approaching forty years. He told me that he was training fifty to sixty horses but wanted to bump that up to about eighty. That was the number that he felt would allow him the opportunity to compete once more at the top level. As for the bad times, he had consigned them to the past. 'Mentally, I got quite down,' he admitted. 'But I've come out of all that now. I've got all of my ambition back – I'm positive.'

The feature was published in the July 2006 issue of *Thoroughbred*

Owner and Breeder magazine. Chris Bourchier's accompanying photographs depict a man who has recovered his mojo. In one, Cecil is reclined in that single armchair, one long leg thrown casually over the other while his hands are crossed in front of him with fingers pointing upwards. His head is turned slightly to one side and the pose captures Cecil to a T. There is effortless style coupled with teak-tough determination. Racing followers always knew about that relaxed demeanour but it's the second-ary element that's more interesting. The way Cecil's jaw was set hinted at reserves and strength that he could call on when he was most up against it.

'Whatever situation he was in, I don't believe that he ever thought he would go under or have to give up,' says Joan Plant. 'He always believed he could come back. The fight to survive in his training was always there. Henry was a very strong man.'

Allied with that was a burning pride. Cecil was very aware of how plenty of folk had written him off. He understood he was the subject of 'dinosaur' jibes. As an innate competitor, such talk struck a nerve. It fuelled his desire to fight back. 'His big thing was, he hated being a has-been,' confirms Lanigan.

Possessing an iron will and an enduring competitive streak were important factors behind why Cecil refused to buckle in the wilderness years. But there was another reason why the man sat across the table from me exuded such a sense of purpose. 'I've got a super girlfriend,' he told me. 'She has been great for me in a lot of ways. I'm no longer struggling.'

Henry Cecil had a woman by his side who believed in him.

Chapter Two

'He never changed who he was but he changed how he was'

For many years above the fireplace in Henry Cecil's study stood a homemade Easter card. It had great sentimental value for the trainer and he chose to show it to people sometimes. The card had come to Warren Place via airmail in 2005.

Its sender had been unable to locate a suitable card to purchase in Dubai where she was working at the time but she duly designed her own. The end product was a motivational work, including several carefully considered messages. One of them read, 'A champion is someone who gets up even when he can't.' Her intention was to raise Cecil's spirits ahead of the coming season and the following words from a short poem were added on the back.

> A Friend's Love says:
> 'If you ever need anything, I'll be there.'
> True Love says:
> 'You'll never need anything, I'll be there.'

The card was from Jane McKeown and accompanied a letter thanking him for a dress he had chosen and sent for her to wear at the upcoming Dubai World Cup.

Jane hails from a racing family. Her father Charlie Guest was a jockey and trainer, while her brothers Richard and Rae both train racehorses. Richard was also once a jockey and rode a Grand National winner – Red Marauder in 2001. Her sister Sally worked for Sir Michael Stoute for many years, riding a considerable number of his stable stars on the home gallops. As a young girl Jane also rode out in her school holidays for Ryan Jarvis but took her career in racing in another direction, working as trainer David Loder's secretary during his rise in the 1990s.

Loder's alliance with Sheikh Mohammed led to him being asked to train the Godolphin two-year-olds in France in 1998. For Jane, moving across the Channel wasn't a straightforward matter as she was a single parent raising a young family. As she weighed up the situation, a secretarial vacancy at Warren Place arose. Jane barely knew Cecil at the time but attended an interview that went well, and a week or two afterwards accepted his job offer. She took up her new position just before Royal Ascot in June. Par for the course in those days, he had around twenty horses to saddle at the Royal meeting. But if that week was a baptism of fire, it couldn't have prepared her for the following five years.

Towards the end of 2000 she and Cecil had grown closer. Around that time he asked her to accompany him to an owner's annual shoot. From that point their relationship developed but the couple would separate in May 2003. Jane went north to

Durham to help her brother Richard, who was training there at the time. A few months later she accepted a position with Godolphin that gave her the opportunity to work in Newmarket during the British flat-racing season and then Dubai during the winter.

She and Cecil never lost touch, despite separating. By the early part of 2005 it seemed that the words from the old maxim held some substance for them both; absence had indeed made the heart grow fonder. The time was right to resume their relationship.

There were changes, though. Jane would return to Warren Place but not in a working capacity. She would remain in her job at Godolphin. Cecil had also stopped drinking, which was important for Jane. It had caused problems when they had first been together and her belief was that he became worse company not better when taking a drink. Cecil reached a point where he held a similar opinion. In an interview a few years later he referenced how drink made him either laugh uncontrollably or become belligerent.

A few weeks before Jane headed back from Dubai she posted the card that Cecil would always treasure. The morning of its receipt he tracked down fellow trainer Ed Vaughan, who had become a tenant at Warren Place at the end of the previous year. A little help was needed with a swift response to the card. It wasn't that Cecil was struggling for the words for his reply, more that he had a technical problem.

'He wanted to send a text message but didn't know how to,' recalls Vaughan, who was asked to carry out the task on Cecil's phone. 'It must have been the first Nokia ever, long before predictive text. You had to press the button x amount of times if you wanted the h. He was dictating to me. We were struggling along with it but I eventually managed to send this message verbatim, which probably took us most of third lot to do!'

Flowers soon arrived in Dubai. The accompanying card saw Cecil repeat the last line of the poem that Jane had quoted: 'True Love says: "You'll never need anything, I'll be there."'

Having Jane back was a game-changer for Cecil. For a start, she steadied the ship when it came to the business's finances. She was behind the redecoration of the handful or so Warren Place cottages that were subsequently rented out to American servicemen. The sizeable building that was once the stable staff hostel was also upgraded and leased out. That, along with the fact that three other trainers were now based at Warren Place, helped balance the books.

Just as importantly, Cecil was no longer lonely. With Jane once again alongside him, he stopped the habit he had fallen into of ringing people late into the evening. 'Henry wasn't someone to be alone,' says Joan Plant. 'I definitely think Jane settled him down. She certainly wanted to help him get the business back on track.'

Vaughan also recognised the steadying qualities Jane brought to Warren Place. The trainer was still happy to play the fool on occasion but all of a sudden there was the right balance to his life that had perhaps been missing in the decline. 'Jane kept him stable, kept him positive and was great with the business side of things as well,' says Vaughan.

Jane is slim and not much more than five feet three inches but there is an inner strength that belies her physique. She has a tireless streak when it comes to work and adopts a practical hands-on approach. She is not a person to shout and scream but is nevertheless persuasive, and very capable of making her point and standing her ground when necessary. In short, she isn't someone to be taken too lightly.

'She got stuck in but in a quiet way,' says Sally Noseda, reflecting on her sister's return to Warren Place. 'She has always been very strong; she brought up her children on her own. And she was always a worker. She gave Henry a bit of tough love as well. He really changed. He was positive and wouldn't have it any other way.'

If Jane brought a work ethic, she also gave regular encouragement. They had one conversation where she offered an opinion that a champion trainer doesn't lose his skills, they are always still there. It's not like the tennis star or ace cricketer for whom age will eventually reduce the level of performance. Training racehorses wasn't reliant on physical attributes and her thoughts were that all of Cecil's genius remained intact. She fully believed in Cecil and that made a very definite impression on him.

'He never changed who he was but he changed how he was,' is the perceptive recollection of Carina McKeown, the youngest of Jane's children who was undertaking a law degree at that time but often stayed at Warren Place. 'He was much more committed to what he was doing but he was still Henry. He liked to do his Mr Bean impressions and play the clown; that side of him never changed, but he definitely had a lot of focus.'

The transformation in Cecil became apparent to those outside Warren Place at the October yearling sales in

Newmarket. In the mornings before the auction began, he would be busily looking at the young horses he had initially identified through pedigrees in the sales catalogue. Occasionally Cecil took a break for a coffee in the restaurant adjacent to the collection ring at Tattersalls. But those minutes would find him with head down, poring over the sales catalogue. His dedication as he toured the boxes, studiously carrying out his homework, showed Jane a side to him that she had not seen before.

'When we used to go to the sales, my experience was that we'd mainly go and sit in the tearoom,' she says. 'He barely seemed to look at a horse. But that Sunday before the sale, I remember it being bitterly cold and thinking we'll be going for a cup of tea soon and he would say to me, "We'll just look at one more." It so wasn't like me to be thinking let's go and have a cup of tea because in previous years I used to do everything to stop him going!'

There was one other person working hard and effectively for Cecil during the sales season: his assistant David Lanigan. He is a natural horseman having been raised on his father's Tullamaine Castle Stud in Fethard, Tipperary. In his school holidays, Lanigan had enjoyed riding out for a clutch of top trainers. As a young man, he enhanced his experience by working at Walmac International, one of the largest breeding and stallion businesses in Kentucky. His ambition was to run his own training business one day and that was what brought him to Warren Place in late 2002. Initially he turned down the assistant's role as rumours about Cecil's demise did the rounds. But the trainer was persistent and Lanigan agreed to drop in to Warren Place during his trip to Europe's premier yearling sale in Newmarket that autumn. Cecil cooked his guest some Newmarket sausages.

'I went to see him, all very hush-hush,' says Lanigan. 'It was only meant to be a chat. Anyway, I accepted the job. No, I hadn't accepted the job – he told me I was doing the job!'

Lanigan recalls how his new boss was very trusting and granted him considerable legroom in the stable. But the assistant knew that he was overseeing a very experienced team of staff and had to go about his role strategically. Industrious by nature, his style was to lead by example rather than shout the odds. Take the time when a decision was made to get rid of the blowers that were used to clean the yard. All the lads were asked to pick up a brush and sweep the place from end to end. There was plenty of moaning for several months as the work was more intensive but Lanigan's hands-on approach ensured everyone fell into line.

'Every day you had to chase them out of the tack room,' says Lanigan. '"C'mon everyone, grab a brush!" If you stand there with your hands on your hips and say, "Right lads, sweep the yard," everybody thinks you're a prick. But if you get out there and sweep the yard yourself they come with you: "Your man is prepared to get his hands dirty, he's sweeping the yard, he can't be that much of a prick." All those sort of things get everybody in on it.'

Lanigan's energetic manner was always evident when the regular delivery of shavings, the horses' bedding, used to arrive late in the morning. The bales from the pallets couldn't just be left out in the yard until evening stables but for staff who had been in since before 6 a.m. an energy-sapping task was the last thing anyone wanted.

'The lads would be moaning but David would be the first in to start putting the bales in the stables,' says groom Shane Fetherstonhaugh. 'He instilled that work ethic: "I'm not going to stand back and expect you to do it, I'll chip in." Once you have someone like that, people stop moaning and you just get on with it.

'What I always liked about David was he's a grafter – a proper hard worker. You bought into it with him as well. When it wasn't good, David was there and he stuck at it. He wanted to do well for Henry, you could see it. He wanted to please Henry and I think that rubbed off on everyone.'

Book 1 of the October Yearling Sale draws many of racing's major players to Tattersalls, just a stone's throw from Newmarket High Street. It can be pure theatre when two or three of the sport's big guns take aim at a young horse in the auction ring. The yearlings are led inside one at a time with an expert auctioneer overseeing proceedings. There are seats banked immediately in front of the auctioneer as well as to his immediate left and right. To the left of where the horses enter is a standing area, a little similar to a mini terrace at a football ground. It is popular with many bidders but others favour different locations including the odd place – a few steps down on the stairwells opposite the auctioneer, for example – that's not always easy to observe. Tattersalls employs a team of spotters to make sure any potential buyer is seen.

A bid can be indicated with a small shake of the sales catalogue, a nod of the head or similar subtle gestures. Often bidders will have a mobile phone fixed to their ear, taking instructions from an owner or advisor. Preparations will have been done from weeks in advance when the catalogue is first available to view. Targets are initially identified through pedigree assessment but the really hard work begins two or three days before the sale. Owners, trainers and bloodstock agents assemble to view the yearlings that are due to sell. The horses are walked back and forth with just about their every step under scrutiny. If all the boxes are ticked in terms of conformation and pedigree then a yearling's value can easily reach a seven-figure sum as it walks round and round the ring. In 2017, one filly was knocked down for four million guineas (a guinea equals £1.05). That year there were sixteen other yearlings that made seven figures over the three days of Book 1.

Owners' sales orders vary, as do to whom they are given. Some use an agent to purchase their stock; others work directly with the trainer. Either way, the agent or trainer will be given a budget and a number of horses to try and secure from the auction ring. Discussions take place about the type of horse the owner wants to target. Maybe he or she dreams of a sharp early type to run at Royal Ascot the following June or they are content to wait on a later-maturing individual with a view to having a Classic contender a couple of seasons later. There are also those owner-breeders who invest in young stock with a view to their secondary career in the breeding shed. Such buyers will perhaps just want to aim for fillies that will one day add to their broodmare band.

There is a plethora of such details to be talked through and the information was once again on Cecil's mind as he attended the sales. For the first time in a long time, Cecil had plenty of orders to fill and it felt good. Also his activity and diligence at the sale would have raised more than a few eyebrows. It sent a message out to the racing industry: Henry Cecil wasn't washed up and on the brink of retirement. He was back in the game.

If there were important decisions for Cecil at the sales that autumn, there were arguably more difficult ones being made closer to home. There had long been gossip that the trainer had almost as many employees as horses and eventually he had to address the imbalance. One morning in late 2005 he gave Lanigan a list of lads that he wanted to see and told him to get on with first lot. One by one at least six employees, including senior staff, were called in and given the sad news by Cecil. 'That was the roughest day of the whole lot,' says Lanigan.

Around the same time, Cecil also privately spoke to his assistant about the future. Despite all the renewed optimism triggered by their success at the yearling sales and the fact that Jane McKeown had helped restore stability in the business, there was no getting away from the fact that Cecil had recorded just twelve victories in 2005. This was a man who once sent out 180 winners in a single season. Cecil made it clear to Lanigan that they must deliver improved results. 'He said that we had to pull the whole thing together or else I was never going to be training and he was going to be retired. And he didn't want that,' says Lanigan.

There was a lot riding on the next season for the trainer but he was determined to turn his stable's fortunes around. He was switched on and full of fight, keen to prove all of his doubters wrong. What Cecil didn't realise was that 2006 would bring a fresh challenge, the biggest one he had ever faced.

★   ★   ★

During our very first interview the following May, Cecil was attentive and active. At one point, to help the photographer, he leapt from his chair and started larking about riding a rocking horse on the stairs. He had earlier explained how he was feeling fit and didn't have a pain in his body. That wasn't entirely the truth.

Around six months or so earlier Jane and he had taken a short holiday in Granada. For three days, he had been confined to his bed with a stomach upset in the historic Andalusian city. Back at Warren Place there was also the odd evening when he would complain to Jane of some discomfort in his stomach as he watched television. Something wasn't right.

One day early in the new season Lanigan and Cecil went to Nottingham where Custodian, a horse joint-owned by the assistant's father, was due to run. As it happened, Custodian got loose and went running round the track with a long lead rein attached to him. Lanigan recalls having to respond to the race-course stewards' summons while a disdainful Cecil sat outside. During the day, the trainer complained that he had been suffer-ing from chronic indigestion. Lanigan recommended some tablets he used and on their return to Newmarket was asked for them by Cecil. Next morning the two men were having coffee when Lanigan discovered his employer had swallowed just about the whole lot. 'You can't eat all those,' Lanigan told him. 'That's like liquid cork!'

Somewhat reluctantly Cecil went to the doctor for tests and was referred for a biopsy. Not that he let the procedure get in the way of his work. Cecil put on his morning suit over the bandages applied after the biopsy and drove himself and Jane to

Royal Ascot. He had just the one runner there that week and was determined not to miss the race. As it materialised, the filly Novellara could only finish eighth of eleven in the Ribblesdale Stakes, doing little to alter the public's perception that Cecil's best days were behind him.

The results from the biopsy, however, were much more worrying than the outcome of any race that Cecil had ever contested at Royal Ascot. The same month it was confirmed at the Nuffield Hospital in Cambridge that he had follicular lymphoma, a type of non-Hodgkin lymphoma. The Macmillan Cancer Support website says: 'In NHL, blood cells called lymphocytes become abnormal. These abnormal lymphocytes are the lymphoma cells. They keep dividing and grow out of the body's control. Over time, there are enough lymphoma cells to make a lump, called a tumour.'

Cecil's disease started with lymph glands enlarging behind the stomach. Jane was sitting with him when Dr Rob Marcus, a consultant haematologist from Addenbrooke's Hospital, informed them of the diagnosis. It was devastating news and her thoughts instantly returned to how Cecil struggled to come to terms with his twin brother's cancer six years earlier. 'When David had cancer, Henry just couldn't and didn't cope with it all,' she says. 'So you think, "How are you going to cope with your own?" I just thought, "This is going to be terrible. How are we going to get through this?" '

Chapter Three

'A goosebump day'

Soon after his diagnosis Henry Cecil had chemotherapy for the first time. He received a cancer drug combination called R–CVP that is used to treat low-grade non-Hodgkin lymphoma. R–CVP are the initials for the four drugs – rituximab, cyclophosphamide, vincristine and prednisolone. The last named is taken as tablets and the rest are given intravenously.

While the first cycle of R–CVP marked the beginning of Cecil's treatment, in his own mind he had already started his fight against the illness. Jane McKeown's deep concerns that he might crumble after the crushing news were not realised. Previously Cecil had always channelled his competitive streak into professional ambitions; now it was redirected towards his very own survival. Cecil never liked finishing second and cancer was an opponent he was going to take on.

'He just decided he was going to overcome it,' says Jane. 'That was how he coped with it; by not letting it overtake his life, in taking control.'

At the outset his illness wasn't publicised. Aside from Jane, there was only one other person who was quickly made aware of it – David Lanigan. 'I've got a tumour the size of a basketball in my gut,' Cecil informed him. The trainer added that only he, Jane and the Irishman knew and it had to stay that way. Lanigan didn't need telling twice. If word had got out at that stage, a couple of months before the annual yearling sales got under-way, the Warren Place assistant felt that the whole thing would have been 'toast, finished'.

While Cecil could count on the support of Jane and Lanigan as he faced up to his most serious challenge, there was some-thing else that proved invaluable: his work. Just a few yards from his back door there were more than fifty horses in the stable and some nice prospects in among them. They were exactly the right sort of distraction for him to wake up to every single day.

'I think the horses were a release,' says jockey Ted Durcan, who rode for Cecil for several seasons from 2005 onwards. 'At least with the horses, he had them out and had his mind work-ing; [they] had him active, active, active. He loved the horses, so I think they were a major factor that he was able to fight the illness as long as he did. Without them he wouldn't have.'

The hectic life of Warren Place meant he had little time to brood about cancer. He had plans for his string, races to win. Training was a way of life for him and he refused to let illness stop him from enjoying what he loved. This was a time for action. Henry Cecil was thinking positively on every front.

During the season, which runs from late March to early November, Cecil's string stepped out on Newmarket Heath six days of the week. Only on a Sunday would the vast majority of the horses remain in their box. Their programme would be divided into cantering and galloping exercise. The latter is termed 'work'. Horses that are in fast work are those that are being prepared for a race, as opposed to 'canterers' who are just doing the steady conditioning (rather than speed exercise) that is the bedrock of their training. During the season plenty of Newmarket trainers will have two work mornings each week for their gallopers – often on Wednesday and Saturday. The bigger stables may have as many as four, not that the same 'workers' will be sent each time.

In general, racehorses are not asked to gallop more than twice a week in their preparations for a race. Most of them, and certainly the bigger colts, are likely to need two pieces of work per week, while lighter-framed types or some fillies may require only one. Certain individuals that are prone to injury are also less likely to be asked to undertake fast work regularly. Trainers face a balancing act with such horses as they aim to get them race fit, while keeping them physically sound.

Each horse is different when it comes to the number of pieces of fast work they need to get them ready to race. A neat two-year-old filly may gallop just three or four times before a debut run. A bigger, thick-winded colt could build up through a dozen or so workouts to get ready. The rest of a racehorse's exercise is trotting and cantering. If they are scheduled to gallop on two mornings in a week, they will canter on the other four. The extent of the cantering work depends on the horse and what stage they are at in terms of their preparation.

Many horses in Newmarket use Warren Hill for their cantering exercise. It is a four-furlong polytrack canter that rises continually from the bottom all the way up. Immature or unfit horses will get found out on it. For many strings Monday and Thursday will be one-canter mornings, while on Tuesday and Friday the horses will be asked to go up it twice. But with race-horses there are no hard and fast rules. Each trainer manages their string as they see fit.

In the season most Newmarket yards spring into life between 6 and 6.30 a.m. Morning stables is routinely divided into three 'lots' and revolves around the grooms taking horses out onto the Heath up until just before midday. First lot is normally for the group of horses that are in a full training and racing programme. Second lot can also include a group whose weekly schedule is based around galloping and cantering but there may also be horses that are undertaking conditioning exercise only and no faster pace action. Third lot is often for less developed horses – usually two-year-olds and known as 'backward' horses – or others that are slowly being eased back into exercise after injury or illness.

Unsurprisingly, the 'lads' – the historic term given to stable staff of both sexes – always look forward to work mornings. They are the most exciting ones for a number of reasons. For a start, there is the exhilaration of sitting on a horse as it powers along at a speed close to its maximum. High-class sprinters and milers can reach speeds of around 40 miles per hour. Also, and especially early in the season when pecking orders are still being established, a work rider can dream of discovering a good one. Hearing the lads chat after a bunch of workers gallop first thing on a spring morning is always entertaining and occasionally informative.

A typical exchange between two lads after a gallop in which they have both ridden could unfold along the following lines.

'This is all right, this,' one groom will say about their mount. 'Nah, mine is no good, so don't bother getting carried away by how yours went,' the other will reply. If it was ever noticed that one horse had worked particularly well, word would soon spread among all the riders. 'That's a Group horse, I'm telling you,' a lad may claim. 'It's a machine,' another might add. That's when a cynic (and there are plenty among the lads) will step in to give a more cautionary verdict: 'Morning glory, that,' a common phrase for a horse that only does its best stuff on the home gallops but never at the races.

Work mornings at Warren Place were a mixture of fun and focus. Cecil flitted between both. Sitting in his car heading to the gallops, he would be humming along to something on a commercial music station and light-heartedly musing, 'I wonder what Mozart or Beethoven would make of this?' A few minutes later he would be alongside his string delivering fine-tuned instructions and looking the very picture of concentration.

Cecil designed each exercise the night before and the details would appear the following morning on the exercise board, which hung on the wall just next to the tack-room door. The trainer grouped the horses in twos or threes and the lads would arrive at the gallops alongside their respective exercise companions.

He usually liked one horse in each group to lead, and a common scenario would be for the other one to be pulled out from the slipstream and complete steady work together, 'upsides' as it's known. 'Join up, smoke a pipe,' Cecil would tell his riders in the briefing just before they cantered down to the start. If he wanted to test them a little bit more the instruction would be something along the lines of 'Join up, make them finish.' In that instance, the grooms were expected to keep niggling away at their respective mount and yet not overly exert. With both situations Cecil often called for a 'dead-heat' or a 'double dead-heat' if there were three workers. There was a third outcome that the trainer would occasionally want: 'Join up and then let him go away.' The lead horse would be eased after being passed, allowing the second horse the positive experience of striding clear.

One thing that Cecil was very specific about was how horses should begin an exercise, whether it was cantering or galloping. He was insistent that horses never jumped off, preferring them to ease into it by jogging a few strides. Cecil's extraordinary eyesight meant he could see from long range what was happening three furlongs away at the bottom of Warren Hill as horses prepared to canter.

'Henry was quite strict,' says Claire Markham, a Derbyshire girl and long-time Warren Place secretary who used to ride out at first lot. 'You had to do what he said. He did everything on the steadier side, on the sensible side. There was no going flat out anywhere – ever. I got a speeding ticket one Monday. There were a few groups of fillies going too fast. We all got called into the tack room and got a bollocking. He wouldn't let it drop if he told you off. He'd tell you off and then tell you off again!'

Dee Deacon has memories of a similar experience from her early days at Warren Place. She got on the wrong side of the guv'nor after a gallop didn't go as he wished on Long Hill. Cecil was riding out with the string on his 'hack' Snowy and told Deacon, who was working in a group of three fillies, to 'make it finish' – only for her to misinterpret the instruction.

'The two in front of me were going much better, so I got down and started driving my filly. She wasn't of their calibre. I didn't realise that, I was so green myself. We got to the top and I'd overdone it with my filly; she started tying up, cramping behind. He came flying up on Snowy: "What are you playing at? What do you think you're doing? You could see you weren't going as good as those so why didn't you just sit still? You can see what's happened; now you're paying the consequences." I knew I'd cocked up. He was bang on the money. I took the filly home, bottom lip well and truly on the floor. But the very next lot I went up to him and said I apologise. "You've learned your lesson, let's get on with it – what are you on now?"'

If a big gallop morning had gone well Cecil's excitement would be very evident. He would jump in his car and make the short journey to where the horses collected after their exercise. 'That chestnut colt worked well, didn't he?' he would say or something similar. 'He could be quite good, couldn't he?' Cecil wasn't inviting you to offer an opinion in response. He was simply airing stream of consciousness thoughts as they raced through his mind. If one of the Warren Place stars had galloped impressively there was almost a force field of pleasure emanating from Cecil.

There was a lot of common sense in Cecil's training style. After exercise he would regularly remind the lads walking back on the colts to slow down. This would ensure that the line of fillies – walking behind the colts for obvious reasons – weren't having to jig-jog to keep up. He would ask for the string to walk back at the pace that suited the slower individuals, reducing stress and strain. And through his tutelage Warren Place horses had a reputation for being 'well mannered', as Markham points out.

'It was just to do with the environment,' she says. 'They were taught to do things gradually and gently from an early age. You wouldn't get many pullers [horses that failed to settle]. They weren't buzzed up, lit up and didn't go flat out. Therefore they were relaxed. They were laidback on the canter and always happy horses coming home.'

Cecil rarely, if ever, missed a beat when he was around his string. For example, a lad could expect to get pulled up for hand-walking a horse on just one rein after a gallop. Cecil felt that horses at exercise were used to two reins governing relatively equal pressure through the bit applied in their mouths. If they were subsequently walked on one rein it led to the bit being pulled almost through the mouth. 'He was always: "two reins", to hold the mouth steady,' says Warren Place farrier Stephen Kielt, who attended just about every gallop morning. 'He had an extreme eye for detail.'

Just about all racing stables run along similar lines in terms of personnel structure. In most mid-sized and large operations the trainer will be supported by an assistant. Some of the biggest stables even employ two. They are expected to take charge of the stable in the trainer's absence, including representation at the racecourse. Assistant trainers may have served in a pupil-assistant capacity early in their working life.

Next in the pecking order are the head lads. Such men and women will have been promoted through the ranks having previously shone as lads. These head grooms have a series of extra responsibilities that are likely to include mixing up the bespoke feeds for horses, dealing with minor ailments and injuries, and bandaging horses prior to exercise. They also fulfil a vital role in the chain of command, liaising directly with the trainer or conveying important information through the assistant.

Each stable will also routinely have a travelling head lad who is in charge of the horses when they are sent to the races. The bigger stables, such as Cecil's, have one or two others as part of their travelling team for those busy summer Saturdays when runners are sent all over the country.

The bulk of the staff is comprised of lads. These are the grooms, whose ages may vary from sixteen to seventy, that ride out the string through the three lots of morning stables as well as carrying out duties around the exercise. They are also kept busy with feeding and brushing over their horses later in the day at evening stables. The lads are invariably allocated two or three horses that are theirs 'to do', catering for every daily need short of medical care. They don't necessarily ride out their three. The trainer decides which grooms are best suited to certain horses, with weight and riding skills being key factors. Lads are expected and usually want to accompany their horses to the races.

Occasionally they are unable to go, requiring another lad to deputise. Those were the circumstances that led to Dee Deacon getting the nod from Cecil to accompany a horse called Multidimensional to France for the Group 2 Prix Guillaume d'Ornano in August 2006.

Multidimensional was a homebred belonging to the Niarchos family. They and Prince Khalid Abdullah were the two major owners who had remained steadfast in their backing throughout the worst years of Cecil's career. There was a handful of others who also kept the faith but it was the two owner-breeders whose staunch patronage of Warren Place really helped Cecil ride out the storm. 'He wouldn't have survived if they hadn't supported him through thick and thin,' says Jane. 'And he was aware of that.'

Stavros Niarchos was a Greek shipping tycoon and also became a leading racehorse owner-breeder. Niarchos acquired Haras de Fresnay-le-Buffard, the stud farm in Normandy once owned by the renowned French entrepreneur Marcel Boussac, and also Oak Tree Farm in Kentucky. He enjoyed tremendous success, not least with horses based at Warren Place. Through the 1980s and early 1990s Cecil trained a series of high-profile winners for him, including five at Royal Ascot.

Niarchos died in 1996 but his daughter Maria took charge of the breeding and racing operation. She and Cecil had already known one another for some time and got on well. The pair quickly developed an excellent working relationship. Alan Cooper, racing manager for the Niarchos family since the 1980s, says, 'There was a unique symbiosis between Henry and Maria. It was very much teamwork.'

Other owners may have deserted Warren Place early in the twenty-first century but that was never a consideration for Maria, according to Cooper. 'I don't think it occurred to Maria to do anything other than have horses with Henry. Undoubtedly, there's a down period in Henry's life but it wasn't something that we sat and discussed because Maria is a team person. You have to believe . . .'

That trust in Cecil's ability was rewarded in 2006 thanks to the feats of Multidimensional. His mother Sacred Song was very competent in Stakes company. This is the highest level of racing, which incorporates Group and Listed races. She won two Group 3s for Cecil and progressed to finish second in a Group 1 – the highest tier of all.

Cooper says Multidimensional was a 'tough little horse and beautifully made'. But like his trainer he had more than his fair share of adversity to overcome. As a two-year-old, the earliest age that flat horses can compete, Multidimensional became very sick and spent time at the Greenwood Ellis veterinary clinic in Newmarket. 'He got a bit of pneumonia at one stage and I remember going to see him in the clinic,' says Cooper. 'He was being drip-fed to keep him right.'

Multidimensional never made it to the racecourse as a juvenile. Indeed his debut wasn't until the end of June the following year but the wait was worth it. His first run was at the July Course in Newmarket and the horse's connections went to the races in positive mood after impressive work on the home gallops. Cecil's assistant David Lanigan was sufficiently confident about the outcome of the mile maiden race that he made one of just two bets that he confesses to having had in his life. It proved a shrewd investment as 10/1 shot Multidimensional slammed the field by three and a half lengths.

It was as convincing a debut display as you could wish to see and raised hopes that he could emulate his mother's feats at Stakes grade. A subsequent course and distance victory next time out in a handicap (races in which a horse's official rating dictates the weight it has to carry) only increased enthusiasm.

Glorious Goodwood, one of racing's most prestigious meetings, arrived a fortnight later and Cecil opted to let Multidimensional run in another handicap. He went off a well-supported 4/1 joint-favourite, no doubt buoyed by money from the many who wanted to see the trainer back in the winner's circle at the picturesque racecourse on the Sussex Downs. Sadly, it wasn't Cecil's or Multidimensional's day. The colt failed to land a telling blow and trailed home last of eight runners. But his jockey Ted Durcan was not as down in the dumps as those who greeted him in the unsaddling enclosure.

'The ground was rock hard and he hated it,' explains Durcan. 'He ran an absolute stinker. After going a hundred yards, I thought to myself, hang on a minute. From halfway I just eased him down. I remember unsaddling him; everyone's faces were just on the floor . . . it was one of them. I was like, "No, relax, don't worry; he wasn't at the races today."'

Durcan's assessment offered hope for the future. Even so, off the back of finishing plumb last in a handicap Cooper didn't expect to have Cecil on the phone a week later proposing to run Multidimensional in a Group 2 contest in France. Not only was the race set to be the horse's third in under a month but it was against much stiffer opposition – and at a new distance of a mile and a quarter. It was a bold move but typified how Cecil would campaign a horse in which he believed.

'It was a little bit of a surprise when Henry rang up and said, "I think we should go to Deauville,"' says Cooper. 'That's part of Henry's genius. He could call up and recommend you do something and you didn't dispute it. You just said, "Great, let's give it a whirl!" Maria always went with him.'

Cecil arrived at the decision to send Multidimensional across the Channel after watching a stunning workout on the Al Bahathri. This was the polytrack gallop favoured by the trainer when the turf on Newmarket Heath was too firm. And there was certainly no way he was going to risk Multidimensional on fast ground after Durcan's post-race analysis at Goodwood.

In the gallop the Niarchos's colt was ridden as usual by Victor Deering. He was led by Sound Of Nature, who was also a three-year-old colt with plenty of potential, albeit never quite fulfilled. Such is horseracing. Dee Deacon was in the saddle of Sound Of Nature and has fond recollections of that piece of work.

'The Al Bahathri is really only a seven-furlong gallop and then you've a furlong to pull up,' she says. 'We went over that – eight furlongs – and were still going coming off the path. That horse got into gear and, oh my God, it was fantastic; the best piece of work. We couldn't pull them up, they were so well.'

Multidimensional's supreme health was at the opposite end of the spectrum to how it had been in the early stages of his two-year-old career. 'He was a sickly child, so ill,' says Deacon when recalling that brush with pneumonia. 'He'd be standing in his box dripping, white with sweat.' There were no such worries as Deacon, along with travelling head lad Michael McGowan, journeyed by land and sea a couple of days before the race in Deauville.

Jane McKeown would travel across on the eve of the race, Saturday 19 August. Cecil remained in Newmarket. The regimen of the trainer's treatment meant that he was having chemotherapy at regular intervals through the summer. It was also the holidays and he was enjoying having his twelve-year-old son Jake to stay at Warren Place.

The Cecil team was owed some good fortune and shortly before Multidimensional's race they received a slice. The feeling was that the horse had been compromised by the fast ground a fortnight earlier at Goodwood but sustained rainfall on the morning of the French race meant the six-strong field faced soft conditions. Multidimensional would subsequently prove just as effective when the going description was good-to-firm but that day connections were pleased that the rain came for him.

'We thought, "Brilliant, that's just what we want, a bit of give in the ground,"' says Deacon. 'The heavens opened. We thought that's somebody saying, "This is yours." As soon as we got in the parade ring it stopped and the sun came out. You couldn't write it.'

The favourite for the race was Carlotamix, a Group 1-winning two-year-old the previous season. He represented the powerful connections of elite French trainer André Fabre and the Aga Khan, one of racing's most influential owner-breeders. Only one of the other runners carried a larger starting price than Multidimensional, whose odds were a fraction under 10/1, but there was a quiet confidence around him, especially after that rainfall. 'Henry had a lot of faith in him, he really did,' says Jane. 'Obviously he wasn't going to send the horse if he didn't think he'd win but I remember him being very keen for me to go.'

The sole English-trained horse in the race was to be ridden for the only time by Christophe Lemaire, the Niarchos family's contracted jockey in France. While the partnership was a brief one, it proved to be successful. Multidimensional was held up by Lemaire through the early part of the mile-and-a-quarter race before being pulled out and asked for an effort in the home straight. The well-named outsider, Boris De Deauville, looked for a while as if he might deliver a surprise result. Having led from way out, the 17/1 shot sustained his run deep into the closing stages but Lemaire had everything under control on Multidimensional.

The horse made relentless headway on the outer and finished his race strongly to win by three-quarters of a length. The victory was Cecil's first victory at Group-race level for four years, fittingly provided by a determined little colt owned by one of his most committed supporters. 'It was a goosebump day,' assesses Cooper. Not long after the race the racing manager tracked down Deacon and McGowan to hand over a large bottle of champagne.

'You could see the relief etched on his face,' says Deacon. 'It meant a lot to him as well. We were all in the winner's enclosure and your face was hurting with grinning. Jane came in absolutely beaming. It was a very special day.'

Jane recalls, 'I think Henry was on the front page of the *Racing Post* the following day, which hadn't happened for a very long time. That meant something – it had been such a long time since he'd had a Group winner. Henry had been working particularly hard to bring things back up. All trainers work hard but it was so nice to get that [win]. Maria was there as well and it was the first time I had really experienced her joy. She was pleased for her team, obviously, but she was especially pleased for Henry.'

For Deacon and McGowan the drinks flowed well into the evening, even though they and Multidimensional had an early departure time scheduled for the next day. Deacon duly stirred at 4.30 a.m. in the bed and breakfast where they were staying but became slightly concerned as she realised there was no sounds coming from McGowan's room. 'I went downstairs to bang on the door: "Mick, Mick!" Nothing. I opened the door, peered round and there's clothes all over the floor. He was still asleep on the bed! That was a damn good night.'

At last the Warren Place team had good reason to celebrate again. A long overdue Group victory, albeit a Group 2, was due reward for the unstinting efforts of everyone connected to the stable, not least Cecil. In his circumstances, the commitment to work was important but it needed to offer encouragement and that is exactly what the Deauville result provided. The win was a timely and significant boost. What Cecil didn't realise that weekend was that it wasn't going to be the only one he would receive in 2006. Less than three months later he himself would be off to France and this time it was for a Group 1 race.

Chapter Four

'Go and have a good steak!'

Multidimensional's wasn't the only important success for Henry Cecil that August. The colt may have generated a few headlines for Warren Place but there was a lower profile victory much closer to home that left Cecil very excited. A two-year-old filly called Passage Of Time had built on a rather disappointing first run by winning a maiden at the July Course on the other side of town from her stable.

On the face of it, the triumph wasn't particularly impressive. She edged home by a mere head in the seven-furlong race. But, as often occurred, Cecil had seen something in the filly that others hadn't. He believed she possessed a touch of class and that her initial win was just a stepping stone to far bigger things in the future.

Passage Of Time's groom was Shane Fetherstonhaugh, a modest, unassuming man who speaks with great depth and insight, and ended up riding the best horse ever seen in British racing.

Cecil and Fetherstonhaugh were not unalike one another. Their backgrounds may have been decidedly different but Cecil had an artist's outlook, which was very much in tune with that

of Fetherstonhaugh's. The two men developed a unique understanding. Between them they produced exceptional work and
Fetherstonhaugh's part in it deserves full recognition.

Fetherstonhaugh is from the Irish seaside town of Skerries,
about twenty miles north of Dublin. No more than five feet
seven inches tall, he is tough with a wiry build and the muscular
lower arms that go with the territory if you ride three horses
every morning. When you study Fetherstonhaugh's face, what
initially strikes you are his pronounced cheekbones. But spend
any length of time with him and the furrows of his brow convey
that his is a thoughtful, intelligent mind.

Racing was part of Fetherstonhaugh's life from an early age.
His father Brian was a racing journalist for the *Irish Press*, a
national newspaper that was published until 1995. Brian's
passion for the sport soon became evident in his son. As a very
young child Shane would go with his father to the races, along
with his two eldest brothers. He was soon captivated by the
scene, especially the animals.

'I was just always taken by the horses, how athletic and well
they looked,' says Fetherstonhaugh. 'I spoke to my brothers
about this afterwards and they were doing other things. They
never really took any notice of the horses while my earliest
memories were of standing watching them in the parade ring
and the jockeys and silks. It caught my imagination.

'I used to go everywhere with my father on weekends, all
over Ireland. My two eldest brothers stopped going as they got
older and found other things to do. But I still wanted to go.
When I was old enough, eleven or twelve, I asked my father to
get me into a stable, weekends and summer holidays. The

nearest yard to us was Peter Casey's and I used to go and just muck out and help. I cycled there. It used to take me an hour or so and an hour back. But I absolutely loved it. I loved being around the older lads in the yard and I loved having the craic.

'They were great people and always gave me a lot of time. I had no knowledge of horses whatsoever. I learned everything from there. They taught me how to ride, which was all I wanted to do. I used to ride a little pony, and learned and gradually stepped up to the quietest horse in the yard or the slow one.'

Fetherstonhaugh didn't just feel drawn to the horses with which he worked; he followed the sport and all of its stories, home and abroad. The racing world had him hooked and with the fearlessness of youth he set off for England aged just sixteen. He was bound for Epsom, the home of the most famous flat race of them all, the Derby.

'I wanted to leave home, go out and do my own thing, so I just came over. I had no set plan of what I was going to do or how it was going to work out. I just decided I wanted to have a bit of fun. I loved my parents but I couldn't wait to get out in the world.'

The teenager found a lively training community in Epsom, working for several yards including Simon Dow and Reg Akehurst. He secured a few rides as an amateur and enjoyed booting home a winner at Salisbury in 1996.

Eventually the pull of Newmarket resulted in him joining trainer Michael Bell in the centre of Newmarket. There he rode out every day on 2005 Derby hero Motivator. To be such a key part of any Classic success, especially the Derby, is what all racing staff yearn for. But months later Fetherstonhaugh had become disillusioned, perhaps a little burnt out, with Newmarket and horses. Aged thirty he was ready to return to Skerries and had it on his mind that he might work with his brother on the fishing boats.

'I'd sort of had enough of racing,' he says. 'After Motivator, I'd got bored with it. I thought that's as good as it's going to get – a Derby winner and all the rest of it. I'd just come to a cross-roads with what I was going to do with my life. I'd half got it into my head that I was going to go home. I was at one of those places where I didn't know what I wanted to do.

'But a friend of mine, John Kelly, who was working at Henry's, said to me, "Before you go back, just go and see Henry, have a chat with him – you'll like him." It was the last thing I was going to do before I left. I'd have probably headed on after that. I went up there . . . it was freezing and a misera-ble, dark evening. I remember walking through the main yard and half the boxes seemed to be empty and it just looked a bit rundown, tired. And I'd seen the string out on the Heath; five or six, that was all.'

Approaching the house at Warren Place he sensed nothing to reignite his innate feel for a racehorse or the life provided by working within a stable. If anything his footsteps across the yard brought home to him what a cold, labour-intensive and thank-less life it could be for a stable lad. There was no scent of Epsom glory that day, no hint of people proudly nurturing champions of the sport. Just a reinforcement of what the town and racing folk thought, that the master of Warren Place was on the way out.

Still, Fetherstonhaugh had an appointment to keep and one he wasn't going to swerve. Stepping out of the midwinter dreich into the house, he was soon hit by its light and warmth. It wasn't all down to the electricity either. A major contributor to the energy supply was the man Fetherstonhaugh had come to meet. Not quite kindred spirits, but Cecil was someone towards whom the sensitive Fetherstonhaugh immediately felt drawn.

'I sat with Henry in his study,' he says. 'He was one of those men – he had something about him. We talked about everything bar coming to work for him. He was showing me his soldiers and this, that and the other. Then he said, "Right, when are you starting?" I said, "Monday." Straightaway, I thought I'll give this a go.

'One other thing I noticed when I started was we had a uniform. I think Jane was probably instrumental in that. There were proper jackets, navy with the pink "HRAC" on the back. They were smart. We only had a small string but we looked the part.'

As his first year at Warren Place unfolded Fetherstonhaugh was struck by the spirit within the staff. Off the back of that dismal 2005 campaign there was no reason for it to be so buoyant. But, months before any big-time winner was on the board, morale was somehow high. The fact that they weren't a big team helped. Everyone knew each other and there was little animosity among the group.

The big yards with the big horses in Newmarket can breed a divided camp, especially if one or two lads end up getting lucky with an owner who looks after them with a few extra quid. Jealousy and resentment too often creep in and spoil a yard's success. But that was far from the case in Fetherstonhaugh's early days at Warren Place. He recalls only around ten staff riding out with a couple or so more lads on the ground in the yard. He says they were 'a tight-knit group' and believes that the special atmosphere stemmed from the man at the helm.

'That season, we won a Listed race at Newmarket [with Novellara] and we all went into the office to watch it,' says Fetherstonhaugh. 'I've worked in big yards and you'd have Group winners and half the lads wouldn't even bother to watch: "Oh that won, did it?" Everyone working for Henry at the time went into the office and we were shouting it home! It was just a Listed race and this was a man who'd trained champions but it meant something. That's when it felt like it was turning. I put that down to Henry. He created that.

'I always felt, you wanted to do well for *him*. I've worked for other trainers, and I'm not saying they're not good trainers or good people, but it wouldn't mean the same. He always went out of his way to come and say, "You're doing a good job with that horse," even if it had won a little race at Bath or a Group 1. He would say thanks.

'It's hard to describe. You just wanted to do well for him. What that creates is, everyone feels the same and goes that little bit further than they usually would. Other jobs, you feel you just do what you have to do and get out, but not at Henry's. I'm not alone in saying this. Most of the lads would come in earlier than they had to and leave later than they had to. There was no making you come in early; it was off your own back, especially in the summer time when you'd get the horses out for a pick [of grass]. You'd come in early and there'd be five lads in before you all thinking the same thing: "I'll get mine out for a bit, ten minutes longer." That's what he created.'

Passage Of Time was a January foal for Prince Khalid Abdullah, whose Juddmonte Farms breeding operation had its European base at Banstead Manor Stud in the village of Cheveley, just outside Newmarket. She was sired by Dansili, a stallion who was on the way up, and was the third foal to race out of a Juddmonte mare called Clepsydra.

Cecil trained Clepsydra, and the grand-dam Quandary had also been under his care. Quandary took time to develop but the trainer was happy to be patient with her. His approach was rewarded when she finally lost her maiden's tag as a four-year-old before signing off her racing career with an impressive Listed victory at Newmarket.

Cecil felt there were benefits to understanding his horses' families. His knowledge of a sibling or a dam would invariably help him. 'It's like with humans, certain traits are passed down,' he told me. 'You've got a filly from a mother who you recall needed time. On the other hand, perhaps a half-sister had a bit of temperament. Or there was one who you'd trained very lightly. The whole thing is like a jigsaw puzzle.'

Clepsydra proved to be no star on the racecourse, winning her maiden at the fifth attempt. That was her sole career success. She didn't fare much better in her early years as a broodmare with her first foal Gems Of Araby, sent to Cecil in 2004 and 2005, failing to get her head in front. The second foal, Sandglass, did at least win a race for trainer Amanda Perrett in June 2006.

By that point Cecil had got going on the home gallops with Passage Of Time even though she had only arrived in the yard in March. She had been deemed not quite ready to come with the rest of the Juddmonte juveniles a few months earlier.

Fetherstonhaugh was the ideal groom for the filly as she was far from straightforward. Tall but noticeably weak still, she would be reluctant on occasion to do what was asked of her during and after her exercise. This would manifest itself in several ways, notably her tendency to plant herself when asked to return to her box. It's not an uncommon trait for a horse and neither is it unusual for a groom to resort to a bit of force to resolve the situation.

Such tactics were always deplored by Cecil, who would have been reassured by Fetherstonhaugh's approach. Like all instinctive horsemen, and there are not as many as one might imagine working in racing stables, he had the skills that gained Passage Of Time's respect and trust. He didn't ride her 'too short', a style adopted by some stable staff wanting to emulate the professional jockeys. Neither did he try to grab hold of her head by resorting to overly tight reins. Consequently, and vitally, he didn't tug with undue force at the filly's mouth. Instead, he helped Passage Of Time build up trust in her rider, which would in turn enable her to learn and flourish through the process of becoming a racehorse.

'Shane had a kind nature,' says Jane. 'He was relaxed and used to ride with a nice length of leg. It was natural, he seemed to have an affinity with every horse he rode. Passage Of Time was a bit wayward; she definitely had a mind of her own. Until Shane started riding her, people used to have trouble getting her on the canter or even back into her box after exercise. He'd rather give her a pat than a kick or a slap. She responded to that better.'

Cecil always liked her. Very early on in her career he felt she had the makings of a Group-race filly. The very first morning I went with him on the gallops, Passage Of Time, then a once-raced maiden, impressed in her work. To my inexperienced eye it wasn't flashy exercise. But something, perhaps the easy athleticism behind the saddle, triggered an excited response in her trainer. On the other hand Fetherstonhaugh had concerns surrounding her attitude shown in fast work.

'Never, at any stage, could I remember her being a good work horse. She was just workmanlike,' he says. 'But Henry had that knack – he could see. I used to question it myself sometimes, especially with her. She'd get upsides her lead horse and wouldn't put her head in front. That would be her, but Henry always believed in her, he'd seen something. Maybe the way she moved, he could just see she was going through the motions.

'Very seldom was he wrong about a horse, what he expected of them. You'd be riding them and questioning him. After a horse had galloped, in your head you'd be thinking, "This just galloped all right, nothing special," and he'd be brimming: "This is a nice horse . . ." You'd go along with it but in the back of my mind, I'd be thinking, "He's got this one wrong – I don't think this is as good as he thinks." But they turn out to be. After a while you don't question it any more. You just go with whatever he says.'

Even Cecil will have been somewhat disheartened after Passage Of Time was well beaten on her debut at Yarmouth in a seven-furlong maiden, a race in which she was sent off the 15/8 favourite. 'She was disappointing first start,' remembers David Lanigan. 'We thought she'd win.' The bookmakers again chalked her up as favourite at Newmarket in mid-August. This time she justified her market position, narrowly winning for jockey Ted Durcan.

'She just scraped home,' says Fetherstonhaugh. 'It wasn't until her following run when she bolted up in a fillies' Listed race [the Montrose Stakes at Newmarket] that it just suddenly all came together for her. Richard Hughes rode and he came in and straightaway said she was an Oaks filly: "She stays all day, just wants to keep galloping."'

The five-length win came in late October at Newmarket's final meeting of the season. Prices for the following season's Oaks were bandied around and that was expected to be that for the year for Passage Of Time. 'She'd had three runs, plenty enough,' says Fetherstonhaugh. But a race for the French title between her owner Prince Khalid and His Highness the Aga Khan led to Cecil being persuaded to run the filly in the Group 1 Critérium de Saint-Cloud staged just two weeks later on Sunday 12 November. Entry for the race had already closed but it had a 'supplementary' stage that enabled connections to pay a significant stake and secure a late berth. All of a sudden Passage Of Time was bound for France,

'Passage Of Time won the Montrose and in normal circum-stances she would probably have been put away,' explains Lord Grimthorpe, the racing manager to Prince Khalid. 'We were in a very close battle with the Aga Khan and I said to Henry, "We're looking for troops to go to raid France — what about if we run this filly in the Group 1?" I think if it had been five years earlier or five years later Henry would probably have said, "No . . . this is a really nice filly, we're going to put her away for the Oaks." But in terms of timing, and because he understood that Prince Khalid had helped him considerably, he liked the idea.'

The same could not be said about her rider Richard Hughes. He simply couldn't understand the decision to run. There wasn't just one reason why he felt it was a bad call – more like a handful. 'She won quite well in Newmarket and I thought we'd have a nice filly for the following year; she was still a little bit weak,' says Hughes, one of the most successful British-based jockeys of his time. 'But I was highly surprised when he said he was running her in France. I thought he'd gone mad! Her coat was gone and I didn't think she'd be strong enough and we were taking on the colts. To be honest, I thought it was going to be a waste of time. If I'd had anything to do with it she wouldn't have been running. I just thought it was a huge, big shot in the dark before I went over.'

Saint-Cloud is half an hour to the west of Paris and accompanying Fetherstonhaugh on the trip there was Michael McGowan. The travelling head man was another relatively new recruit to the Warren Place staff and needed a little more persuasion to join than his colleague did. McGowan had been working for another trainer in the town and heard all the chat on the Heath that it wouldn't be long before Cecil finished for good.

'I had to ask him, was he going to pack in, retire?' says McGowan, a Liverpudlian raised in Fazakerley not far from Aintree, the home of the Grand National steeplechase. 'He said he never would. "I'll never be champion trainer again but I want to train nice winners."'

They were the words McGowan wanted to hear. He felt reassured. But, in accepting the position, McGowan had his own challenge with which to deal. His natural shyness around Cecil early on, especially at the races, was something he had to overcome, despite having acquired extensive experience with prominent trainers such as Barry Hills and Peter Chapple-Hyam. 'I grew up and Henry was champion trainer year after year after year,' says McGowan. 'He was more of a legend than an employer. I did get nervous that first six months, saddling up with him, but he taught me a lot. He made me a better person.'

Days such as the one in France were what McGowan signed up for. They were also what Cecil had been striving for: the opportunity to saddle a winner at the highest level. He and Jane flew out early that Sunday morning to join up with the advance party. There were to be thirteen runners in the mile-and-a-quarter contest; the biggest field since it had been upgraded to Group 1 status in 1987.

Only one filly had won it in the previous nineteen renewals and in 2006 many of the shouts around the course's overnight stabling block were about an imposing colt trained by Aidan O'Brien called Soldier Of Fortune. 'They thought it was their Derby horse,' says McGowan. Indeed, the following summer Soldier Of Fortune did turn out to be a Derby winner, albeit in Ireland after being well beaten at Epsom. But it wasn't to be his day in Saint-Cloud.

The group for lunch included top Irish trainer Dermot Weld, due to run Consul General in opposition to Passage Of Time later that afternoon. He was accompanied by his son Chris who, it turned out, was an ardent Henry Cecil fan. If that was a good omen, so too was Hughes's reaction on gauging the condition of the track at Saint-Cloud. 'I had it in my head that the ground was going to be very soft and it turned out it wasn't,' he says. 'It was really nice ground.'

Getting Passage Of Time out onto the racecourse, however, was proving problematic. She had always been a filly with a strong sense of her own individuality, which can be a positive for a racehorse. But in this instance she took exception to an archway that the horses had to go through in the preliminaries. Her old habit of simply digging her heels in when she didn't fancy going somewhere had resurfaced at just the wrong time.

'She was tricky enough, a bit of a madam,' says Fetherstonhaugh. 'She wouldn't walk into the parade ring. You walk through a little archway and she wouldn't go through. She stood there, planted herself. We ended up saddling her outside the parade ring and eventually got her in. She had to turn around and we walked her in backwards.'

It would have been a long way for connections to have travelled for Passage Of Time not to go to post. But in the end she consented, with Cecil showing his renowned touch with fillies. She responded to Cecil's sympathetic encouragement. 'Henry was mollycoddling her,' recalls Fetherstonhaugh.

The short-priced favourite at 13/10 for the race was the French-trained Spirit One. He deserved his lofty spot in the betting, having been beaten by just a head in a Group 1, the one-mile Critérium International, a fortnight earlier. Passage Of Time, though, wasn't far behind in the market. The manner of her Montrose Stakes success clearly had captured the punters' imagination. Accordingly, she was a 16/5 shot, coupled with Prince Khalid's other runner, Consul General, who was facing a distinct step up in class after winning a maiden contest in Ireland on his only other outing. Passage Of Time was joined in the race by just one other filly, the German-trained Meridia.

While Soldier Of Fortune was touted as O'Brien's hope for the following year's Derby, it was his other runner, Red Rock Canyon, who showed in front early on. Spirit One soon took up the running and Passage Of Time, although relatively prominent, was settled in fifth spot – one place behind Soldier Of Fortune. As they forged on up the straight, Hughes appeared to be sat suffering with no clear run for Passage Of Time to deliver her challenge. Conversely, Soldier Of Fortune had no such problems and grabbed the lead off Spirit One with just over a furlong to go. It seemed as if the big Derby prospect would deliver. But crucially, the race was about to open up for Hughes and Passage Of Time.

'I rode her very patiently and had nowhere to go at one particular point in the race; probably the most important time I had nowhere to go,' says Hughes. 'So I left her where I was until the gap opened, rather than switching course. She wasn't a filly that was going to take much of a bang, so to speak, in among the colts. I couldn't have made room on her, put it that way – she was too slight. I bit my lip, waited for my gap and it came. She came through lovely.'

According to the form book, Passage Of Time burst to the front with 150 yards to go and went on to prevail by three-quarters of a length from Soldier Of Fortune. McGowan stood watching the action unfold, close to the O'Brien travelling team. He chuckles when recalling those decisive moments. 'She'd skipped away coming up the straight. After the race their head lad turned round to me and he went, "Where did you get her from?" They couldn't believe it.'

Up in the stands, Jane McKeown could hardly contain her pleasure and pride in her partner's achievement. Her faith in him and his ability during the dark days had been vindicated. 'Richard did give her a lovely ride, but it wasn't an on-the-line race,' she says. 'You could just see that Passage was going to win. I was just jumping all over the place! Henry didn't really show a lot of emotion in a race, and I can't say that he really did that day. Obviously he was really pleased but he was controlled and composed.'

For Cecil it was his first Group 1 victory since Beat Hollow landed the Grand Prix de Paris in 2000. Passage Of Time: the horse could not have been more aptly named. For Lord Grimthorpe, whose idea it was to approach Cecil about swiftly backing up the filly after her Newmarket win, there was great satisfaction and no doubt a little relief. Victory ensured his boss Prince Khalid secured the French owners' title for the year.

In the barren years no owner had shown more belief in Cecil than the Prince. The 2006 *Horses in Training* publication confirmed that. Cecil had fifty-five horses listed and seventeen belonged to Prince Khalid. Passage Of Time wasn't even among the seventeen as she had not arrived at Warren Place when the list was submitted. Her rise and victory in France vindicated her owner's steadfast allegiance.

THE TRIUMPH OF HENRY CECIL

'The fact she'd done it gave a huge boost to the yard. It was Henry back,' says Lord Grimthorpe, an avuncular man known as Teddy to all his friends and colleagues. 'I never doubted his hunger, his sheer determination. Prince Khalid never had any great worries about him. We had lots of conversations about the wellbeing and everything of Henry, of course we did. But in terms of doubting, I don't think so. Certainly I never heard anything to say, "We're not going to send horses there." Nothing like that ever occurred.'

Then there was Richard Hughes, who had thought the whole trip was a lost cause from the outset. But it ended up giving him an opportunity to show his skill in the saddle with one of those perfectly timed rides that would become his trademark on the big days for trainer Richard Hannon. And Group 1 wins don't come along all that often – even if, for Cecil, it once must have felt as if they did. Hughes knew the importance of this one for the trainer. 'It was definitely the turning point,' he says.

The victory was one to savour too for Fetherstonhaugh. He had begun the year mulling over whether to finish with horseracing, but as the 2006 flat season drew to a close, he was leading up a Group 1 winner.

There's a deep sense of satisfaction around such moments for racing people. Hard work doesn't guarantee you success in racing. So on those rare occasions when everything slots into place the warm glow it triggers is justified.

Fetherstonhaugh saw his own pleasure at the success reflected in Cecil when they spoke after the post-race presentation. 'It just looked like a big winner, his first Group 1 in years,' says

Fetherstonhaugh. 'He's brought a filly over and she'd won with her ears pricked. And he's just won the Prince the championship. He was so happy – it mattered, big time.'

Cecil made sure his men weren't forgotten in the hubbub. It was a time for gratitude and he marked it in generous if slightly comical fashion, albeit in keeping with his own unusual style. 'What's always stuck in my mind, Henry came down to the yard afterwards and gave me and Mick fifty quid each,' says the groom. 'He told us to go have steak and chips . . . "Go and have a good steak!"'

That day meant much to Jane. She remembers it, of course, for Passage Of Time's victory and what it meant for Henry Cecil and Warren Place. But she also treasures it for his words at the end of that long, long day. Touchingly he chose to thank her. He said that it wouldn't have happened without her. 'I obviously laughed it off as I laugh it off now as well,' she says, dismissing the whole notion out of hand. Yet rewind eighteen or so months and it's hard to imagine such an outcome had Jane not returned to offer the stability and encouragement Cecil so badly needed. Similarly, if he had been alone when told of his cancer earlier in 2006, would he have responded with such unrelenting positivity? One thing is certain: having Jane alongside him to enjoy that special afternoon mattered to Cecil. He wanted her to be part of it.

It was why he woke her at the crack of dawn the next morning, rushing into their bedroom with the paper. He wasn't especially interested in the report about Passage Of Time. Much more important to him at that moment was that the picture accompanying the jubilant post-race scenes included Jane. 'That gave him a lot of pleasure,' she smiles. It was confirmed in black and white: they were now a winning team on the racecourse as well as off it and that photograph captured the moment perfectly.

It wasn't only Cecil who was inundated with congratulatory messages the next morning. When his lads rode out, they were whooped by staff from other strings on the Heath. 'People were saying, "Well done with your filly,"' says Fetherstonhaugh. 'Of course, it gave everyone a lift. You go out on the Heath and you're proud. We were back.' While stables sometimes pay lip-service to one another's big wins, this was one time that the shouts and goodwill messages were heartfelt.

Just as he was popular among the racing public, Cecil was looked upon in an often affectionate and just about always respectful manner by Newmarket's racing folk, a fair few of whom had worked for him over the decades. Even many of the whisperers and gossips who had written him off in previous years were chuffed. Mind you, they were also probably the same ones who were claiming that morning they had never lost faith in the guv'nor . . .

Back at Warren Place, Ed Vaughan dropped by the breakfast room to offer his congratulations. The phone never stopped ringing as they tried to find a few minutes to share a coffee and a chat. Cecil replaced the telephone on its handset and turned to Vaughan with something of a sheepish expression on his face.

'All Henry kept saying was, "I'm so embarrassed . . . I'm really embarrassed it has taken me so long to win a Group 1 again,"' says Vaughan. 'But he was so chuffed and he knew he was back. That filly just really lit him up. I'll never forget that day. I learned my biggest lesson in life, which was never to give up. It was the beginning of the greatest comeback that I feel anybody had witnessed in the history of the sport.'

It was always the ritual at Warren Place for the flag with the family coat of arms to be hoisted whenever the stables recorded a Group 1 success. At times during the 1980s and 1990s Cecil might as well have just left it up, so often was he saddling top-class winners. But that Monday, after such a lengthy period in storage, it's understandable if there was the odd crease or two on the Horn of Leys. Indeed, Cecil himself was quick to make a joke about the flag during one of that long line of calls he received. 'There's not much breeze here this morning, and it looks rather like a damp dishcloth,' the *Independent* reported him as saying in an article published on 14 November.

It was a classic Cecil line. The article was very upbeat. 'We're all very optimistic for next year,' he added. Of course, on the face of it, this was exactly the sort of talk you would expect in such circumstances. Passage Of Time was now the favourite for the following year's Oaks and an increased yearling intake meant Cecil was closing in on a string size of eighty, markedly up from the start of 2006.

Yet there was no mention of his illness due to the fact that he was still all but keeping it to himself. Between July and October, he had six cycles of R–CVP treatment but it had brought about only a partial response. Just two days after Passage Of Time's heartening success, Henry Cecil walked into hospital to start receiving a different chemotherapy-based drugs combination.

Chapter Five

'Three cheers for Henry'

David Lanigan succinctly sums up Henry Cecil's response to chemotherapy treatment: 'He was as hard as nails.' The Warren Place assistant admits he was worried at the outset about how his boss would react to his illness. After all, Cecil had previously taken himself off to bed for days when he had the flu. Lanigan wondered if he would ever see him once treatment started – but it turned out the opposite was the case.

The trainer used to attend first and second lot on the dates when he was scheduled for outpatient treatment. First thing the next day, he would be back in the yard. Lanigan would occasionally forget and greet him with a breezy 'Morning!' only to receive a somewhat sharp reply. 'You had to remind yourself that he had chemotherapy yesterday,' says the Irishman.

In November and December 2006 Cecil was given fludarabine, adriamycin and dexamethasone, a drug combination known as FAD. In general, he didn't complain. He just got on with his work even if he was suffering from the effects. But that winter there was one early morning when he called on Lanigan for assistance as the horses were limbering up inside the covered ride.

'He was leaning up against the door while they were doing their trot and said to me, "Get the car". His legs felt like jelly. He told me one day his whole body would feel like jelly the day after he'd had the chemotherapy.'

Overall, Cecil took his treatment very well. Of course, it would have an impact but he forced himself to push on, push through. 'The most important thing is that every day you think happy thoughts, put the bad stuff behind – and you get up,' he told Lanigan. 'The more sleep you get the more you need.'

Quietly Cecil had begun to let people know about his illness. It wasn't something about which he made a fuss. If anything, the suggestion was that it was an irritation rather than a life-threatening disease. 'I've got this thing in my stomach. It's being reduced, we'll beat it,' he said one day to Lord Grimthorpe.

Towards the end of the winter the media were told about Cecil's cancer via a statement. The trainer made it clear that it was going to be business as usual. In fact, his stable strength had greatly benefited from 2006's successes, which was reflected by the Warren Place horses-in-training card. This was the under-stated but still faintly stylish small booklet that Cecil produced for stable connections at the start of the season. Its front page carried his silks; predominantly pink with two vertical white stripes and grey cap. Under the silks were the names of the stable's key personnel, while the horses for that year were listed inside on the folded card.

The booklet had been restored for 2007 after several seasons of dormancy. Its publication was another indication that Warren Place was once again on the up. The card detailed more than eighty horses, close to doubling the number from eighteen months or so earlier. The key drafts from Juddmonte Farms and the Niarchos family had increased, while the size of the support from Gerhard Schoeningh's Ennismore Racing was also significant. Plantation Stud and Ballygallon Stud were two other welcome additions to the yard. There was a host of horses to excite Cecil as he started preparations for the new season. 'That year, we went into it thinking we could do anything,' says Lanigan, summing up the confidence that once again had begun to sweep through Warren Place.

'Henry had realised things were swinging around,' says Ted Durcan, whose name was one of two stable jockeys referenced on the front page of the Warren Place card. 'His eye was in and he was enthusiastic. People like André Fabre, Michael Stoute and Henry Cecil, they need nice horses to have them interested. These potential stars are what make their enthusiasm tick. It gets the mind going; the plotting, the planning.'

Cecil's starting point was to take his string to the Waterhall grass gallop, a fairly remote exercise ground that the big stables only tend to use in early spring before the adjoining Limekilns opens. He visited Waterhall twice for what he termed 'sensible work'. The Al Bahathri was Cecil's other favoured destination for his gallopers that March and early April as ideas began to formulate and crystallise in his mind. 'The horses are on the whole coming along nicely and hopefully we will have our first runners around Craven week,' he wrote in a set of notes for the website. 'Overall, I'm happy with things and looking forward to the season.'

Craven week is a colloquial reference for fixtures that take place at Newmarket and Newbury just after the middle of April.

The Craven meeting is staged over three days at Newmarket followed by the two-day spring meeting at Newbury. Both offer opportunities for older horses as well as early season Classic trials. Just as importantly for Cecil, the meetings also provided a range of maidens and the odd handicap that allowed him to weigh up his three-year-olds.

With another winter behind them and their first pieces of exercise done, he would already have a very good idea of the pecking order within Warren Place, but the meetings at Newmarket and Newbury allowed him to evaluate their ability when pitted against the strings from across the town and beyond. 'That was why he felt it was vital to get so many of his horses out that week,' says Stephen Kielt. 'It really allowed him to finalise his plans at an early juncture.'

Cecil would say to his farrier: 'There's no point in me thinking of a Derby prep if the horse isn't good enough or thinking of a handicap if he's better. I need to get out and see where we are.'

Aside from the plotting for the weeks and months ahead, there were personal challenges around that spring. Cecil had to put up with his first inpatient stint just before Warren Place's season got underway. He told Lanigan that his upcoming treatment would be like having 'a bomb in the middle of the tumour . . . it explodes and kills everything'. The trainer returned after a few days away and went straight back to work, determined not to be kept from his work for a minute longer than he needed to be.

Around that time, Lanigan was reading Lance Armstrong's book, which detailed the cyclist's cancer battle. The Warren

'Why should I retire just because people think I should?' Cecil pictured in the author's first interview with him in May 2006. *(Chris Bourchier)*

Cecil pictured in his beloved rose garden at Warren Place in 2006. *(Chris Bourchier)*

Jockey Ted Durcan in full cry as he boots home Light Shift in the 2007 Oaks. *(Steve Cargill)*

Three cheers for Henry! Emotional scenes in the Epsom winner's enclosure after Light Shift's Oaks victory – Cecil's first in a Classic for seven years. *(Steve Cargill)*

David Lanigan – Cecil's assistant at Warren Place for six seasons, until 2007.
(Hugh Routledge / REX / Shutterstock)

Jane and Henry Cecil at the Tattersalls Yearling Sales in Newmarket. The couple were married in June 2008. *(Chris Bourchier)*

Twice Over and Tom Queally head to the winner's enclosure after the 2009 Champion Stakes. Near side, travelling head man Michael McGowan keeps step. *(Steve Cargill)*

Groom Shane Fetherstonhaugh congratulates Midday after her Yorkshire Oaks victory at York in 2010. 'She was a tough hardy mare – she never shirked,' says Fetherstonhaugh. *(Steve Cargill)*

Frankel's debut on a soaking wet night in August 2010 at Newmarket; he just gets the better of Nathaniel. The pair would meet again in their final race more than two years later. *(Steve Cargill)*

Cecil with the author (to his right) and members of the media at a gallops event in Newmarket. Cecil said he was always happy 'to do my bit' to promote major race days. *(Chris Bourchier)*

People ran to the winner's enclosure to greet Frankel after his breathtaking victory in the 2,000 Guineas. 'That's when you know you've got a good one, a special one; people run,' says Michael Prosser, Newmarket's director of racing. *(Steve Cargill)*

Prince Khalid Abdullah and Henry Cecil at Newmarket – 'It was a friendship,' says the Prince's racing manager Lord Grimthorpe. 'They got on tremendously well.' *(Chris Bourchier)*

Stephen Kielt was one of many members of staff who played a key part in the Warren Place revival. As well as his farrier duties, Kielt made the most of his time working alongside Henry Cecil. *(Tony Rushmer)*

Henry and Jane enjoying the famed Warren Place roses on the weekend in June 2011 that the trainer's knighthood was announced. Cecil was hosting a charity event in his garden that day.
(Chris Bourchier)

Place assistant was struck by how weakened Armstrong became during his extensive chemotherapy cycles. That brought into sharp focus for Lanigan how Cecil seemed to be shrugging off the treatment he had just received in hospital. 'They told him to take it easy; he was out at first lot the next day.'

For all of Cecil's anticipation, it hadn't been plain sailing with the horses either. Multidimensional encouraged with his early work and Cecil had in mind a Group 2 for him at the Craven meeting. But the Niarchos family's colt, aged four at that stage, suffered a stress fracture, which would require a long convalescence programme.

There was better news for the same owner regarding a three-year-old filly called Light Shift, a maiden winner the previous campaign. There had always been something of a buzz about her. She was a Niarchos homebred by their very influential sire Kingmambo, himself the first foal out of the brilliant miler Miesque. Light Shift's mother was Lingerie who was out of the Niarchos's Prix de Diane (French Oaks) winner Northern Trick.

Lingerie was already doing well as a broodmare and, as with Passage Of Time, Cecil had a good knowledge of her family. He had previously trained a couple of her daughters with some success. One of the pair, Shiva, triumphed in a Group 1 in Ireland in 1999, while a year later her sibling Burning Sunset was also a winner for Warren Place.

Cecil had seen Light Shift as a yearling when Maria Niarchos commented that the filly could be an Oaks prospect for him. It was a remark of exceptional foresight and, according to Alan Cooper, one that outlined the understanding that existed between the owner-breeder and trainer. 'That's a Henry horse,' was Maria's feeling and so, when they were allocating young stock to their roster of trainers, Light Shift was duly sent to Warren Place.

She was always a very capable and athletic filly, allowing Cecil to get on with her training relatively early as a two-year-old. In late June 2006, she was second on her debut over six furlongs at Newmarket and finished third at the same course the following month. The runs were encouraging enough but left something of a question mark as to the level she might one day reach.

Cecil decided to give her a short break and only brought her back for one more run that season, in the second half of September. He also stepped her up in distance to a mile for a fillies' maiden at Newmarket. Light Shift was the 15/8 favourite and won by half a length.

'In true Henry fashion he gave her some experience,' says Cooper. 'She won on her third start but he didn't over-face her at two because the family on the maternal side was more three-year-old and older.'

The trainer's call to back off rather than go for a grander prize at the back end of the season was typical of his training style, and it showed that his touch was back. There was no rush. Instead, he was already imagining the type of filly she would become with another winter behind her. Light Shift is an example of Cecil's sympathetic approach to his work and his patience with her would be rewarded in spades.

Sure enough she was ready when Cecil began priming his first wave of runners for the 2007 season. He had her inked in to start off her campaign at Newbury's opening day, Friday 19 April. Stablemates Phoenix Tower, Brisk Breeze and Tempelstern were also due to run there and it would turn out to be a very satisfactory afternoon.

Light Shift's first race of the year had been a bone of contention between Cecil and Lanigan. She was rated 81, a figure that they both knew was a major underestimation of her talent. Lanigan and Light Shift's jockey Ted Durcan were keen to go for a handicap, while Cecil wanted to test her against better horses in a mile-and-a-quarter conditions race – which was where she ended up.

'At the time Ted and I were into just getting winners on the board,' says Lanigan. 'We were both there going, "This filly will run well, be placed and she'll go up to 95." She went and pissed up!'

Durcan rode her differently to how he had done as a two-year-old. He held her up towards the rear through much of the race, whereas previously she had been asked to take a more prominent early position. The combination of those tactics and the increase in distance, along with the fact that she had improved with age, resulted in an impressive final two furlongs. The 7/1 shot ran on in great style, leaving her seven rivals behind her to win by a length and a quarter.

'The way she won at Newbury was very exciting,' says Cooper. 'It gave me the feeling that we did have something; that she was going to go up the ladder. It was a very exciting spring.'

On the same card, Phoenix Tower made it two wins from two career starts with a four-length romp in a handicap while

Tempelstern and Brisk Breeze both finished second. Warren Place had picked up where it had left off the previous season with Passage Of Time, who had wintered as the Oaks favourite. There was real momentum and everyone in the team could sense it, not least Cecil.

'The horses have run well and shown promise,' he wrote at the very end of April. 'They should improve from their races and quite a few have indicated that they will benefit from a slight step up in trip. Light Shift ran a good race at Newbury and hopefully she will be able to have a tilt at the Cheshire Oaks.'

The Cheshire Oaks is an Oaks trial but Listed-class status conveys that it's not as strong in that capacity as the Group 3 Musidora Stakes at York, for example. Even so, it was a definite rise in class for Light Shift who was the 11/8 favourite in the eleven-runner field at Chester. With the left-hand turning nature of the track and the race distance being only half a furlong less than the mile and a half of the Oaks, 9 May's assignment was going to be a proper test of Light Shift's credentials.

Once again she was ridden by Durcan. The man from County Mayo was also her regular partner in fast work at home and had developed an excellent understanding with the filly. This was highlighted when he gave her a peach of a ride at Chester, even if those connected to her experienced a few moments of concern during the race.

Early on Light Shift was held up towards the back of the field, some distance off the frontrunners. Durcan knew what made her tick by this stage, conscious that she might be tempted to over-race if she travelled in the pack. Unlike Passage Of Time she was the opposite of a lazy type. Her tendency was to want to do too much too soon, especially if she was immersed in the hurly-burly of a race. Durcan was very mindful of such a possibility and was content to drop her out, allowing her to switch off and travel smoothly into her race. It made perfect sense and shows the rider's horsemanship as well as his tactical nous.

With Cecil absent at Chester, the stable was represented by Lanigan. As the field made its way onto the back straight of the sharp track, the assistant trainer was feeling none too optimistic about Light Shift's prospects. In his opinion it looked as if she had an awful lot to do to get competitive. 'I thought, "This is going to be lapped . . . can't win from there, no chance." '

It all felt very different to the man in the saddle. Durcan was getting all the right signs from Light Shift and wasn't overly worried about his position in the race. He had preserved her energy. Durcan was confident that he would get the right response when he chose to ask the question of the filly. And the rider was right.

The home straight at Chester isn't long and it helps if you're on a nimble-footed and agile horse, just like Light Shift. Durcan delivered her with a perfectly timed challenge and the pair sped round the final turn. A cluster of rivals were fighting it out upfront approaching the last furlong but Light Shift arrived on the scene with purpose to pip the lot of them. The victory margin was three-quarters of a length.

'When Light Shift went to the Cheshire Oaks we really fancied her,' recalls Durcan. 'We thought it would suit her around there; she'd got a nice turn of foot and we thought everything was right. I never even gave her a smack that day. People said she flew home and was only up on the line. But she never looked like losing and she beat two really smart mares, one of Aidan O'Brien's called All My Loving and a Peter Savill-owned filly [Fashion Statement].

'People said, "Oh, you were a long way out of your ground on her." But she was one of those, after a hundred yards in a race, you had to just settle. If you went handy, she'd become lit up. She was a little bit out of her ground early on going round there but riding her I was never worried. She was going round hard-held, running away. I always thought I'd win. I pulled her out and off she went. If you watch the replay, I was hands and heels.'

Aside from the victory, the other key development from the day was that Cecil now had two serious contenders for the Oaks, which was to be run just over three weeks later on Friday 1 June. Light Shift had emerged as a 10/1 chance for Epsom, while Passage Of Time still headed the market at 3/1. The latter was due to make her seasonal reappearance the following week at York but Durcan was clear in his own mind about which of the two fillies he preferred for the upcoming Classic.

As Lanigan and Durcan returned south to Newmarket, the jockey was speaking to a journalist on the phone when the very subject came up. Durcan gave nothing away in the call but once he had hung up it was a different story. He turned to Lanigan and said: 'I know which one I'd like to ride.' And the name on his lips was not Cecil's ante-post favourite.

Durcan felt Passage Of Time had been slow to come to herself that spring. While a tall filly, in his eyes she was lean and hanging onto her winter coat. Lanigan also had negative thoughts about her condition. He recalls being almost 'border-line embarrassed' at the way she looked for her York date.

The 2006 Group 1 winner still carried Cecil's full confidence but his notes ahead of her seasonal bow in the Musidora Stakes were rather contradictory. 'Passage Of Time seems fine and working nicely. Although like last year she works on the lazy side.' Another worry emerged after she duly recorded a narrow win by a neck at York. Cecil referenced how Passage Of Time had a throat abscess, adding, 'they can be a nuisance'.

The main thing that day at York was she won. Her support-ers in and out of the stable were entitled to believe that the race would bring her on considerably for the Oaks just over a fort-night later. The onset of a bit of early summer sun wouldn't do any harm either. And if anyone could bring a filly to peak condition for the big day it was Cecil. He had already won the Oaks on seven occasions; Passage Of Time was in the best possible hands. Equally, so was Light Shift.

Friday 1 June, 2007, will always be a red-letter day for Ted Durcan. Funnily enough it was exactly two years on from when he had ridden his first winner for Henry Cecil. That was a horse called Akimbo in front of a weekday crowd at Yarmouth. Not long before that, Durcan had started riding work for Cecil, who was then deep into his slump.

By contrast the jockey, in his early thirties, was on the way up. He had been champion rider in the United Arab Emirates on multiple occasions and was steadily rising through the ranks in Britain too. His first two Royal Ascot winners arrived in

2005, while there was a Group 1 success that year aboard a Mick Channon-trained filly in France. Durcan's main early morning commitments in Newmarket were with the powerful Godolphin operation but he was pleased to add to his network and help out Cecil with the Warren Place gallopers.

'I very much enjoyed it,' says the jockey. 'Even in the lean years there was always four or five nice potential horses. You were just hoping he would unearth one just to help him out of it.

'It was great, great fun – always was, even the first year when there were no horses and we weren't having winners. Henry made it great fun. I was amazed how relaxed he was over everything. I loved being in his company. He had a lovely way with everyone. He was a natural charmer and had so much patience with everyone. Small little things that might annoy you, he could just let go over his head. He was just so likeable. That's why people were always willing to support him, even in the bad years.'

Durcan's work for the Warren Place cause was rewarded with an increasing amount of rides for Cecil. The jockey had become a key ally as the stable's resurgence gathered momentum. Now he had a chance in a Classic for the trainer, who was saddling two of the first four in the betting at Epsom.

Light Shift's big-race preparations hadn't passed without a hitch. She had an ankle joint flare up after her gallop the week before the Oaks. It was 'a big scare' according to Lanigan, and Cecil duly had to back off the filly for a few days. He was frustrated as he had been aiming to get one more piece of work into her. His concern at missing out on it will have been eased by the fact that Light Shift was a naturally fit individual who didn't need to do as much at home as other horses in the string.

The trainer woke even earlier than usual on the day of the Oaks. Not long after 4 a.m. he was in the yard with the tireless Lanigan who was doing his usual feeding rounds. Later that morning, he would head to Cambridge Airport and fly by heli-copter to Epsom along with Jane and his thirteen-year-old son Jake.

'Henry wasn't that keen as he'd once had a bad experience in a small aircraft,' recalls Jane. 'He told me how he'd seen the eyes of a pilot in another aircraft that had popped out of a cloud! So he looked a little nervous before the helicopter flight as did my sister Rita who came with us. But everything went smoothly and Henry was in good form as we flew across London.

'When we arrived at the racecourse the support for Henry was immediately evident. You could tell that so many people really wanted him to win. They kept coming up to let him know that they were rooting for him. I know he'd had all those lean years but you could just tell that the racing public still believed. Likewise, he received loads of good-luck messages beforehand – on my mobile phone as he barely ever carried one.'

Lanigan finished his morning stables duties before driving to Epsom with his fiancée Amy. Also travelling with the couple were Cecil's long-time book-keeper Joan Plant and Claire Markham, who had only started as the stable secretary a couple of months earlier. Lanigan was cautious about Passage Of Time and Light Shift's chances.

'When we got there Amy said to me, "It would be great if we had a winner, wouldn't it?" I turned round and said, "Fairy-tales don't happen in racing. The great thing is we got them here in one piece." I was saying it to myself to a certain degree.'

Lanigan may only have travelled in hope rather than confidence but he was sure of one thing: Light Shift would run well. He favoured her chances over Passage Of Time's, despite the Musidora Stakes raising hopes in the yard that perhaps she was one of those who upped her game at the racecourse. There have been many top horses over the years that have looked after themselves on the training grounds and then deliver when it mattered most on race day. Even so, Lanigan had no doubts over which of the pair he thought would fare best that afternoon around the unique challenge that is Epsom Downs Racecourse.

The left-handed layout is an extraordinary test of a horse's capabilities and has been for well over two hundred years. The first Oaks was staged there in 1779, a year before the inaugural Derby. Both races are staged over a mile and a half and require the winner to demonstrate a series of qualities, including tactical speed, stamina and balance. The bumper crowd and general hoopla, especially on Derby day, also ask stern questions of a horse's temperament.

Epsom starts with a lengthy climb from the starting stalls. There is a slight turn to the right after a couple of furlongs and it is important not to be shuffled too far back as jockeys seek a decent early position. The pronounced descent starts from around seven furlongs out, turning into the home straight at Tattenham Corner. What's left is an exciting run-in of just

under four furlongs in which the field must cope with a noticeable camber from right to left. Inside the final furlong is a slight
upward incline that calls on a horse to dig deep to have a chance
of being first past the post.

'Light Shift would put her heart on the line for you,' says
Durcan. 'She was just one of those genuine sweethearts. We
knew that Epsom wouldn't be an issue to her. If you watched
her go round Chester, I thought, "She's made for Epsom."

'The only thing about her was, and it was always in everyone's mind, she was kind of light framed and a little bit small.
You just wouldn't want to get in a barging match with her. The
other thing with her was, in other races, if anyone was upsides
her it would light her up, even in her homework. So you had
to be mindful she would go from nought to a hundred a little
bit faster than you wanted. Rather than go and get in the hustle
and bustle you'd be better off forfeiting maybe a few lengths but
getting a nice smooth run with her.'

Durcan felt that Light Shift came into the race somewhat
beneath the radar, her Cheshire Oaks form underestimated. But
in his mind she was a very definite contender, the first real 'live'
one he'd had for either of the Classics at Epsom. He had ridden
in two Oaks and two Derbies before but never threatened to
get a piece of it. The closest Durcan came was in the 2003 Oaks
when he had been aboard 100/1 outsider Thingmebob who
was eighth of fifteen, finishing just over five lengths behind the
winner Casual Look.

Always an intelligent rider, those previous experiences were
never going to be wasted on him. Along with his accumulated
knowledge of Light Shift, they will have been factored into his

pre-race planning along with Cecil's advisory words. True to form, the trainer kept it simple. He told Durcan that the good-to-soft ground would be ideal for Light Shift before adding that there was no need to be in any hurry early on. 'Just make sure you get her nice and settled going up the hill and then ride your own race,' said Cecil.

At the post Passage Of Time was the 9/4 favourite, while All My Loving – behind Light Shift at Chester – was next in at 5/1 alongside the John Oxx-trained Four Sins, who had won a Group 3 race in Ireland a fortnight earlier. Light Shift's price had fluctuated in the minutes prior to the race before she was sent off at 13/2. Cecil felt positive about Warren Place's chances as he stood on the steps close to the winner's enclosure. He was sufficiently confident in Passage Of Time and Light Shift to even suggest a forecast bet to Jane's sister Rita.

Also in the fourteen-strong field was a 20/1 shot called Peeping Fawn, trained by Aidan O'Brien. This filly was having her sixth run of the season and had been in action just the week-end before when placed in the Irish 1,000 Guineas.

When the starting gates flew open Durcan recalls how Light Shift broke 'like a rocket . . . going fifth gear'. The jockey remained unflustered and eased her back towards mid-pack as they made the ascent. On the face of it, Light Shift appeared to be a little wider than ideal but Durcan was focused on ensuring that his mount stayed free of traffic problems. Meanwhile Passage Of Time, ridden by Richard Hughes, was more promi-nent as she settled not far behind the heels of the early leaders.

'I got popped out a little bit wider than I wanted to be but she was a hundred per cent switched off, so I was happy where

I was,' says Durcan. 'She was travelling round and that's what you need. You don't handle Epsom if you don't travel well and I was travelling. The only thing that was in my mind was, "Don't get in a ruck with this filly." I knew she'd over-race.'

The early pace dropped to slower fractions as they closed out the opening half mile or so before the long descent. Durcan sensed that the pack was stacking up and kept his distance, aware that the inner was likely to be the haunt of a potential hard-luck story or two. Where Light Shift was positioned, he was always going to be able to dictate when he wanted to make his move, rather than having to wait for a gap to open up.

Passage Of Time was also where her backers would want her to be as they swung for home around Tattenham Corner. But it soon became clear that it was Light Shift who was going best of the Cecil pair. She had surged on the outer and had only two or three rivals in front just inside the final half mile. Light Shift was moving like a dream, almost too well in fact. So adeptly was she handling Epsom that she quickly mastered Four Sins and All My Loving and found herself in the lead. The concern was there were still about two furlongs to go and now she was the target for any potential 'closers' – those horses held up for a late challenge.

'Light Shift, with the revs up a little bit, has taken me there so smoothly,' says Durcan. 'All of a sudden I'm arriving at the two-marker or maybe inside; she's absolutely running away. In hindsight I got there a hundred yards earlier than I expected and wanted.'

From towards the rear emerged one fast-finisher, Peeping Fawn. She had not enjoyed the smoothest of passages but when jockey Martin Dwyer launched her she came with a withering run. It was a stunning move and for several seconds there was an inevitable look about it.

'If a stand was going to fall down, the Niarchos team might have caused it to,' laughs Cooper as he recalls the lung-busting roar that connections and the thousands of Cecil fans let rip with in the closing stages. 'The last five or six strides, if we could have brought the stand down shouting we would have! Where was that winning post?'

Up on the steps, not far from Cecil, stood David Lanigan. He had seen Peeping Fawn's blistering progress, processed it and come to the conclusion that it appeared to be one of those runs that results in the horse getting up on the line to score. Thrilling if you're connected to the chaser, agony if your horse is the one being hunted down. 'I remember thinking, "Please don't do that,"' recalls Lanigan in a quiet manner that is much more powerful than if he had volubly emphasised the point.

That afternoon his plea was answered. Peeping Fawn's bid was also slightly wayward. She edged across from the centre of the track and down the camber towards the inner. Perhaps the overall effort taken to get to within a neck or so of heading Light Shift had begun to take its toll. After all, it was Peeping Fawn's second Classic in the space of five days; tiredness was entitled to be kicking in.

'The excitement through the final furlong or so was almost unbearable, especially when Peeping Fawn loomed up,' says Jane. 'Light Shift was definitely smaller and you just feared Peeping Fawn brushing her to one side. But Light Shift showed just how gutsy she was – she relished the battle it seemed.'

The Niarchos's filly was re-energised when she felt the Irish challenger threatening her supremacy. Durcan got her organised for one last effort and, honest trier that she always was, Light Shift reasserted to win by a half-length.

'I think Light Shift was idling a bit because when Peeping Fawn arrived upsides her, I switched leads [changed her stride pattern] and off she went again,' says Durcan. 'At the line she was actually heading away from her. On that day, though Peeping Fawn ended up an absolute superstar, I don't think she would have ever beaten Light Shift. Light Shift was primed. Henry had her spot-on.'

Watching on from his eyrie on the top floor of the Queen's Stand was course commentator Richard Hoiles. He had called the dramatic conclusion to the race in astute fashion, pinpointing the head-to-head between two powerhouse operations – Warren Place and O'Brien's Ballydoyle stable. The fact that there was only Light Shift and Peeping Fawn fighting out the finish meant that Hoiles was able to present that narrative before declaring an eighth Cecil-trained winner of the Oaks.

It dawned on Hoiles that perhaps he had just witnessed a glorious last hurrah from Cecil. He also considered that it was rather apt that the runner-up that afternoon was the man destined to become as dominant a force in the sport as the Newmarket trainer had once been. Such thoughts were running through his mind as he spotted the two men way beneath him almost immediately after the race.

'Just before Light Shift came back in, Aidan O'Brien walked into the winner's enclosure and shook hands with Henry,' says Hoiles. 'I always remember that image – it was like the crossover of two dynasties in a way. It lasted, I don't know, a matter of seconds. It was wonderful, one of those where you can still see it in your mind's eye. You're aware of what's going to happen because of the way one moves to the other. They were slightly separate, it wasn't in a scrum. It was just a really magnificent moment. Actually, you thought that might be the full stop of the career really. I think most people did. You were penning those tributes for the final time. Journalistically, everyone writing stories was thinking of what a great finale to a career.'

There was a huge swell of emotion around the racecourse with the hub being the winner's circle where Light Shift had arrived. Cecil, in a dark navy suit over a pale yellow shirt that caught a shade in his tie, was the focus of everyone's attention. Close by was Jake, whose jubilation at the moment of victory was captured by a television camera.

If anyone ever doubted just how much Cecil meant to the sport of racing then it was reinforced that day. The respect he was held in by his fellow trainers was exemplified by O'Brien's handshake. As for the public, they roared a salute of 'Three cheers for Henry' ahead of the trophy presentation. Cecil's bottom lip wobbled.

Durcan had missed much of the celebratory scenes due to the obligatory weigh-in following the race. But the size of the achievement for all associated with Warren Place began to seep through him as he sat with winning connections in the post-race media conference that took place in a room at the foot of the grandstand.

'When you're looking at Maria Niarchos, Alan Cooper and Henry and how much it meant, that was special,' he says. 'That element was magnificent. When you're young and come into racing as a lad or work-rider, the people I'd have idolised then would have been all the legends. I'd never have dreamed I'd have a Classic winner for one of them.

'There are hundreds of better riders in weighing rooms around the world that are never lucky enough to win a Classic. To win one, you never expect that. So when it happened, great. But it was Henry's day and to be part of it was special.'

Cooper feels similarly and possesses several mementoes. He even bought a painting to commemorate Light Shift's victory, but it's not a portrait of the filly or a racing scene of her last-furlong duel with Peeping Fawn. It's a painting of a blue moon – fittingly, there happened to be one at the time of Light Shift's triumph. 'The once-in-a-blue-moon expression came through for us,' he smiles. For years Cooper even held onto the gipsy's lucky rose that he bought as he walked into Epsom. He kept it until it dissolved. Much more enduring are his memories.

'I'll never forget the joy Maria took from Light Shift winning the Oaks,' he says. 'She was just so happy for Henry to have won the race. There was the extraordinary "three cheers for Henry". Even now I get a frisson. It was such a confirmation of all the emotion that was around the winner's circle that day. Tears were in a lot of people's eyes.'

Back at Warren Place there was uncontained delight. Many of the staff had been glued to the television in a small room at the side of the canteen. Emotions were running just as high as they were a hundred miles away at Epsom.

'It was a room that was six feet by six – you'd be surprised how many lads you could fit,' says Dee Deacon. 'We all watched and, bar the race being absolutely fantastic, the most moving part was when Henry came to receive his trophy and the bottom lip went. That got us all. We had to take in a breath and swallow. Everybody was choked to see that because it meant so much. Not just to Henry, but to the whole yard. It was the stamp that said, "We're back!" '

Such a monumental result for the stable wasn't going to be allowed to pass without the lads savouring the moment. Once evening stables was finished they headed en masse to the Shoes, the stable-staff pub at the bottom of the hill into Newmarket. It was soon chocka and full of good cheer. In fact, there were so many lads that they spilled out onto the road. All of them were waiting, waiting. They knew that Cecil had to drive by that pub on his way home and they were keen to show their affection for him on such a landmark day for Warren Place. There was no way his car was going to be allowed to pass that early summer's evening.

'Everybody swamped it,' says Deacon. 'You'd think he was a movie star. We were cheering, shouting, applause, the lot. We were leaning through the window giving him a kiss. It was just fantastic. Then he drove away and he'd literally gone ten yards when he stopped the car. We thought, "What's the matter?" He reversed and dropped a load of money out of the window. "Go and get champagne, not beer, champagne!" So a couple of lads and I popped down Threshers [the nearby off-licence] and just bought them out of their champagne. And we toasted that man all night! That's the man he was.'

Back at the yard that night, however, one of Cecil's staff

needed consoling. For all of the elation that the Warren Place team was basking in, Shane Fetherstonhaugh's hopes had been shattered. Passage Of Time had finished eighth, some twenty-one lengths behind Light Shift. Her chance had been compromised by the lingering throat abscess. Cecil would later say that the filly 'couldn't really breathe'. It was a desperate disappointment to Passage Of Time's lad despite all the conjecture about the abscess in the build-up. That evening Fetherstonhaugh's emotions were in sharp contrast to those of his colleagues and also to how he had felt after Passage Of Time's victory in France the previous November.

'I know we'd won the race but I was probably the only one attached to the yard that was devastated,' he says. 'It was hard. You had to put on a brave face: "It doesn't matter, the other filly won." But it wasn't like that at all – I was gutted. She's trailed in, ran no race. I remember leading her back down the track and your world has fallen in. Everyone asked me to go out that night but I made my excuses.

'Henry came to see me the same night. He'd come down to the stable, I think Jane was with him. "Don't worry about it. We'll get her back. We'll have another day with her." How many other trainers would have done that? He'd just won the Oaks with the other filly and he went out of his way to come down and see me, the lad.'

Cecil was known for his sixth sense when it came to horses but his own life had taught him about the contrasting emotions that surrounded racing. The wave of pleasure that a victory can produce is a unique high. The sense of satisfaction is immense. Similarly, when things don't work out in a race, the disappointment is crushing. All that time invested, all that input, and for what? So that evening he understood Fetherstonhaugh's despair.

He experienced a range of feelings himself that long day. Firstly, there was professional satisfaction. After seven years he had managed to win a Classic again, the twenty-fourth of his career. The 'has-been' whispers had all but been dampened down the previous season but Light Shift's win reinforced that any Cecil runner on the big stage was once again a force with which to be reckoned.

The widespread delight at his resurgence also made an impression on him. When we sat in his rose garden on the Sunday morning, he told me that he was 'overwhelmed' by the public's reaction at Epsom and all the coverage in the media. It was almost as if he was mystified by the warmth extended towards him. 'He couldn't get his head round it,' recalls David Lanigan, who had brought in some newspapers carrying reports that were full of generosity towards Cecil. HURRAY FOR HENRY was the headline in the *Daily Mail* summing up the mood in the media.

'I said, "That's what you're thought of around the place,"' continues Lanigan. 'I don't think he actually knew.'

He may not have quite understood why he had such strong public support but he had certainly appreciated it that previous afternoon in Surrey. The trembling lip revealed how Henry Cecil felt inside.

'Henry undoubtedly was moved; he was close to tears,' says Jane. 'I think he might even have shed a tear. I don't think you'd ever seen him do that before. He'd won Oaks, Derbies, but that day did mean an awful lot to him.

'The emotion after the win was huge. To get to that point after all the obstacles and all the work that Henry and everyone at Warren Place had put in felt almost overwhelming. It was just phenomenal, really. I know Henry was thrilled to win but he was also relieved as there was a lot of expectation.

'He had been having treatment as well so there was a lot to take in on that day when you're not a hundred per cent anyway. You could sort of feel the love . . . actually sense how everyone was so pleased for Henry.'

His cancer fight made the victory all the more poignant. Certainly it added an extra dimension for the media in their coverage. Likewise, the public's pleasure was intensified by his bravery in the face of illness. Cecil didn't speak about his cancer that day so it's hard to estimate just how much consideration he gave it in among everything else that unfolded. His Oaks victory demonstrated one thing though: he was not going to let cancer get in the way of his work.

It was to prove a recurring theme.

Chapter Six

'I'm afraid I'm going to be around for some time yet!'

Light Shift would face Peeping Fawn twice more in the summer of 2007. On both occasions she ran with great credit but the Oaks runner-up was on a steep upward curve. The Epsom heroine finished second to the Aidan O'Brien-trained filly in the Irish Oaks and then third behind her in the Nassau Stakes.

If the order among the top-class three-year-old fillies changed that summer, so was there transition at Warren Place. The assistant David Lanigan was leaving with Henry Cecil's encouragement to become a trainer in his own right. He was to set up in Newmarket on the Hamilton Road, the other side of the town.

To Lanigan, life at Warren Place had become like working for family. It meant a great deal to him. Departing was a wrench for the Irishman, not least because he was concerned about doing so while his boss was struggling with cancer. The subject came up one afternoon when the two men were speaking in the trainer's study.

'I've got something on my mind, it's bothering me a bit,' said Lanigan. 'I haven't rented the yard yet, signed on it or anything like that. If you want me to abandon plans for another year or two I'm not going to leave you in the shit.'

Cecil had long known about Lanigan's ambition to train and wasn't about to let his own situation prevent his loyal right-hand man from moving on. He realised the time was right.

'No,' he replied. 'Everything is lined up for you to start. Nothing has changed on that. It has to happen this year.'

There was a further indication of Cecil appreciating Lanigan's years of enthusiastic work for the stable. When a press release was finalised with news of the Warren Place assistant striking out under his own name, Cecil insisted on calling journalists to offer his own glowing endorsement of Lanigan's skills. It was a personal touch: an element that Cecil offered with no calculation or angle. If he could support a friend then he always would. He and Lanigan would remain great allies in the years ahead. Often Cecil would drop in unannounced on the younger man for a coffee and a catch-up.

The assistant's role at Warren Place was taken on late in the 2007 season by Mike Marshall, who joined from Godolphin where he had been a head man. He was older than Lanigan and came with a lot of experience that included time as an apprentice jockey at Ian Balding's stables. Another key role in the yard had to be filled that year after the death of much-respected farrier Fred Wray: it was then that Stephen Kielt, a Northern Irishman in his mid-twenties, joined the Warren Place team.

He had come across to Newmarket in 2003 for an agreed two-year period, working for O. A. Curtis and Sons, a farriery business of long standing. Kielt was the son of a farrier and grew up loving horses. But it was only as he immersed himself into

life in Newmarket that he started to develop an endless fascination with racing stock.

That initial two years were never going to be enough to
satisfy his curiosity and in the autumn of 2007 he was excited to
be contacted about the opening at Cecil's. He had been working for David Elsworth, another Newmarket-based trainer,
when Marshall called him. The two men were previously
acquainted at Godolphin where Kielt had a short stint.

In due course Kielt went to meet Cecil for the first time. It
was to prove an illuminating and thrilling experience for the
young farrier. Like many before and others after, Kielt received
that extraordinary Warren Place baptism in the study. He was
swept along by the trainer's positivity and charisma.

'I want you to come and be part of the team,' Cecil told him.
'We used to be up here; then we were down here and had some
quiet years,' added the trainer with gesticulatory arm gestures to
illustrate the fluctuation in his fortunes. 'But I'm on the way
back. I want to win more Group 1s, more Classics. We're going
to attract new owners. Come and be part of it all. You look
after my good horses, and I'll look after you.'

Kielt didn't need to be asked twice. 'I can remember what he
said and how special he made me feel,' says Kielt.

Cecil duly included him in many aspects of stable life. The
farrier would attend just about every gallop morning, seeing not
only a host of top-class horses but also getting to study his
employer's methods. Kielt would go racing with him and be
privy to conversations between the trainer and his owners. 'It
was just an amazing time,' he says. 'I had this unique insight
into how he thought, how he worked, what he did.'

Marshall and Kielt were to prove two important and reliable additions to the growing number of staff that were once again required at Warren Place. Cecil had another new ally too; someone whom he would later refer to as his 'best friend'. The individual possessed a presence, a somewhat dignified bearing. In short, he had class. His name was Twice Over and he was another choicely bred horse from Juddmonte Farms. Cecil knew the colt's family very well. Like Passage Of Time his grand-dam was Quandary, while his mother was Double Crossed, who won for the trainer in Listed class as a three-year-old.

Cecil's affection for Twice Over began while he was a two-year-old and it would only grow through the six seasons he would spend in training at Warren Place. 'I love a broad, honest head with a good eye – he is blessed with these qualities,' he once wrote, summing up his admiration for the imposing-looking son of Juddmonte stallion Observatory.

Twice Over was given time to develop into his frame as a two-year-old. As a consequence, he didn't start off at the racecourse until lining up at Newmarket in early October 2007, appearing again at the same venue a month later. Cecil's charge created a very favourable impression when winning a maiden race on his debut and his reputation soared after he followed up with a victory in a mile-and-a-quarter conditions race. The manner of his wins, the obvious potential for significant physical progression and the fact that he was being tutored by Cecil resulted in him wintering as second favourite in the ante-post betting for the 2008 Derby.

Twice Over's twin successes helped Warren Place register forty-five victories on the domestic front for the 2007 season; twenty more than the previous year and almost four times as many as the 2005 nadir. Light Shift's earnings of £222,350 at Epsom was, of course, a hefty contributor to overall prize money of £732,000 but the strike-rate of 21 per cent was the best achieved by the yard since 2000 and demonstrated that Cecil's horses were running well across the board. Typically Cecil's end-of-season website notes barely referenced the triumphs of the previous months; he was already focused on what the future might offer.

'Next season we will hopefully have a potentially stronger team with an increase of around 20-something horses,' he wrote. 'This is a good manageable number and helps [us] to be more competitive. The yearlings are gradually coming in and quite a few are now ridden away. Feel there are going to be about 50 . . . and there are some very nice ones among them. As usual we are going to have more fillies than colts but nowadays this always seems to be the case.'

The winners were flowing and the size of the string was growing. No doubt about it, Henry Cecil was back. Not to the extent of his yesteryear dominance but he was once again recognised as a major player by the racing industry, the media and the public. Cecil's brightness about the prospects for the following season was fully understandable.

The marked upturn in the trainer's professional fortunes contrasted with a sizeable increase in concern for his health. On Tuesday 27 November of a year that delivered so much achievement, it was confirmed that he had suffered a relapse in his cancer fight. The mass behind his abdomen remained a challenge.

On 10 December he received a cycle of IVE chemotherapy treatment (ifosfamide, VP-16 [etoposide], epirubicin), which was repeated four weeks later. Halfway between the two, at Christmas, Cecil proposed to Jane. Their engagement was a ray of sunshine amid the toughest of times. There was only a minor response to the treatment, not enough to fulfil criteria for a 50 per cent reduction.

The quest to regain control in the face of the lymphoma led to radiotherapy treatment. In March 2008, he ventured abroad to the Mayo Clinic in Minnesota. After that a decision was made to treat Cecil with Zevalin, the trade name of a radio-labelled antibody, ibritumomab tiuxetan. But the months passed by and the light at the end of the tunnel was proving elusive: Cecil's disease was progressing.

The trainer remained stoic and optimistic. This was evident to Jane during their meetings with the consultant. If a treatment had not produced the hoped-for response Cecil wouldn't show any disappointment even if he felt it. Instead, he would swiftly be pressing for another solution, another course of action. 'He'd be, "Well, what are you going to do? There must be something else,"' recalls Jane. 'He wasn't prepared to accept that there wasn't anything. That was partly why he was receptive to me giving him a juice concoction – I'm a believer in juicing.'

After first lot, she would head to the Warren Place vegetable garden and dig up whatever organic produce was in season. Carrots, spinach, broccoli and asparagus were among the ingredients for a beetroot-based blend that she would make for Cecil every day. Visitors to the Warren Place breakfast table would notice him consuming the glassful, although not always without a grimace! The trainer still smoked – no longer indoors, now on the steps by the back door – and still drank more coffee than Jane probably wanted him to, but he was open to her suggestions regarding some dietary changes that could benefit his health.

Her care and support wasn't flashy but was practical and had substance. Plus, it was given in such a way that Cecil was comfortable with it. 'He didn't like a lot of sympathy, he didn't like being mollycoddled,' says Jane. 'I think he liked the fact that I did things for him but he didn't want me fussing around him like he was an invalid. I'm better at that approach anyway so it suited me as well.'

Cecil and Jane were married on 30 May 2008. A couple of weeks afterwards, the Saturday prior to Royal Ascot, family and friends were invited to attend a blessing at St Agnes Church on Bury Road. In his best man's speech, Gerhard Schoeningh referenced Jane's understated but effective style. 'Since Jane came back from Dubai she has been a tremendous support to Henry in her calm, unassuming way,' the racehorse owner at Warren Place told those assembled.

Schoeningh kindly sent me his speech, which is both respectful and witty. In it there's a particular story that conveyed much about the groom. Schoeningh noted that the trainer was always looking to amuse and had a 'seemingly endless supply of jokes and observations'. One that especially stuck in the German's mind revolved around Cecil's outlook when it came to his illness and enquiries regarding progress with treatment. 'I'm afraid I'm going to be around for some time yet!' would be the trainer's standard response, blending defiance and levity.

It was with a similar frame of mind that Cecil spoke to a large gathering of media on 8 October 2008, a week and a half before the Champion Stakes in which Twice Over would be the Warren Place challenger at Newmarket. It was my first year as the retained racing PR manager for the racecourse and I had found the role far more challenging than I had anticipated. Champions' Day was our final big meeting of the season. With key sponsors it was important that we delivered some strong build-up coverage. A gallops morning with Cecil was guaranteed to provide exactly that.

The day itself was an early autumn stunner. We gathered by the Al Bahathri around 7 a.m. – it was still just about dark. Barely half an hour or so later we had witnessed a couple of 'shots' of Cecil workers, listened to a string of his asides and the sun had emerged to light up a perfect Newmarket morning. Cecil had a captive audience after sending the horses back to Warren Place.

He shared thoughts about the season: 'On the whole the horses have run well . . . it would have been nice to have won at least one Group 1 by now.' The sixty-five-year-old also offered an insight on how he viewed the latest stage of his career: 'I've enjoyed it much more over the last two years than I have for years.' And Cecil gave a typically upbeat update on how he was confronting cancer. He referred to his ongoing chemotherapy as 'a nuisance' and explained that he hadn't won the battle, 'but you've got to keep positive'. At that point Cecil was being treated with gemcitabine and cisplatin, receiving two chemotherapy cycles during September and October.

There was a host of articles and some television coverage stemming from the morning. The newspaper story that resonated most with me was written by Paul Haigh in the *Racing Post*, 9 October 2008. It neatly summed up the mood in our party as we headed back for breakfast after enjoying the early morning in the company of Cecil: 'Off we shuffle, all of us glad we had been there, some reflecting that anyone who began to take an interest in racing just a decade ago would have no real understanding of how this man once bestrode it like a colossus; at least one thinking what a shame it is we so often waste the description "living legend" on people who are nothing of the sort.'

Cecil had been planning to run two horses in the Champion Stakes – Phoenix Tower alongside his younger stablemate, Twice Over. The four-year-old exercised on the media morning but days before the race his retirement was announced as a result of a tendon injury. It was the final setback in what was a luckless campaign for Phoenix Tower, who had come second in four Group 1s.

The season would also bring to an end Ted Durcan's time as Cecil's go-to jockey. When I spoke to Durcan about why the alliance finished, his reply was offered swiftly and with honesty: 'Too many seconds.' Phoenix Tower's name was brought up moments later by the rider, who was aboard him for the four runner-up finishes in 2008. In three of them the Juddmonte horse had gone down by less than a length. Indeed, the margin of defeat was just a short head at Sandown in the Coral Eclipse Stakes.

'Phoenix Tower lost a shoe halfway up the hill at Sandown,' said Durcan. 'I'm not making excuses, it's racing, but he was in front a stride before the line and a stride after the line. If he had won it might have been different. It might not have been, I don't know. But we had a year when we had a lot of nearly horses. They were nice horses but they weren't consistent Group 1 horses. For whatever reason, we were falling a little bit short.'

Tom Queally was asked to partner Twice Over in the Champion Stakes. He had just turned twenty-four. His initial ride for Cecil was in late 2006 and a strong working relationship developed as Queally became a regular on Warren Place work mornings. His first winner for the yard arrived the following season but it was in 2008 that he began to receive a series of high-profile opportunities for Cecil. For starters there was a spring success on Phoenix Tower in a Group race at Newmarket. After that, he would get a chance on other big bullets from the string such as Multidimensional, Many Volumes, Tempelstern and Tranquil Tiger. But the Champion Stakes was to be the first time he had ridden Twice Over in a race.

The colt had enjoyed a very good season without turning out to be the Classic contender the hype machine suggested he might become. He had won a Group 3 on his first start in 2008, beating Raven's Pass who would develop into a top-class horse in Britain and America. A first career defeat in the Dante Stakes at York on his next start meant there would be no Derby tilt. Instead, he dropped back in trip to finish third at Royal Ascot in the Group 1 St James's Palace Stakes, a race landed by the 2,000 Guineas winner Henrythenavigator.

Twice Over regained the winning thread in a Group 2 race at Maisons-Laffitte in midsummer. He would return to France as the favourite for another Group 2 contest at the end of August but finished seventh of eight. It might have appeared a tall order asking the horse to run in the Champion Stakes next time out. Twice Over, though, had no luck whatsoever on that trip across the Channel, twice being hampered in the race. Also Cecil knew that his horse was still maturing and improving. Hence Cecil wasn't afraid to give Twice Over the chance to prove himself against his elders in the prestigious Group 1 at Newmarket.

As it turned out, he ran exceptionally well in defeat to that year's Derby winner New Approach. Twice Over again didn't enjoy a straightforward passage but once in the clear he sustained a strong gallop to the line. He had signed off for 2008 by finishing a gallant second in one of British racing's showpieces. All in all it was a pretty encouraging end to Twice Over's season – and his relationship with the Champion Stakes had only just begun.

The 2009 season would bring a clutch of magnificent victories for a revitalised Henry Cecil. And revitalised is exactly the right word to describe the trainer, for the best result of the year for Warren Place wasn't one that arrived on a racecourse. The disease behind his abdomen was under control. He had come through a worrying winter in which he received radiotherapy. That, along with chemotherapy, had resulted in a sizeable reduction to the mass behind his stomach.

'He had an awful lot of therapy to get to a proper remission. Then he had a decent period of remission,' says Doctor Charles

Crawley, the clinical director for haemato-oncology at Addenbrooke's and the man who became Cecil's consultant in early 2008 after Rob Marcus took up a position at King's College Hospital in London.

Cecil never told me that he was in remission nor did he say that around the stable. But the facts were that, after a particularly gruelling stretch, he was definitely in a much more positive position health-wise, despite unsuccessful attempts to strengthen the situation with an autologous stem cell transplant in 2009. From June that year, his illness timeline shows how he started receiving rituximab maintenance. As outlined on www. lymphomas.org.uk, 'Rituximab is an antibody therapy given as maintenance treatment to people with advanced low-grade non-Hodgkin lymphoma who go into remission after chemotherapy.' Every few months for the next couple of years or so, Cecil would be given rituximab as his illness was kept in check.

Another development in the spring of 2009 was Jane's return to work on a full-time basis at Warren Place after she left her position at Godolphin. That June she was alongside Cecil as he recorded his first victory at Royal Ascot in seven years. Father Time, a full brother to Passage Of Time, won the King Edward VII Stakes by four lengths. It was the trainer's seventy-first success at the world-famous meeting.

Less than six weeks later, Cecil was on target at the highest level at Glorious Goodwood thanks to a talented filly called Midday. She had been beaten by a head in the Oaks that year but secured a deserved first triumph at Group 1 level in the Nassau Stakes.

Heavy rain blew in beforehand accompanied by a sea fret,

and Cecil was concerned about the ever-softening ground before opting to give the race a go rather than pull out at the last minute. Recalling the race preliminaries, Michael McGowan says, 'Henry was walking over with the saddle and one trainer turned round to him and said, "Does the filly run?" Henry has looked at him and looked at the saddle and just walked away!'

Aside from worries triggered by the inclement weather, the travelling head man's other recollection of the day was how Midday was not at her most amenable as she was boxed across from the Goodwood stabling block to the course. McGowan says she's 'probably the most difficult filly I've dealt with', and on that occasion wouldn't let him or her groom Shane Fetherstonhaugh reapply a piece of tack.

'She's trouble,' McGowan said to Cecil as they went about final preparations. Between them they saddled her in record time before she went and stormed to a comfortable victory. It was the first Group 1 winner that Queally rode for Cecil, but it would be far from the last that would be heard of Midday, yet another star performer from the Juddmonte Farms breeding business.

Just about everything was running smoothly at Warren Place. Except, that is, 2009's anticipated stable flag-bearer Twice Over appeared to be regressing. The likelihood of the now four-year-old colt fulfilling his sizeable potential was in some doubt. Approaching the end of the summer he was winless from four runs, albeit three of them were in top company.

The fourth race of his season, the Eclipse Stakes, was by far and away the most depressing for connections as he trailed in some seventeen-and-a-half lengths behind the magnificent three-year-old Sea The Stars, who was enjoying a stunning 2009. After the race at Sandown, questions were definitely being asked about Twice Over. 'We were perhaps starting to think he was just below what we hoped he was,' says Stephen Kielt.

But it wasn't that Cecil's charge had all of a sudden lost his appetite for racing – which is not that uncommon among race-horses from all ability levels. He wasn't struggling with his soundness either. There was no escaping the fact, however, that Twice Over wasn't delivering the results for which all at Warren Place had hoped. It was time for a rethink.

Twice Over had gone a year without a win and, while it's highly questionable how much any horse is aware of finishing first, he would certainly not have been in a position where he had been asserting his authority in a race. In the early part of his career Twice Over had got used to the experience of mastering his rivals. That was no longer the case. Twice Over was finding himself mastered by others and finishing behind them.

Cecil felt that the horse needed to find the winning rhythm again. In short, he required a confidence boost. It wasn't quite back to the drawing board, but Cecil chose to forget about Group 1s for Twice Over for the time being; instead, it was time to search out an opportunity in a lower grade of racing for him.

Certain trainers employ a racing secretary or commission a specialist race planner to pinpoint targets for their string but Cecil did it all himself. Some mornings, I would arrive just after 6 a.m. and find him sitting at the breakfast-room table, gently humming as he peered down through black-framed glasses at the contents of a large leather folder. There was a sheet with the following week's entries and another with a list of all his horses and their current ratings. Next to the folder was an open *Racing Calendar*, the weekly publication that details all the upcoming races, their conditions as well as the entry fees and dates. In it he would jot down the names of horses alongside specific races. During his early morning research he discovered the perfect spot for Twice Over, a Class 2 conditions stakes on 9 September at Doncaster's St Leger meeting.

The race would mark the first occasion in which he had run in a new shoe, for Stephen Kielt had also done plenty of thinking of his own in the days after the Eclipse. Twice Over was a heavy-topped horse with delicate feet and was prone to corns and heel pain. 'If you have no foot, you have no horse' is the old saying and you won't find a trainer that disagrees. Throughout that summer Kielt was determined to do his bit to help Twice Over regain the winning thread.

Shoeing him was a problem as there was very little nailing room available in the horse's hoof walls. Twice Over was flat-soled and traditional glue-on shoes didn't suit him either. They left him very sore in his heels. Kielt wasn't about to give up. He had heard about a different type of glue-on shoe produced in America that he felt had a chance of offering comfort to Twice Over and in turn boost performance. It had rubber to greatly assist with cushioning at the heel and was glued on at the side of the hoof wall with little tabs as opposed to the bottom of the foot. Correspondence between the shoemaker and Kielt led to an adjusted version being shipped to Newmarket as Cecil had agreed to give it a try. The Northern Irishman's conscientiousness was rewarded: the somewhat bespoke 'Savile Row' solution brought about the desired results.

'When we applied the shoes with rubber, and no nails or pressure on the bottom of his feet, he strode out further,' says Kielt. 'It's key to remember Twice Over was sound nearly always but when he had the special shoes he increased his stride length and, as a result, covered more ground, galloped better. Henry liked them. He felt Twice Over moved so much better in them.'

It's a prime example of the problem solving and attention to detail you will find in all the top racing stables. They don't just receive special care for the horses' feet either. Around the racing industry there are back specialists, equine dentists, nutritionists and equine masseurs among other expert services that are available.

Their dietary requirements are managed on an individual basis and intake is closely monitored. Horses are unlikely to do well physically and in their exercise without getting the right amount of fuel into them in the first place.

At Warren Place there were essentially three feeding times: early mornings pre-5 a.m., after exercise and then again at evening stables. This programme, however, wasn't set in stone for all of the Cecil string. There was the odd individual or two – invariably fillies – who would be picky with their feed, especially if confronted with a sizeable portion. Such horses might be given four smaller feeds, the last of which perhaps required a lad to pop in during the late evening. But in general there was no requirement for a night feed. Cecil believed in letting his horses rest without unnecessary distractions.

Twice Over was kept sweet with extra goodies supplied by

his lad John Fletcher. Like the horse, Fletch was a Warren Place stalwart and one of its great characters. The story goes that Fletch had never sat on a horse until he was sixteen and jumped on a loose one in his street in his hometown of Doncaster in the mid-1980s. He joined Cecil's team in the second half of the 1990s and looked after Twice Over's mother Double Crossed before building up a great rapport with her son.

There's little doubt that a groom has a key part to play when it comes to the wellbeing of a horse, and Fletch ensured that Twice Over received the best of care. The Yorkshireman would stop by the market on Saturday mornings at 5.30 a.m. to collect a bag of apples for the big colt who could be a little grumpy on occasion. In general, Fletch kept him happy with a steady stream of treats. 'He loved his apples, carrots and Polos,' says the lad. 'He always knew that you had stuff for him.'

All the effort put into Twice Over by Cecil, Kielt, Fletcher and the horse's regular exercise-rider Graham Purse – known as Percy – was repaid in the closing months of the 2009 season, starting with a convincing victory at Doncaster. That was followed by a similar outcome in a slightly higher level of race at Goodwood a couple of weeks later.

With back-to-back successes under his belt it was time for Twice Over to be stepped right back up in class to contest the Champion Stakes at Newmarket for the second time. Derby runner-up Fame And Glory was the hot favourite, while the French-trained Never On Sunday was a previous Group 1 winner who had been well backed. Oaks heroine Sariska was another of the fancied runners in opposition.

Despite his own recent resurgence Twice Over was

unconsidered by most punters. Some bookies in the betting ring even offered him at 20/1 before he was sent off at a starting price of 14/1, almost double the odds that he had been for the same race a year earlier. But as stable lads are fond of telling you, a horse never knows what price he is. Even if he had been interested, Cecil wouldn't have given the betting a second glance: he knew Twice Over was in prime form, running on perfect ground at a track that the horse had always shown a strong liking for. That afternoon the colt would prove once and for all that he belonged in Group 1 company.

Tom Queally did a fine job early in the race as his quiet hands allowed Twice Over to settle into a relaxed rhythm. Kielt was watching on in satisfaction as the horse extended in a manner that suggested he was completely at home in those made-to-measure racing plates. Racecourse commentator Jim McGrath could also see it. With approaching three furlongs left to travel he referred to how well Twice Over was going.

Queally patiently engaged the Warren Place horse, who hit the front with a quarter of a mile to travel – but it wasn't plain sailing for either of them from there on in. The Rowley Mile has its fabled Dip just inside the two-furlong marker where a horse can often become unbalanced. Twice Over started to edge towards the far side before Queally sought a corrective right-hand drive.

The pair subsequently hit the line with three-quarters of a length in hand from Mawatheeq but the drama was not over. A stewards' enquiry took place into Twice Over drifting towards the right at a key time in the race when the runner-up was coming up to challenge from just behind. The stewards deemed that Queally caused interference (he was given a one-day ban) but decided that it hadn't improved his position so the result was not overturned. Cecil had won the Champion Stakes for the third time and Twice Over, at long last, had a top-class victory on his CV.

'This horse deserves it,' Queally said, in the Racenews Racecourse Service report. 'We got his confidence right back up with the last couple of runs and it paid off today. Henry could see it in his work in the mornings and he was bullish coming into the race, even though he was a big price. There were better fancied horses but Henry obviously saw something that nobody else did.'

Just like his trainer, Twice Over was 'going to be around for some time yet'. As for that season, he faced one more challenge – the Breeders' Cup Classic at Santa Anita Park in Arcadia, a city not far north of downtown Los Angeles and in the shadow of the San Gabriel mountains.

The Breeders' Cup is staged every autumn in America and sees a series of championship races on dirt and turf over back-to-back days. The meeting, inaugurated in 1984, sees many of Europe's equine stars head across the Atlantic to tackle home favourites and is billed as a chance to see 'the world's greatest thorough-breds'. The location often switches year-on-year (although Santa Anita hosted five between 2008 and 2014), but all Breeders' Cups have been in the US apart from the 1996 renewal, which was held at Woodbine in Canada. All the races were initially staged on one card before it expanded to a two-day meeting in 2007.

Aidan O'Brien's Ballydoyle team annually targets the meeting. It is very important for Sheikh Mohammed's Godolphin operation, too. Other European trainers such as Sir Michael

Stoute and André Fabre have also enjoyed notable success at the Breeders' Cup. But Cecil, even in his Championship years of the 1980s and 1990s, was sparsely represented at the meeting. He was a traditionalist at heart and the biggest prizes in European racing, especially in England, were always the priority when he planned campaigns for his best horses.

By 2009, he had sent only six horses to the Breeders' Cup: Indian Skimmer, Distant View, Eltish, Dushyantor, Royal Anthem and Passage Of Time. The closest he had come to a winner was Eltish finishing second in the Juvenile. So, seasoned Warren Place-watchers might have raised an eyebrow when the trainer decided to head Stateside with Twice Over, Midday and Father Time – a veritable army by Cecil's standards – in early November of that year.

On the opening day Father Time was a well-beaten favourite in the Breeders' Cup Marathon. On the same card Midday was scheduled to contest the Filly and Mare Turf.

Just over a month earlier, she had finished third in the Group 1 Prix de l'Opéra at Longchamp. That had been her first run back after winning the Nassau Stakes in high summer and Cecil was immediately left wondering whether he had left her a little light in terms of fast work prior to France.

'In the paddock I remember Henry being a bit disappointed,' says Jane Cecil. 'He thought he had her right, but after the race felt he'd maybe been a bit easy on her. He made a joke, saying something like: "Wasn't a bad prep race for the Breeders' Cup." But that actually did put her spot-on for it.'

Midday was the sole European raider for the Filly and Mare Turf at Santa Anita and Michael McGowan recalls that the Americans weren't convinced by her credentials. The night before the race, he had decided to walk back to the hotel from the stabling block. It had been a hot day so he popped into a bar for a drink. Breeders' Cup fever had hit Arcadia, including the bar, which was staging a preview event. A celebrity tipster was holding court.

'Just as I've walked in they are on about the Filly and Mare Turf, going through horse by horse,' says McGowan. 'It got to Midday and he said: "Midday, GB, we won't even talk about her, she's got no chance," and they went on to the next horse. I just put my glass of Coke down and as I've gone past him said, "You're talking shit," and walked out.'

McGowan knew best, but it still required a ride of courage and confidence from Queally to deliver Cecil's only Breeders' Cup victory. The jockey made light of a wide draw by bringing Midday to the inner rail as soon as the race was underway. He was in the right place to respond when long-time leader Visit injected some pace into the race early into the back stretch. Lastly, and most tellingly, as Visit turned into the home straight a gap opened up on the inner and Midday – stoked up by Queally just moments beforehand – was brilliant enough to speed through it with a furlong to go.

As she made her move Stephen Kielt and Warren Place groom Leah Black were out of their seats close to the winning post. They had seen enough to know the outcome. 'We were celebrating long before the line as we knew she wouldn't get caught,' he says. 'It was a magical night.'

It was also unforgettable for McGowan. 'Probably one of the best moments I've had in racing,' he says. 'To win a Breeders' Cup is absolutely fantastic.' And, of course, he had to return to the bar where Midday's chances had been so dismissively written off. There he discovered that his strong response to the big-shot pundit had left a marked impression on the regulars. The bar-lady bought him a drink and said, 'We all backed your horse!'

A Breeders' Cup victory was reported in the media as Cecil filling in one of the few notable gaps on his CV. 'It wasn't a burning ambition but it gave him a sense of great satisfaction,' says Jane.

Cecil probably wouldn't have reflected too long on such a point. More important for him was the undeniable fact that Warren Place horses were once again regularly winning on the biggest stages and simply giving him an enormous amount of pleasure. The route back hadn't been easy; the successes were the result of hard work and determination in a time of adversity. And that's what gave everyone involved at Warren Place an extra glow of satisfaction, not least Cecil who was back among the top-ten of British trainers for the first time in nine years.

The day after Midday's win, Twice Over gave another typically bold effort. Racing for the first time on the Pro-Ride artificial surface he finished third to the superb mare Zenyatta in the Breeders' Cup Classic. Twice Over's share of the prize money was just over £380,000, almost £170,000 more than he had earned his connections for winning the Champion Stakes the previous month.

After the low point of being beaten almost out of sight in the Eclipse Stakes, Twice Over had been restored to top form by a man who himself had returned firing on full cylinders. The colt's feats summed up the buoyancy in the camp as 2009 came to a close.

'Henry was back, the horses were good and the staff had a bit of a swagger,' says Kielt. 'Things were working in total harmony.'

Chapter Seven

'Until they set foot on a racecourse no one truly knows'

It was late morning on a summer's day in 2010 and Henry Cecil and Ed Vaughan were engaged in an amiable chat on Warren Hill. There was nothing unusual about the occurrence; the two trainers would often see each other at third lot and spend a bit of time together. The conversations would tend to be about something and nothing. Almost without fail there would be laughter as the two men had similar glass-half-full outlooks and the ability to entertain one another.

They were firm friends. Once I was organising a supper for media and trainers at Newmarket Racecourse and Cecil agreed to attend as long as he could be seated 'next to Eddie Vaughan'. Indeed, Jane Cecil used to joke that she might have become slightly green-eyed if 'Vaughany' had happened to have been a girl.

That August day the chat was about upcoming runners. Vaughan was preparing to head down to Newbury where he had one to saddle later on. Cecil was staying much closer to home as he had a horse lined up to make its debut in a mile maiden race at the evening meeting on Newmarket's July Course.

'He was normally one to talk one down,' says Vaughan, but it was very different that morning. The Irishman was struck by the conviction with which Cecil spoke about the unraced colt he would be introducing that night.

'I'm running a two-year-old today at Newmarket and I think this is a very good horse,' he told Vaughan. 'It's the best horse I've got and it might be the best horse I've ever had.'

It was an extraordinary statement given all that Cecil had achieved. More than forty years with a training licence and ten champion trainer crowns to his name, yet here he was claiming he might just have one who could potentially become his greatest.

Vaughan was unlikely to forget his friend's words about the colt. 'He was convinced that he was the real deal,' says Ed. 'I know it's a big statement for a man who trained so many greats but he was really so high on that horse.'

That evening Vaughan made sure he caught the Newmarket race on television. He watched it with his friend and fellow trainer Charlie Hills, who he happened to be staying with in Lambourn. 'Henry said he's got a horse that he thinks is the next coming!' Vaughan joked with Hills.

Moments later, the gates on the starting stalls cracked open and Frankel began his racing career.

Frankel was foaled on 11 February 2008 at Banstead Manor Stud, the European headquarters of Juddmonte Farms' breeding operation. He was a horse that had many admirers long before he got anywhere near a racecourse. 'We thought him special from a pretty early age,' confirms Prince Khalid Abdullah's racing manager Lord Grimthorpe.

Frankel was the product of a mating between outstanding Coolmore stallion Galileo and a Juddmonte mare called Kind, who was a Listed-class winner in her racing days. At the time, the two parties had in place a foal share agreement that saw ten of Juddmonte's mares visit Coolmore's leading stallions. Instead of paying a six-figure stud fee for each covering, Juddmonte would share the foals with Coolmore on an alternate-pick basis. Of those foaled in 2008 under the arrangement, it was Juddmonte who had first choice.

'Frankel was nice as a foal; no question he was a very nice foal,' says Grimthorpe. 'He was our number-one pick, but by the time he'd got to July of his yearling year he was certainly looking pretty interesting. By the time we got a saddle on him in September, October, he'd started the pulses racing.'

Not long afterwards the decision was made by Prince Khalid to send his premier yearling of 2009 into training with Henry Cecil. Like the Niarchos family, the Saudi prince would have been thrilled at the significant upturn in Warren Place's fortunes. Cecil and Prince Khalid was an enduring alliance fuelled by great mutual respect and an excellent rapport.

'It was a friendship,' explains Lord Grimthorpe. 'They got on tremendously well. I'm sure Henry made Prince Khalid laugh but it was much more than that. Henry made him believe that the horses were going to be good and what he was doing was the right thing. I think Prince Khalid always had that tremendous confidence in him.'

Jane Cecil also recognised similar elements in their friendship – how Prince Khalid 'set a lot of faith in Henry's judgement'. She recalls how her husband was always respectful about Prince

Khalid's royal status but that there wasn't any stiffness or overt formality about their association, especially if the trainer had good news to share from the gallops.

'There was no set routine, nothing like that,' she says. 'If Henry saw something he liked he couldn't wait to ring on the landline. If he knew he was in Saudi he would write out an email in longhand [for Claire Markham to forward]. Henry wouldn't know how to send an email.'

Jane also understood just how grateful Cecil was for the Prince's support through the worst of times at Warren Place. He was 'massively appreciative', according to her, aware how he probably wouldn't have got through without it. Such loyalty was rewarded with the Group 1 victories provided by Passage Of Time, Twice Over and Midday – three horses instrumental in the Cecil revival.

Their successes, especially those of Twice Over and Midday, would have been fresh in the owner-breeder's mind when he was making plans for his young stock late in 2009. The Prince's roster of trainers at the time included several of the very best in the business: men such as Sir Michael Stoute, André Fabre, John Gosden and Dermot Weld. But he chose Cecil for Frankel, and the timing couldn't have been better. Professionally, the trainer was well into a sustained revival of his fortunes and health-wise there were no urgent concerns.

'It was a real alignment,' says Lord Grimthorpe. 'Frankel was born in 2008. Imagine if he'd been born four years earlier, even three. Would he have gone to Henry? If he'd been born four years later it would have been too late; even three years – if he'd been born in 2010 – two years later. I'm not saying he wouldn't have gone there but the horse himself wouldn't have had the benefit of Henry. Or nearly enough benefit. Not the benefit that he got.'

That winter Cecil confided in Stephen Kielt that he felt he was once again receiving the nicest of Juddmonte Farms' yearlings. The allocation of the horse named after Bobby Frankel served to back up his supposition.

In terms of prize money won and Group 1 victories, the American Bobby Frankel was Prince Khalid's greatest trainer. The New Yorker died in November 2009. To celebrate Bobby Frankel's life and career the decision was taken to give his name to Juddmonte's best yearling from the crop set to start training in 2010.

It was a bold move, simply because the life of a racehorse can be so unpredictable. So many horses fail to live up to expectations. The best of looks and the best of bloodlines don't always add up to high achievement on the racecourse. A will to win has to exist alongside talent. Also, so often things happen to a racehorse that are out of a trainer's hands. One false step can trigger serious injury or compromise potential. So to honour Bobby Frankel in such a fashion was poignant but not without risk. As Lord Grimthorpe says, it was 'a pretty brave call'.

Frankel came to Henry Cecil on Thursday 14 January, 2010. At the time he was still unnamed and known as the 'Kind colt', referencing his mother. It's very common in stables for a trainer and the lads to use either the sire or the dam's name to describe young horses, even those that have recently been named. Warren Place already had a Kind colt in the yard called Bullet Train but Frankel's elder sibling was by Sadler's Wells, the pre-eminent stallion at the time (Galileo is a son of Sadler's Wells). The three-year-old Bullet Train had made only one racecourse appearance at that stage, winning a maiden by a short head at Yarmouth. He was well regarded in the yard and so there was plenty of initial interest in his younger brother.

It's not always easy for lads to tell if they are sitting on a future champion or not, and Michael McGowan tells a story about how he wrongly evaluated Frankel's ability at the start of the horse's days in training. Colleague Billy Aldridge, who was a head man for decades at Cecil's, was busy lining up his horses for the stable's 'ten to follow'. This was the annual tipping competition for staff that the trainer ran, carrying sizeable prizes for first, second and third, while the lad that finished last would be given a bottle of wine for consolatory purposes. Each entry had to include at least two unraced two-year-olds, which meant that a bit of early season investigation might be required, hence Billy picking the brains of McGowan on an occasion in early 2010.

'I rode Frankel, his first canter up Warren Hill,' says McGowan. 'Billy said to me, "What's that Kind colt like?" I just said, "Billy, it goes up there too well. I don't think it will be any good." The ones that take you up there like that on the first canter are usually on their nerves.'

McGowan is an experienced and respected horseman. He has ridden countless young horses up Warren Hill and knows exactly what a good one – and a bad one – feels like. But he chuckles as he recalls that sizeable misinterpretation of how the Kind colt had carried him up the stiff four-furlong incline. It wasn't the cheap speed of a runaway nervous horse destined for burnout. Instead it was the first indication of an almighty engine the like of which he had never encountered before.

'A lot of the two-year-olds that do go up there very well, when the others catch them up they stay at that level,' says McGowan. 'But obviously he was very, very good. He was straight as a die and didn't change his stride, the first canter.'

Cecil chose Dan de Haan to ride Frankel in his early pieces of educational routine exercise. Taller and more robust than many lads, de Haan came from a jumping background. He had switched to Warren Place for a six-month stint from trainer Paul Nicholls after Kauto Star won the Gold Cup at Cheltenham in 2009. The Newmarket air proved agreeable to de Haan and he stayed. His horsemanship in helping settle free-going types didn't go unnoticed by his new employer. So, when Cecil felt Frankel's early exuberance needed to be channelled in the right way, he called on de Haan.

'He used to try and pull himself out to the left-hand side and just run away, gone,' de Haan recalls. 'Henry said, "Would you start riding this for me?" I'd already been riding horses that had been pulling and they'd seemed OK. So he put me on. When I first rode him he was strong, oh God he was strong. But in the end he started to settle more.'

The groom did such a solid job that Cecil partnered him with Frankel for the vast majority of his exercise for the rest of the season. There were hiccups; with horses there invariably are. But by the end of March the trainer's excitement about the Juddmonte-owned colt's progress was growing. McGowan realised this when he overheard a conversation between Cecil and Lord Grimthorpe in Dubai a day or so before the Dubai World Cup, in which Twice Over was due to compete.

'I was riding Twice Over round the barn and Teddy and Henry were having a chat before I was taking him out for an exercise,' says McGowan. 'As I've walked past, Henry turned to Teddy and said, "I think we've got a special two-year-old – the Kind colt." I thought to myself, "That's that one I rode up the Hill and told Billy was no good!"'

Along with his fellow two-year-olds Frankel was given time to strengthen up and get used to life as a horse in training at Warren Place before anything other than routine trotting and cantering was considered. But when spring was thinking about making way for summer Cecil began to take the young colt across to the Al Bahathri to continue his education. Initially de Haan just followed along on Frankel in solo style, behind all the workers. The horse would barely be out of cantering pace under his attentive rider. It was a necessary part of Cecil's educational process for the potential star pupil. The trainer aimed to very gradually step up the workload with young horses, as he explained to Kielt one day as they were watching the two-year-olds breeze.

'He went into quite a lot of depth on how he did it,' says Kielt. 'He liked firstly to introduce them to the Al Bahathri without galloping them. Basically he would just let the horses lob up, so they wouldn't have been blowing when they came off. Maybe from what he saw in a combination of those canters, he would then start organising them into groups, trying to put equally gifted individuals together. Then he would gently up their work, switching the groups around if he thought one was struggling.'

One day Cecil decided it was the right moment to ask a more exacting question of Frankel. Michael McGowan took him from Warren Place to the gallops for what he recalls was the colt's first little piece of fast work. He jumped off, making way for a jockey to ride in the exercise, in which Frankel would travel in behind a couple of other horses. McGowan was on hand to hear his boss issuing his customary clear-cut instructions.

'Henry said to her, "If he is a bit keen, just stay behind. But if he is nicely settled then join." She brought him out and joined and you could just see he was in second gear and they were in fifth!'

Preparations for Frankel's racecourse bow were gradually stepped up and there were a couple of turf gallops that stand out in the minds of those who were around the horse. The first came on Racecourse Side when he shone alongside fellow two-year-olds Midsummer Sun and First Mohican in a workout on the Watered Gallop, a strip that comes into its own during dry spells.

'It was about a month, six weeks off his debut,' says Kielt. 'You hear some people say First Mohican beat him but it was one of Henry's dead heats, upsides. And I can guarantee you there was no horse travelling better than Frankel. I phoned a friend and said: "I think we've a colt that could win the Derby next year."'

Also thinking about the following year's Classic equation was de Haan, who watched the work with Kielt. He was sufficiently impressed to back his judgement in the markets for the 2,000 Guineas and the Derby. 'That was the bit of work,' says de

Haan, referring to the moments that convinced him of the horse's enormous potential. 'He settled brilliantly.'

Cecil entered the horse for his debut in Newmarket's mile maiden on Friday 13 August. But before the race he gave his charge one last piece of work to ensure he was tuned up and ready to go. This time the venue was the vast acres of the Limekilns that open out at the intersection of the Bury Road and the old Norwich Road as vehicles leave Newmarket. Those present for the exercise were left in no doubt about Frankel's huge raw talent.

'Frankel was working with a horse called Kings Bayonet [who was a year older and officially rated in the early 80s at the time],' says Kielt. 'He was a seven-furlong horse who probably worked better than he delivered. Frankel absolutely pulverised him about twenty lengths, hard held off level weights. It was seriously impressive.'

Jane was another of the amazed onlookers. She had been aware of the growing stable buzz around the horse and also Henry's belief in him. But Frankel's exercise that morning demonstrated to her that all the enthusiasm was justified and more.

'Frankel's gallop on the Limekilns just before his debut was unreal,' she says. 'All of us watching were just a little bit stunned. Almost, "Did that really just happen?" For an unraced two-year-old to gallop with such power and intensity made you want to rub your eyes in disbelief. It was just exceptional.

'At that time and in the lead-up to Frankel's first race I'd never seen Henry that excited about a horse. I'd regularly seen his optimism about promising horses before – and sometimes he could be over-optimistic. But I could sense from him an extra level of anticipation ahead of Frankel's first race.'

The place was packed to the rafters for Frankel's debut, but it was nothing to do with the talented young horse's first public appearance. The July Course was hosting one of its 'Newmarket Nights' concerts and Westlife were due to play.

After-racing concerts have become part of the scene at British racecourses through summertime, but the weather was anything but seasonal that night. A warm day had broken up into a wet and hazy evening. The persistent rain had got into the ground, which was described as 'soft' by the time the horses were in the paddock for the third race on the card.

Word of Frankel's spellbinding training had got out to those in the know and he was duly chalked up as the favourite. But the Warren Place colt was still odds against in the betting and that was due to the fact that there was also strong support for the John Gosden-trained newcomer Nathaniel, also a son of champion sire Galileo.

'I was amazed he wasn't odds on, I couldn't believe it,' says Lord Grimthorpe, reflecting on Frankel's 7/4 starting price. 'I mean, his homework . . . he just blew everything away. I was shocked. I knew that Nathaniel had been backed but you get so blinkered.

'Several years later a punter came up to me and said, "I want to tell you a story, have you got a moment?" He said. "I'd heard there was a great Galileo colt in Newmarket – at John Gosden's. And I backed this thing like nothing on earth." And he was right. He was a great Galileo colt. He said, "I just had to pick the one race in the one year that Frankel turned up!"'

The two powerhouse stables were conscious of the other's contender, both of whom were carrying entries for defining races in the last part of the season. 'There was a big build-up all day,' says Michael McGowan. 'Gosden's lads were backing theirs and our lads were backing our horse.'

Shane Fetherstonhaugh recalls that the pre-race mood at Warren Place was a suitably positive one. 'There was the usual sort of banter that you get. "You can have a bet on this, this'll win."'

If only it was that cast-iron. Lord Grimthorpe's many years in horseracing had taught him that no debutant can ever be considered a certainty, however dazzling their homework may have been. The first-time out horse is often compared to a child having his first day at school. There is so much to take on board that the challenge can prove all too daunting. Races can be lost in the paddock if nerves surface and needed energy is prematurely tapped.

'We've all been through morning glories and until they set foot on a racecourse no one truly knows,' says Prince Khalid's racing manager. 'The racecourse environment, the way the horse gets to the races, behaves at the races; all that is a huge learning curve for every thoroughbred. How they take that on is a big part of what happens, actually, in the race.'

Lord Grimthorpe's vantage point that night was not anywhere near the winning line, nor was he berthed in front of a big screen at the racecourse. In fact, he watched the race on a small screen in a hotel room in Deauville where he was attending the yearling sales. The distance between himself and Newmarket did little, if anything, to dampen his anticipation ahead of

Frankel's big moment. 'My wife said to me, "I've never seen you so nervous before a race." I said, "This may be something – come and sit down and we'll watch."'

I was also expectantly monitoring Frankel's racecourse debut on a small screen, only I was in the Press Room at the July Course. It was a working night for me, providing the analysis of each of the seven races on the card for the following day's *Racing Post*. Deadlines are so tight in such situations that I would have to conduct all my preparations before racing commenced. With maidens, especially one in which there were plenty of debutants, I would be relying on pedigrees and the previous achievements of siblings to help develop my copy. I would normally try and nip down to the paddock for a two-year-old maiden race to assess the horses' fitness, scope for future development and their behaviour. That night the heavy rain, not to mention the work from the two earlier races on the card, stopped me making the less-than-straightforward journey through the large crowd from the Press Room to the paddock.

Frankel was towards the rear in the opening phase of the race, having been slower to break than most of the other eleven horses in opposition. Even so, he was not far off the early leader Dortmund as there was understandably no attempt by any jockey to set a stiff gallop in what were particularly taxing ground conditions for young horses.

Racecourse commentator Derek Thompson soon spotted that jockey Tom Queally and Frankel were tracking Nathaniel towards the outer of the field. As the tempo increased several horses began to flounder but not Frankel or Nathaniel, who took up the baton with around a quarter of a mile to run. It was quickly apparent that the pair would have the stage to themselves through the closing strides. But it was an unusual conclusion to study from an analyst's perspective. Frankel arrived in such an assertive fashion with less than a furlong to go that it appeared as if the race would be settled in four or five strides.

That didn't materialise. Nathaniel wasn't about to wilt even after Frankel edged in front. Consequently what ensued was a much closer finish than had looked likely, although the market favourite did seem to come back on the bridle for the last moments of his half-length victory, suggesting additional reserves were available if required. That was the aspect of Frankel's debut that McGowan most recalls. Not so much for the impression that the horse seemed to have extra to give but more for the impact his racing style had on race-goers.

'That was a strange night,' says McGowan. 'He quickened twice and then came back on the bridle! The whole place went silent. They were all cheering and cheering, then nothing. I think it was because he came back on the bridle – everybody was stunned. They started cheering again just before the line.'

Up in the Press Room I was feeling similarly excited. Had we just seen a horse quicken twice on demand? Good horses can provide an injection of pace when asked by their jockey, but the July Course seemed to witness not one but two exciting push-button moves of acceleration from Frankel.

As is the norm for an analysis writer, I immediately re-watched the race three or four times to assess it in greater depth. The structure and tone for such copy is necessarily formulaic, but my enthusiasm for what I had witnessed was evident in the words that I sent across thirty-odd minutes after Frankel crossed the line.

'It wouldn't be the greatest surprise in the world to see Frankel and Nathaniel clashing at the end of the season, such was the favourable impression they created,' I wrote, alluding to their respective Group-race entries.

There was half a length between them at the line with a further five lengths back to the third in a field full of promising types.

Frankel is closely related to the stable's Lingfield Derby Trial winner and out of a Listed winner. A February foal, the manner in which he travelled up to challenge the eventual second was visually impressive. Barely off the bridle, he only needed to be nudged out by his rider to settle this and will have learnt plenty from the experience. He is in the Royal Lodge Stakes and, with the Programme Book not full of options for a horse who certainly won't have been missed by the handicapper, that could be an interesting target.

Nathaniel, closely related to Playful Act and Percussionist, looks sure to enhance the family's reputation. If it hadn't been for Frankel, he'd have been a five-length Newmarket maiden winner and grabbing the headlines himself. He is undoubtedly a smart prospect and, on breeding, looks sure to improve as he matures from this very pleasing debut.

For racing professionals, form-book students and racing fans alike it can be easy to upgrade what you have witnessed on the racecourse. In particular, I would always want a maiden race to offer up a horse or two about which to wax lyrical. I can't deny that plenty of maidens have lit me up over the years, but only two have triggered a rush of excitement; made me feel that I may just have seen something remarkable. One was the John Gosden-trained colt Kingman, who gave a dazzling debut run in 2013, also on the July Course. The other was Frankel's first racecourse appearance.

Pop band Westlife may have been billed as the headline act that night and I don't doubt they were very good, but I didn't stick around to check. Instead, I was in my car not long after the last race. As I drove home I was sure that I had seen a colt of huge potential. What I could never have imagined were the extraordinary feats that Frankel would go on to deliver in the following two-and-a-quarter years.

There was probably only one person who may just have had an idea of the heights the horse would scale. And that was Henry Cecil.

Chapter Eight

'He might be the best horse anyone has owned'

The summer of 2010 was just like the good old days at Warren Place. Frankel may have been hinting at future stardom but Henry Cecil had two proven Group 1 horses in Twice Over and Midday that were running up to their very best. A year after Twice Over had laboured among the stragglers in the Eclipse Stakes he returned to Sandown for the same race and won by half a length, demonstrating talent and courage in abundance. As for Midday, she was in the form of her life. In the space of just six weeks she would win no less than three Group 1s.

The first of those victories came in the Nassau Stakes at Glorious Goodwood. Now a four-year-old, Midday defeated the highly regarded French filly Stacelita by a length and a quarter to land the Nassau for the second successive season.

The quality of her pre-race work under groom Shane Fetherstonhaugh was such that those around her were brimming with belief. Indeed, confidence was running so high among those who travelled from Warren Place to Goodwood that they even uncorked the champagne on the eve of the race. It might have looked like bravado to the outsider but the gesture neatly captured the feelgood mood within the stable that summer. Cecil's team were anticipating another big-race triumph and weren't afraid to show it, even to the French rival Stacelita's grooms.

'Shane, Becky Quorn, a girl who looked after another Cecil runner at the meeting, and I went to a club the night before,' says Stephen Kielt. 'The French guys were there and convinced their filly would win. We were already drinking champagne and offered them some as we were also certain Midday would not get beaten.'

Nobody was enjoying the flow of winners more than Cecil. Earlier the same week Kielt had witnessed a candid moment that revealed just how much the stable resurgence meant to the trainer. Cecil was represented on the opening day of Glorious Goodwood by Lord Shanakill in the Group 2 Lennox Stakes.

The horse, a Group 1 winner the previous season, had been switched to Warren Place for his four-year-old campaign. Lord Shanakill's first few runs for his new yard had been promising enough but he hadn't quite managed to find his best form. Taking a similar approach to the one he had successfully used for Twice Over the previous year, Cecil decided that a drop in class was required just to get Lord Shanakill's head in front once more. A Listed race at Chester in the first half of July was identified and sure enough he justified his favourite's tag, only needing to be pushed out by Tom Queally to win in straightforward fashion.

Two-and-a-half weeks later, a fully restored Lord Shanakill went to Goodwood for a much tougher challenge. Kielt watched the race in the Warren Place office along with the stable's book-keeper Joan Plant. The seven-furlong contest proved to be an exciting spectacle and Lord Shanakill was never far away. As the field thundered through the closing stages Queally drove out his mount, who got up to win by a head.

'Next thing, Henry, who I didn't know was in the house, came bursting through into the office, right past me,' says Kielt. 'He didn't notice me as he went round to the right where Joan was. He grabbed her, almost twirled her round and was like a kid. Then he realised I was there: "Brilliant, bloody brilliant." He was gone as quick as he came in.

'It was a rare glimpse of what it meant to him. It wasn't a Group 1 winner but there might have been a certain amount of pressure to do well with the horse. It had come in [to Warren Place that season] and he wanted to revive its fortunes. So when it won that day he felt massive elation.'

Cecil went into the final couple of months of the 2010 season with big plans for all of his stable stars. With Frankel he was targeting the Group 2 Royal Lodge Stakes at Ascot on the final Saturday in September. But before he would allow the debut winner to take his chance in such a good race Cecil wanted to build up his experience. In keeping with his method, the trainer was keen to ensure that Frankel's ascent unfolded step by step.

It wasn't his style to ask a horse to do too much too soon. That was why he chose to head to Doncaster for a conditions race a couple of weeks before the Royal Lodge Stakes. Frankel's second start was a furlong less distance-wise than the mile he had faced on his debut. That may not have been ideal but, with the upcoming Ascot engagement in mind, race options were limited within the timeframe to which Cecil was working. Anyway, Frankel had so much natural speed that nobody at Warren Place was concerned about him running over seven furlongs. Kielt did touch on the subject with assistant trainer Mike Marshall, only to receive an emphatic response. 'Mike said, "You haven't seen a horse like this – don't worry about that."'

Frankel's maiden victory four weeks earlier and subsequent growing reputation meant that only four horses were declared for the Frank Whittle Partnership Conditions Stakes. Frankel was the 1/2 favourite with the Godolphin runner Farhh next in the betting. Like the Warren Place runner, Farhh had been an impressive debut winner at Newmarket on his only other start.

Before the Doncaster race Michael McGowan was chatting with his opposite number at Godolphin, Tommy Burns, about their respective runners. Farhh, he discovered, was indeed well thought of within the rival camp. But the quietly spoken McGowan was quick to respond with his own succinct summary of Frankel's chance: 'Tommy, you won't beat this fella.'

The evaluations continued in the parade ring as the jockeys arrived to be legged up. Frankie Dettori was heard speaking positively about his upcoming ride on Farhh. McGowan remembers that Burns then asked the jockey about their chances of getting the better of Frankel. 'He looked over at our horse and said nothing,' says McGowan.

As it materialised the expected duel between Frankel and Farhh never played out. Or it didn't that day; the pair would eventually clash a couple of summers later. At Doncaster the Godolphin horse became unruly in the stalls and was withdrawn, making Frankel's task that much easier. He duly tracked Diamond Geezah until the final furlong pole was in sight at which point Tom Queally unleashed him. It was a spectacular scene; the first time the public had seen Frankel bounding lengths clear of his opposition.

'Tom was told to get after him, make sure he has had a race because he was going for the Group 2 at Ascot after that,' says McGowan. 'So, Tom has chased him and he has gone past us, half a furlong from the line. Tommy [Burns] looked over: "I tell you what, that horse will do himself an injury the way he lets himself down."

'He just took off. Every time Tom [Queally] is asking him, he's just giving him more. A lot of horses will probably look about, but him – head down, just wanting to gallop.'

Frankel won by thirteen lengths. The two-strong opposition may not have been anything special but the visual impression he created that day meant his stock was rapidly rising. As a result of his victory he climbed to the top of the bookies' lists for the following year's 2,000 Guineas and Derby. 'He's got a long way to go,' said Cecil in a comment reported by the Racenews Racecourse Service on 10 September, but a clear indicator of how he viewed the horse's potential soon surfaced. 'It has been a long time since I had a two-year-old as promising as him,' he offered. 'He could be special but he isn't yet.'

Queally was more than impressed by Frankel's sustained galloping prowess at Doncaster. It seemed as if there was a bit of amazement in his reaction and that was unusual. As Shane Fetherstonhaugh says, 'Tom doesn't get overly excited about things.' A couple of days after the Doncaster demolition, however, the two men were at Longchamp and Fetherstonhaugh spoke to Queally as he led him around on Midday before the Group 1 Prix Vermeille. 'I asked, "How good was that two-year-old then?" He said, "Shane, you wouldn't believe it." This was two days afterwards and he was still a bit gobsmacked by him.'

An air of invincibility had started to surround the horse – certainly at Warren Place. For the lads, it wasn't a question of whether he would win the Royal Lodge Stakes; they were only debating what the margin of victory would be. 'There was a massive amount of confidence and a lot of excitement,' says Kielt about the build-up to 25 September's race on the round mile at Ascot. 'The lads were now backing on distances – five lengths I think the bookies were offering – and that's where some of them were putting their money.'

This wasn't just another low-key conditions race that members of Cecil's staff were bullishly punting on. Frankel was heading to the one-mile Group 2 Royal Lodge Stakes, a £125,000 contest that had previously been won by future 2,000 Guineas and Derby heroes. Indeed, in the race that afternoon was Treasure Beach, who would come second in the following year's Epsom Derby and subsequently win the Irish Derby. He never got near to Frankel on the home straight at Ascot, nor could any of the other three runners. The distance-backers at Warren Place got paid out that day as Frankel won by ten lengths with a headline-grabbing performance.

The margin was great enough, but it was more the fashion of his victory and an astonishing move just after the halfway point that left seasoned race-goers shaking their heads at what they had just witnessed. Having sat last of the five runners for the opening half a mile, Queally angled out on Frankel. In a matter of a few giant strides he powered around the opposition, going from last to first. What made the move all the more amazing was that it seemed to require the minimum of effort as the colt remained hard held on the bridle. Comparisons were drawn with Arazi's last-to-first manoeuvre in the 1991 Breeders' Cup Juvenile – for some, the most dramatic big-race surge.

Having asserted himself, Frankel proceeded to stretch clear of his rivals. The BBC commentator Jim McGrath conveyed what everyone watching at Ascot or at home was surely thinking when he declared: 'By Golly, he looks a champion!'

Cecil was as excited as anyone as he made his way from the stands down to the winner's enclosure. 'I think he's the best I've trained,' he said to Jane Cecil. He stopped short of sharing the same opinion with the press but only just. Instead he told them that not since his 1975 champion Wollow had he trained a better two-year-old.

'Afterwards he complained that there was a lot of hype,' says Jane, laughing. 'And I always said to him, "But it's your fault . . . you cranked it up!"'

In the post-race furore Cecil bumped into Jane Chapple-Hyam, trainer of the runner-up Klammer. 'You've got a freak,' was her verdict. Klammer wasn't a top-class horse but he was very smart. Either side of the Royal Lodge Stakes he won a Listed race in France and a Group 3 at Newbury. Against Frankel, he had offered no answer to that devastating turn of foot.

'That ten-length display was just amazing,' says Chapple-Hyam. 'I know I'm only a yellow and red spot in the distance but I still get goosebumps when I see the replay of that race. The last time I saw a horse win by such a long way was Secretariat [the 1973 Triple Crown winner in the US]. They don't come round very often but when they do you sit back and you know – you know they're good. I'm proud to finish second to Frankel. Not many people can say they finished second to him.'

The Royal Lodge Stakes victory revealed Frankel's explosive ability to a wider audience. At Newmarket he had given a very eye-catching debut display but there are plenty of those in maidens every season. That had been followed by a straightforward success in a three-runner race at Doncaster. This was different; it was a proper statement, a performance of undoubted authority that was broadcast on national television on a Saturday afternoon. Just three races into his career 'Frankel the Freak' was the talk of racing and beyond.

Henry Cecil relished the challenge of training Frankel but it was a job that brought an increasing amount of pressure. There were also a few hitches along the way. One problem that emerged immediately after the Royal Lodge Stakes was the horse's stabling. In his early days in the yard when he was known only as 'the Kind colt', he was under Dee Deacon's care in the House Barn, located a mere few yards from Cecil's home. Many of the yearlings or young horses started their time at Warren Place in the House Barn.

From there Cecil moved Frankel to the Garage, a relatively modern eleven-box addition to the stabling at Warren Place. It was located in an area of the yard that was far busier than other parts, close to a few of the cottages. There was often a lot of human and equine activity to observe from the Garage. It provided a room with a view, so to speak; at least it did for half of the boxes that had a window out into the heart of the yard. Frankel's box was the second on the left and suited him to a T.

'The Garage just seemed to fit,' says Deacon. 'He could turn inwards and had horses quite close to him. He could stick his head out of the window and watch the world go by. He loved it.'

The Garage, however, wasn't quite perfect. The boxes, while very acceptable in any racing yard, weren't thought of as up there with the best at Warren Place, plus Cecil couldn't see the barn from his house. By contrast the Main Yard was right next door to where he lived and had more spacious stabling. It was considered the most prestigious location, certainly for the top colts in Cecil's string. Twice Over was housed there, as had been many stars down the decades.

Therefore it was more than understandable that Cecil wanted to switch Frankel to the Main Yard. After the Royal Lodge Stakes a box was prepared halfway along the row closest to the house and the talented two-year-old duly moved across. The horse, however, rejected the upgrade from the moment he arrived at his new abode. By the Sunday morning he had loosened a plate and the situation didn't improve in the next day or two. Frankel was no longer the relaxed horse that he had been. He was box walking and banging the door.

Cecil had been closely monitoring matters, hoping his young star would settle into his new surroundings. But by Thursday of that week he decided that the increasingly fractious Frankel should return to the Garage.

'Henry didn't really want him in there because it wasn't really one of the top parts of the yard,' says Deacon. 'But at the end of the day Henry did what was best for the horse.'

Frankel wasn't the only one who had been anxious during his brief stay in the Main Yard. The lads chose to bolt the top door across his box on the Thursday morning out of concern that the strong-minded colt might even try to jump out. But human and equine worries alike were allayed by Frankel's move back to his former 'home'. He was a completely different horse once restored in the Garage, as Stephen Kielt saw. 'No word of a lie, he went and took a big drink of water, ate his food after exercise and lay down,' he recalls.

Even so Cecil was rather frustrated by the chain of events and Kielt served as a sounding board later that day when the two men were in the Fillies' Yard. 'I've had to move him back,' said the perplexed trainer. 'He just didn't like it in there. It was far better for him but if he doesn't like it . . .'

It wasn't to be the only time that Cecil wanted to install Frankel in a box nearer the house. He also tried to base him in an area known as the Dip, a few seconds' walk from the train-er's back door. Again, Frankel expressed his dissatisfaction at the move. So that was that: Cecil accepted the horse would remain in the Garage during his time at Warren Place.

The Dewhurst Stakes on the Rowley Mile racecourse at Newmarket is always keenly anticipated. Every season the seven-furlong Group 1 is recognised as a defining race for each generation of two-year-olds. It brings together different form lines, and not just those from English racing. The top Irish juveniles invariably line up; likewise French trainers consider heading across the Channel if they have a very good one.

A horse that wins the Dewhurst stands a strong chance of being named as Europe's champion two-year-old. That was certainly the case in 2010 when six runners were declared for the race. The Ballydoyle contender was Roderic O'Connor, a horse that would win a Group 1 as a two-year-old and a Classic at three. Also from Ireland came the Jim Bolger-trained Glor Na Mara, beaten by half a length a couple of months earlier that season in the Group 1 Phoenix Stakes. On the Monday prior to the race, Godolphin made the £20,000 supplementary entry for their unbeaten colt Saamidd, winner of the Group 2 Champagne Stakes at Doncaster a month before.

The only horse in the race to have achieved top-class success at that stage was Dream Ahead. Trained in Newmarket by David Simcock, Dream Ahead had followed a Group 1 win in France with victory by no less than nine lengths in a soft-ground renewal of the Middle Park Stakes on 1 October at the Rowley Mile. His connections were determined to make a swift return to the scene for a shot at the Middle Park–Dewhurst double, a very rare feat for a horse to pull off. It was a daunting task in itself but became a greater one in Simcock's mind after he witnessed a gallop on the Heath a week before the race.

'We knew Dream Ahead was obviously pretty special because he had won Group 1s on his second and third starts,' says Simcock. 'So he had achieved more than any horse in the field. I was excited about running him and then the week before I remember being on Racecourse Side on the turf and seeing this horse going upwards of ten lengths clear of a lead horse.

'I didn't know whether the horse had just run off or what had happened but it was outstanding and it was Frankel. It was exciting to watch but I knew my horse couldn't work like that.'

Cecil's horse was working with a three-year-old called Capital Attraction, who was rated 100 at the time. Frankel was given an official figure of 123 on the back of winning the Royal Lodge Stakes but, even so, the manner in which he asserted his authority over his elder that morning was remarkable. Having been hard held in behind Capital Attraction, he was eased out before shooting clear in what seemed like a couple of seconds to onlookers. 'It was tremendously impressive,' says Stephen Kielt. 'It took your breath away.'

Champions' Day at Newmarket on Saturday 16 October, 2010 would be unforgettable for many race-goers – and certainly for Cecil. It wasn't all about Frankel either. Twice Over was back to contest the Champion Stakes a year on from his victory in the race.

While the ground was on the soft side it was a glorious early autumn afternoon after a damp start to the day. The sun shone and helped temperatures rise into the teens as a crowd of 14,000 packed the grandstand. Many of them were Cecil devotees, hoping to see fresh fireworks from the young buck Frankel and the usual class from the ever-dependable Twice Over. They weren't to be disappointed on either account.

Frankel wasn't as explosive as he had been at Ascot but it was a fourth race in a busy two months for the two-year-old. Also, he was hampered shortly after breaking from the stalls and jockey Tom Queally reported that he had received a bump early on, which didn't help. As a result, Frankel was engaged through the opening exchanges much more than his trainer wanted. Even so, the outcome never looked in doubt once Queally allowed him to challenge with over a quarter of a mile to travel.

The 4/6 favourite soon closed in on the long-time leader Roderic O'Connor and second favourite Dream Ahead wasn't able to go with him, while Saamidd never looked like playing a part in the finish. Frankel cruised through to seize control entering the Dip, just over a furlong from the line. There was no hint of him weakening on meeting the rising ground and he galloped out well without Queally having to use his whip. It may not have been the wide-margin triumph of Ascot but Frankel still had two-and-a-quarter lengths to spare – and that in his very first Group 1.

After the race people were running to the winner's enclosure so that they could secure a good position to see the horse being led in. That was the first time I had noticed such a level of fanaticism in my time working for Newmarket Racecourses. And, of course, there was the Henry Cecil factor. All of his winners in my years at Newmarket received a warm reception that underlined the affection in which he was held by the everyday race-goer. But the ovation that he was given on Champions' Day was sustained, loud and boisterous.

The swell of support from the crowd will have resonated with Cecil and he was in great form with the throng of attending media after Frankel's win. 'I've never had a two-year-old who works like him,' he said, as reported by the Racenews Racecourse Service. 'If he was a Formula One car, he'd win everything, so long as I didn't drive him!'

In fact, there were two emotional ovations for Cecil that afternoon because Twice Over lived up to his name. Twelve months after a first Champion Stakes win, he successfully defended his crown. Cecil responded by calling Twice Over his favourite horse, but it must have been a close-run thing due to the thrill that the trainer was getting from bringing through Frankel.

The two horses delivered almost £400,000 of prize money that day, helping Warren Place smash through the £2 million mark for the domestic season. It was the first time that Cecil had reached that figure since 1999, a year in which he saddled three of the UK's five Classic winners. It had been an extraordinary return to racing's top table by one of its most enduringly popular heroes.

'It was a wonderful day and both Frankel and Twice Over did us proud,' wrote Cecil in his reflections for the website. 'Frankel unfortunately got a nasty bump after leaving the stalls. This gave him quite a shock and the result was he ran very free for the first part of the race. Things do not always go just as one hopes . . . I do not think the ground helped either.

'Twice Over is a real stable star and ran such a good race on ground which I feel was softer than he now prefers. We love him dearly and he really has done us proud. He will have a rest and he says that he would like to have another crack at the Dubai World Cup. Who am I to argue with him?'

It wasn't just Cecil who had claimed both of the feature races on Champions' Day. So had jockey Tom Queally, who was now established as one of the weighing room's biggest stars. Also, of course, Prince Khalid Abdullah owned both Twice

Over and Frankel. For him and his Juddmonte Farms organisation it had been an afternoon of spectacular success.

Five-year-old Twice Over had claimed a third Group 1 victory and was an undoubted star by that point in his life. But it was the new kid on the block who was suddenly the main event, commanding most of the attention. The flying start that Frankel had made to his career was underlined that autumn day at Newmarket.

'The day of the Dewhurst was almost the changing of the guard at Warren Place,' assesses Lord Grimthorpe. 'The realisation that Frankel was going to be a champion . . . this was the future. A pressman came up to me after the Dewhurst: "Is this the best horse that Prince Khalid has ever owned?" And I said, "He might be the best horse anyone has owned." And you really felt that. It wasn't a bravado thing. We really believed in him.'

And so did a rapidly increasing number of the public. But the Henry Cecil and Frankel story was only just beginning.

Chapter Nine

'Go with them – do not try and make them go with you'

Shane Fetherstonhaugh was in the Dominican Republic in late 2010, relaxing after another busy season. The filly he looked after, Midday, had well and truly flourished as a four-year-old. She had won three of her five races, finishing second in the other two. Yes, it had been a good year all right.

Holidaying with him was his girlfriend Claire Markham, secretary to Henry Cecil. Both were dedicated to Warren Place life and the place was never far from their thoughts, even when they were on an island almost 4500 miles away. One day while they were relaxing, the subject of Frankel came up. Markham, an inquisitive person with an active mind, asked her boyfriend if he had ever ridden the horse. The answer was in the negative, in more ways than one. 'Never,' said Fetherstonhaugh. 'I don't want to be involved. No, I'd gladly not ride him. As much as he is a lovely horse and all that, I just wouldn't want the hassle.'

He had not been back long from the Caribbean when he was pulled to one side by Cecil. Straightaway Cecil came to the point. He wanted Fetherstonhaugh to partner Frankel in his daily training exercise and so one of the most famous Newmarket

Heath alliances was born. 'Once he asked, I would never say I wouldn't ride any horse,' says Fetherstonhaugh.

The initial reluctance he had outlined to Markham on the beach that day was in many ways understandable. Frankel had already been crowned a champion – how do you improve on that? Fetherstonhaugh envisaged a situation down the line where those who favoured hindsight wisdom would get their chance to pipe up.

'I remember thinking, "There's nothing to gain from riding the horse,"' explains Fetherstonhaugh. 'He'd already proven himself. It's different if you ride a horse from day one and you go along with how he progresses. But to ride a horse that's already proven himself a champion two-year-old, you think it can only really go one way. Something will go wrong and it will be, "They shouldn't have changed it, what was Henry thinking? Why didn't he leave the lad who was riding him before?"'

Cecil was a strong advocate of Dan de Haan's work on Frankel through 2010. He wrote in a set of notes in autumn of that year how the groom 'had done a marvellous job getting him to settle really well'. But it had become a question of weight. 'I was just too heavy,' says de Haan, who is much taller and more powerful-looking than the average lad.

Cecil wanted someone lighter to ride Frankel in his early spring work as Tom Queally was set to have big-race commitments on Twice Over in Dubai. Who better for the job than Fetherstonhaugh? Everyone connected to the yard knew how skilful a rider he was. Likewise he had the respect of all of his colleagues for his natural empathy with horses.

Fetherstonhaugh first sat on Frankel during the period either side of Christmas when Cecil always trotted his string in the covered ride at Warren Place. What struck the groom from the outset was how he rode like a horse that seemed a hand bigger than he looked. Fetherstonhaugh also noticed just how wide the colt was when he was in the saddle.

'He was a giant to sit on. I've ridden proper big horses, big jumpers and what have you. People talk about a presence or whatever; I'd be sceptical of things like that. But there was something about him. It's hard to put into words.'

The assiduous groom also knew that working with this horse was going to be a challenge. Traditionally Cecil would start his string back cantering from 1 February and those first few mornings on Warren Hill weren't stress-free for Fetherstonhaugh. While it's almost expected that a horse will be boisterous on returning to more purposeful exercise after winter quarters, Frankel – now a three-year-old – was much too eager to get on with things for his rider's liking.

'The first few times I cantered him he was mad-fresh. He was very, very keen. "What have I got myself into here?" It was a struggle. It took a couple of weeks just to get a bit of confidence with him. The first couple of weeks I wasn't sure; was it going to work or not?'

Fetherstonhaugh was thirty-five by this stage and had ridden racehorses for more than twenty years. All of the experience he had gained was needed through the early spring as he tried different tricks of the trade in his quest to help Frankel settle better. Gradually an understanding was forged. Frankel, while still enthusiastic, was willing to work with his rider.

Cecil knew that in Fetherstonhaugh he had put a key piece of the jigsaw in place. 'Frankel, so far, is pleasing me,' he wrote a couple of months into 2011. 'He has grown and seems to have matured mentally and settled down well.'

The horse's first major target of the season was to be the 2,000 Guineas, the first of the five Classic races held for the three-year-old generation. Inaugurated in 1809, it had been won by many legends of the turf including the likes of Nijinsky, Brigadier Gerard and Dancing Brave. The 2,000 Guineas is a stallion-making race. Beat the best of your age group over the Rowley Mile at Newmarket and a future at stud, a role in which millions of pounds can be generated in covering fees, is all but guaranteed.

To ensure that Frankel was ready for that challenge, Cecil felt that the horse should contest a prep race; specifically the Group 3 Greenham Stakes at Newbury. This step might be considered essential, in the way that football teams play pre-season friendly matches, but many a Guineas has been won by a horse making a first appearance of the season. Only two years before, the great Sea The Stars came straight from the training grounds to run out a convincing winner of the race.

The benefits or otherwise of a prep race are a subject for discussion at the start of every season as the principal Guineas contenders emerge from winter quarters. There is also conjecture over whether very good juveniles have trained on into their three-year-old campaign. Was it just precocity that allowed them to excel at two? Perhaps others may catch them up.

Also, a previously unheralded or even unraced horse might emerge at the start of the season and swiftly rise to become a

Classic contender. Just twelve months earlier, the unbeaten Aidan O'Brien-trained St Nicholas Abbey was sent off the even money favourite for the 2,000 Guineas, but finished sixth. The winner was 33/1 shot Makfi, who'd had just two previous starts, and neither of them above Group 3 status, before striking at the very highest level.

The racing public will have been pondering such matters as trials week at Newmarket and then Newbury came towards its close with Frankel's seasonal return in the Greenham Stakes. Many had been waiting six months, for such had been the excitement generated by the colt in 2010. The media further heightened the sense of anticipation. During the spring, a story in the *Racing Post* revealed how Frankel had out-galloped a train. The Al Bahathri polytrack is adjacent to the line that links Bury to Newmarket, and Cecil's star worked better than two trains, one on the track and the other his lead horse, Bullet Train.

The hype machine continued apace in the build-up to the seven-furlong contest at Newbury. There were endless words and discussion in the media. No wonder there were nerves in the Cecil camp that mid-April afternoon.

'You put all that work in over the winter and you're hoping he's going to jump off, put his head down and relax,' says Fetherstonhaugh. 'It wasn't the case. He has gone there fresh and full of himself.'

Frankel was noticeably strong in Queally's hands in the opening couple of furlongs. Cecil had opted to run stablemate Picture Editor as a pacemaker in the six-runner race and he was barely quick enough for the task. Frankel ended up at the front with well over a quarter of a mile to go but his early freshness didn't hinder his ability to close out the race, which he won by four lengths. In fact, the general feeling was the further he went, the better he went. That was reassuring, given that Frankel's next task a fortnight later was to be the 2,000 Guineas, staged over a straight mile.

And Cecil just *knew*. If there was a hint of ring-rustiness at Newbury it would be gone by Newmarket. That freshness the horse displayed, it was understandable, wasn't it? The horse would tighten up physically for his seasonal bow and mentally he would come on as well. Others may have still been a little bit edgy, but not the trainer, as Fetherstonhaugh recalls.

'Henry was much more relaxed about it. "That was his prep; that will put him right." He had done it a million times before and he knew what he was doing.'

Had he ever trained better? All his expertise was apparent as he plotted the way forward with this brilliant colt. Jane Cecil's words that she had shared with Cecil in the doldrums years of how a champion trainer never lost his skills seemed to ring truer than ever. He proved it in the days leading up to the 2,000 Guineas. Plenty of thought went into the preparations and, perhaps more importantly, he demonstrated his unique feel for a racehorse.

On the Saturday in between the Greenham and the Guineas, the trainer took Frankel to gallop with a lead horse on Racecourse Side. Frankel finished in front but after the exercise Fetherstonhaugh wasn't entirely happy with how it had panned out. He explained to Cecil how Frankel's keen-going tendencies surfaced early; he had taken a real tug. But the rider also outlined that when the horse eventually settled into his stride and went past his lead horse, he had relaxed. Cecil thought for a moment, drawing a couple of times on his cigarette, and said: 'Well, we'll just make the running with him.'

It was probably just an off-the-cuff remark – Cecil was adept at those. As a rule, he wouldn't have wanted his horses to break from the gates and lead. Also, he and Fetherstonhaugh had been tutoring Frankel to switch off and travel in behind his exercise companion. It was hardly ideal to switch from the routine. Prince Khalid Abdullah's colt Rerouted, trained by Barry Hills, was in the Guineas and would ensure they went at a strong enough gallop to allow Frankel to travel smoothly into the race, rather than use up energy reserves by pulling.

Even so, one morning the following week Cecil swapped Frankel and Bullet Train around in a routine canter on Warren Hill. Fetherstonhaugh was asked to lead on the 2,000 Guineas favourite, while the elder horse moved into his slipstream.

'The horse had never led in his life,' says Fetherstonhaugh. 'He was a bit unsettled; he didn't know what was going on. We'd spent all that time keeping him in behind other horses and now all of a sudden, "Well, I'm leading now, what's this all about?" He was all right. I don't know what would have happened had he taken off up the gallop flat out!'

Cecil may have had reservations about asking Frankel to make his own running but the publication of the draw just over forty-eight hours before the race brought such a plan into sharp focus. The colt and his intended pacemaker Rerouted had been drawn on opposite sides of the field.

Frankel was in stall one and Rerouted in thirteen. From those positions there was next to no way that Frankel could satisfactorily take a lead from him. Frankel would just have to jump out and be allowed to go at the pace that suited him. If that meant leading from start to finish, so be it. Cecil knew his charge possessed a giant stride; to break it would be to lose an enormous advantage. It wasn't a time to complicate matters. Frankel was the best horse, just let him go and re-emphasise the point.

'I'm pretty sure Henry talked to Tom plenty,' says Lord Grimthorpe regarding race tactics for Queally. 'The main thing he didn't want him to do was to take back or fight him. But the underlying aspect is that we had huge confidence in the horse. It's hard to go into a race feeling any better about a horse. It would have been unthinkable to see him get beaten in the Guineas the way he had been going beforehand. As with all his races, really.'

Lord Grimthorpe, like many of Frankel's fans, simply couldn't give credence to thoughts of the colt losing. It would take something out of the ordinary or, heaven forbid, an injury to stop Frankel, such was the belief in his unique aptitude. 'Once he'd settled into his stride and started travelling you knew what was going to happen,' he says. 'With other horses you certainly are hopeful and confident in their wellbeing but you don't have that same feeling of inevitability.'

There was a crowd of approaching 16,000 – up by 11 per cent on the previous year – for Frankel's attempt at Classic glory in the 2,000 Guineas. Saturday 30 April, 2011 was a big day for racing and not just because of the much-touted appearance of the brightest star at Warren Place. Newmarket was the scene for the launch of the inaugural British Champions Series, a model that comprised thirty-five premier flat races. Its climax was to be at Ascot in October with the £3 million British Champions Day, the richest race day ever staged in the United Kingdom.

Hard work and vision had gone into building the British Champions Series, which had attracted Qatar-based private investment company QIPCO as a sponsor. But what it needed early on was a star. If the British Champions Series could build momentum around a developing story then it could not only consolidate within the racing industry but reach out to a wider audience.

'There was investment in the Champions Series in the belief that we needed to shine a light on the best races in the flat season and create a new finale for the sport in October,' says Rod Street, the enthusiastic chief executive of the British Champions Series. 'The series was structured before we had a sponsor. Serendipitously QIPCO appeared looking to invest in the sport in a meaningful way and we'd created a structure which was perfect for their aspirations. So, very soon after creating the series, we had QIPCO as a long-term sponsor which was fantastic.

'But of course what you need to make anything work, and for anything to get some traction, is stories. And the stories come from the horses, the jockeys and those other participants in the sport. You couldn't have dreamed or written a better start than the one that we had at the beginning of the Champions Series: the 2,000 Guineas, Frankel coming to Newmarket with this amazing reputation from his two-year-old days and some stunning performances.'

If Street and everyone else at Newmarket was buzzing with anticipation, nothing could have prepared them for the fireworks that Frankel provided that afternoon. It wasn't an absolute top-notch renewal of the Guineas in terms of depth, but there were still Group 1 winners in opposition to Frankel. Roderic O'Connor, second to Frankel in the Dewhurst Stakes, had gone on to triumph at the top level. So too had Casamento, who was successful in the Racing Post Trophy. Neither saw which way Frankel went in the 2,000 Guineas.

The 1/2 favourite broke smartly from the stalls and was soon showing tremendous early speed. After the Greenham Stakes at Newbury, Queally had felt that pulling the horse about was costing them lengths. Better just to let him bowl along without restraint, allow him to use that wonderful length of stride. The tactics delivered a truly dramatic display on the Rowley Mile. In an assertion of authority, he quickly put distance between himself and his twelve rivals. Frankel had them all out of their comfort zone, even proven Group 1 winner Casamento who had forlornly tried to follow him into the race under Frankie Dettori.

The comments of several of the jockeys in the immediate aftermath of the race, as reported by the Racenews Racecourse Service, tell the story best. Robert Havlin, who rode ninth-placed Loving Spirit, remarked how Frankel 'took us along at a merry gallop'. Champion jockey Ryan Moore, not a man known to be overly gushing, said, 'I have never seen anything like that!' after trailing home a distant eleventh on Roderic O'Connor. Happy Today's rider Martin Dwyer reported, 'It was an exceptional race – I thought we were riding in the Abbaye for the first couple of furlongs!' The latter remark was a reference to the five-furlong Group 1 speed test, the Prix de l'Abbaye, staged at Paris Longchamp every autumn. His jokey words neatly summed up the unbelievable speed fractions set by Frankel.

The incredulity of the jockeys was matched by the race-day commentator Ian Bartlett. Having stated that Frankel was 'almost ten lengths clear' at the halfway stage, Bartlett's excitement and astonishment came to the fore as he expressed the opinion that the horse was 'fifteen lengths clear' at the Bushes, a Rowley Mile historical reference point around two-and-a-half furlongs from the line.

Michael Prosser, Newmarket's experienced and sage director of racing, isn't quite so convinced about just how far Frankel led by at that stage. His view was that the horse held an advantage of around ten lengths approaching the final quarter of a mile. Even so, Prosser was astonished by what he witnessed from the stewards' box on the second floor of the grandstand. Frankel's bold front-running performance was so unexpected that jaws were dropping right, left and centre.

'Frankel jumped and made his own running at a frighteningly quick speed to the point at halfway where you thought, "Is he really going to keep this up, is it feasible to keep it up?"' says Prosser. 'It wasn't that he was pulling Tom's arms out . . . he got him into his long raking stride. Frankie was following, but Casamento was almost a broken horse after four furlongs and he's a Group 1 winner. He has just destroyed them. It's very rare that you see that at any level.'

My vantage point, as Newmarket's racing PR manager, was the same as Prosser's, the side-on stewards' box. It is always a place of serious work, with the stewards present to ensure adherence to the rules of racing. On those few occasions when I watched a race from the box I knew my place and kept quiet. That day as Queally unleashed Frankel and that enormous lead opened up, two emotions were rising within me: elation and fear. I couldn't help but feel thrilled by the spectacle but a flash of concern went through me that the unthinkable might occur: the horse would falter and get caught on meeting the rising ground in the final furlong. 'Keep him going, Tom,' I cried out aloud, casting aside any attempt to maintain due propriety.

I'm not sure if anyone around me noticed or cared. Outside a huge round of applause was reaching its crescendo as Frankel comfortably ran out the winner, making a mockery of my moment of concern for the horse. Many in the crowd had actually started clapping with the best part of two furlongs left to race. It was the first time I had seen that in a Classic. As we made our way down, plenty of folk were dashing towards the winner's enclosure, ready to greet the champion horse. 'That's when you know you've got a good one, a special one: people run,' says Prosser.

Everyone was searching for superlatives to describe what they had just seen, even the official handicapper for mile races. The Racenews Racecourse Service reported Dominic Gardiner-Hill as saying, 'Frankel's performance can only be described as awesome. I don't think I have ever seen a Guineas performance like that and I am not entirely sure I have ever seen a performance like that. He had them beat at half-way – he was on the bridle and the jockeys on the others were all shoving or pushing.'

The disbelief that was apparent on people's faces just after the race had quickly been replaced by joy. And perhaps the broadest smile seen in the paddock was the one on Rod Street's face. A central aspiration of the British Champions Series was that it would showcase the very best the sport of racing had to offer. In their wildest dreams the organisers couldn't have hoped for a more spectacular display than Frankel's in the 2,000 Guineas, the very first race of the nascent series. This was a horse to set pulses racing in the manner of Usain Bolt, Lionel Messi and Tiger Woods. The British Champions Series had their flag-bearer.

'I was watching the race on the big screen in the paddock and saw people silenced,' says Street. 'People who've been in racing a long time were just open mouthed at this performance. About two furlongs out, people started clapping – it was quite something. Frankel then became the thread that pulled together the series for the next two years.'

How fitting too that Henry Cecil trained the winner of the first race run under the British Champions Series. The champion trainer who had always resonated with the people received a roar of appreciation after the twenty-fifth and, as it turned out, final Classic success of his career.

At the heart of the triumph, Cecil's third in the 2,000 Guineas, was the master trainer's understanding of the thoroughbred racehorse. 'Go with them – do not try and make them go with you,' he would often say. Cecil instinctively knew what was right for Frankel that day. It was unconventional to say the least to let an odds-on favourite dominate from the starting gate and especially unusual for one from Cecil's string. He preferred his horses to jump out, 'get a lead' from a rival early on and preserve energy for the closing stages of a race. But he realised that the only possible way Frankel could be defeated that day was if he beat himself by pulling for his head, held up off a false pace. Far better to let Frankel make the running, relax into a rhythm and stretch out at a tempo only his enormous ability could sustain for the duration of the race.

It wasn't necessarily a strategy that many of his fellow trainers would have chosen if they had been faced with similar circumstances, but then Cecil wasn't exactly a conformist. The portrait of him that hangs in the Jockey Club Rooms in Newmarket is testament to that. Cecil wore blue jeans and a florid patterned shirt when he sat for artist Felicity Gill. So to win the 2,000 Guineas in somewhat unconventional fashion is likely to have added to the customary thrill of such an achievement. Jane Cecil agrees. 'I think he was pleased that those unusual tactics had worked to such effect,' she says. The race will be talked about for as long as they race horses at Newmarket.

For the Warren Place team, Frankel's latest win was worthy of another celebration. As was often the case during the revival years, a group of the staff congregated in the Shoes. That was the night they came up with the Frankel Jägerbomb Challenge. One bright spark decided that for each length the horse had triumphed by in the Guineas everyone should consume a shot of Jägermeister dropped into a glass of energy drink. One or two would wake up the next morning crying never again, but the Frankel Jägerbomb Challenge was to become a custom through the colt's three-year-old campaign.

One man who wasn't at the track or carousing in the Shoes was Shane Fetherstonhaugh. He had watched the race on his own at home before reporting as usual at the yard for evening stables. Of course, his role in Frankel's heroics had been significant and it was not missed by Tom Queally. According to the Racenews Racecourse Service, amid the post-race hubbub the jockey outlined how Fetherstonhaugh had done 'a mighty job'.

The groom's overriding emotion at the race result is likely to have been relief. Months earlier he had been trusted by Cecil to take on the huge responsibility of riding a champion. That meant unrelenting daily pressure for Fetherstonhaugh. But by the end of April it was a case of so far, so good. Frankel had become a Classic winner. And while Fetherstonhaugh may not have witnessed the 2,000 Guineas or raised a glass to toast the victory, he, as much as his boss, had a glow of satisfaction that evening.

Intriguingly, Fetherstonhaugh pinpoints the race as one that was integral to the making of the finished article. He felt that the horse became more respectful after his scintillating 2,000 Guineas victory. 'I think it put manners on him in a funny sort of way,' explains Fetherstonhaugh. 'He had a hard race, there's no two ways about it. Maybe it just got to the bottom of him a tiny bit. He was never as keen again after that.'

Chapter Ten

'He was a man that liked to give people chances; he liked the underdog'

Frankel's victory at Newmarket and his likely next race were the talk of the first few days of May 2011. Those perhaps with a romantic streak dreamed of a daring Derby bid over Epsom's unique mile-and-a-half challenge on the first Saturday in June. Others felt that the speed shown in the 2,000 Guineas could be put to dazzling effect in the six-furlong July Cup at Newmarket. There was even the odd doubter out there. One trainer I spoke to on the Heath suggested that Frankel's racing style on the Rowley Mile was not a formula for long-term success. Try that a couple more times and the colt would be running on fumes was the gist of what he was saying.

Luckily, the one person who wasn't getting carried away was Henry Cecil; or Sir Henry Cecil as he was about to become. A letter had arrived at Warren Place outlining that he was to receive a knighthood. Many in racing thought that such recognition of his extraordinary career was long overdue. But Cecil was as amazed as he was honoured.

Still, he had plenty of work to do before attending Buckingham Palace in November 2011. He had 139 horses on the books in

181

the spring of that season – about 100 more than five years earlier. He had barely ever been more fashionable. On the annual H. R. A. Cecil card that was printed every April there were forty-seven different owners listed.

The renaissance of his career could no longer be questioned by anyone. And like all the best sportsmen when they are in top form, Henry Cecil was making it look effortless. Yes, this was racing and of course that meant setbacks, but to the onlooker it appeared as if there was a real balance and poise to Cecil that season. Like the cricketer that switches off in between deliveries, only to refocus and ease the perfect cover drive to the boundary, Cecil would relax with his jockeys before a key gallops morning and then seamlessly switch into work mode. The instructions would be given before he would stand in splendid isolation to watch the small groups of horses approach and pass him.

Without being at all aware of it, Cecil was in the zone. At such times, there was an artistry about Cecil on the Heath as he enjoyed his work and the company of those who carried out their roles alongside him. Everything just seemed to be well in the world on those mornings. Certainly he was making good decisions, a sign of a clear and settled mind. In consultation with Prince Khalid Abdullah and Lord Grimthorpe, it was agreed that Frankel would not be sent down the route of the Dante Stakes followed by the Derby. He would be trained for Royal Ascot and the St James's Palace Stakes, traditionally a race that brought together the top three-year-old form lines for milers.

'We feel it is better to give him a chance and forget about an attempt at the Derby,' wrote Cecil. 'He would really have to run in the Dante Stakes if Epsom was still a thought but it comes too early after Newmarket. I really believe that he will get a mile and a quarter but have my reservations about him getting further. I feel it makes much more sense at this stage to stick to a mile and work towards the St James's Palace Stakes. After that, he will be entered in the top mile races against the older horses and will also have entries in mile and a quarter races such as the Juddmonte International and so on.'

It was a sound plan. Cecil didn't entertain a single thought about Frankel coming back in distance for a shot at the leading sprint prizes. In his mind, he had never envisaged such a path for the horse. Equally Cecil could see from the Greenham and the Guineas that Frankel's strong desire to go forward early in a race meant that staying the Derby trip would be difficult. Doing what was best for the horse and keeping to a mile for the time being was the right move. Even so, the St James's Palace Stakes turned out to be anything but a smooth ride for all connected to Frankel. In fact, it was an extraordinary race, as seemed always to be the case whenever the horse set foot on the track.

Of the nine horses in the field, five were Group 1 winners. Rerouted was also once again declared to run and this time he took on the pacemaking duties, albeit at a furious tempo that saw him open up a similar sort of early lead to the one that Frankel established in the Guineas. The rest of the runners initially looked content to let Rerouted do his own thing in front as the pace was such that he would inevitably come back to them long before the finish. But with more than half of the race left to run, Tom Queally chose to send Frankel in pursuit.

At first, it appeared to be business as usual. The pair quickly closed down Rerouted and for a moment or two it looked as if the outcome would be a carbon copy of their ten-length victory charge in the Royal Lodge Stakes at Ascot almost nine months earlier. The exertions of Frankel's sustained mid-race move seemed to catch up with him, however, as the final furlong saw his advantage diminish by the stride. From the back of the pack came the Irish 2,000 Guineas winner Zoffany, who produced an unrelenting challenge. Deep into the closing strides Frankel looked vulnerable but the line came in time and he won by three parts of a length.

Cecil told the press that rather than tiring late on his charge was more idling after being out in front for a long time, similar to the Guineas when the horse's huge lead was reduced in the closing quarter of a mile. His face – captured by the television cameras at the conclusion of the race – indicated his real feelings. 'It was like the horse had got beaten; that was his reaction to it,' says Jane Cecil. 'He was not happy.'

Cecil's inner frustration centred on the pacemaker and how Queally rode Frankel. But there may well have been a more telling factor in the horse's perfect record coming under such a threat late in the race. Around the time of Royal Ascot that year, Cecil's string was fighting a low-grade virus. The infection wasn't anywhere near as serious as the one that blighted the horses for so long around a decade earlier but it was there, just about invisible in routine exercise but surfacing under the duress of racing conditions.

'A lot of people blame Tom but our horses were sick that week,' says travelling head man Michael McGowan. 'They had something on them. For me, Frankel was too quiet to deal with that day. After the race he was feeling sorry for himself. His head was on the floor. He looked a sick horse when he came in. I turned round to Mike Marshall and said, "He's not the same, this fella." We got away with it, basically.'

Head groom Dee Deacon tells a similar story. She remembers how the horses weren't quite spot-on and how it wasn't the usual Frankel that contested the St James's Palace Stakes. 'He did keep battling but he only just held,' says Deacon. 'I think if he was a hundred and ten per cent on his game he'd have felt that horse coming – he'd have gone into seventh gear, whereas he was, "This is all I've got to give at the moment." He was under the weather. We had a cloud over the whole yard and he was obviously holding it as well. But the trouble is, being at home and doing his usual regular work, it didn't show. It's surprising how much more they can show when they are put under race conditions. You are asking that little bit extra. Henry never really pushed them at home, so you couldn't get a true reading.

'Obviously he was at his limit that day. But still, big heart, he battled it out to the end. If he really was on his true form it wouldn't have got that close. He would have been well clear.'

If the St James's Palace Stakes was the least satisfying performance of Frankel's career it was followed by one of his most memorable. It was the 2011 Sussex Stakes in which he was asked to compete against older horses for the first time. He also held an entry for the mile-and-a-quarter Juddmonte International Stakes at York but Cecil was adamant that the colt should be kept to a mile. This wasn't the time to be stepping up in distance:

the next challenge for Frankel was to take on his elders and that should be done over a trip that he was used to and proven at. Besides, Cecil had Twice Over and Midday to aim at the Juddmonte International and he had every chance of landing York's biggest race of the year with one of them. Plus, he genuinely believed he would win the Juddmonte with Frankel the following season. Meanwhile, in the high summer of Frankel's three-year-old campaign, in Cecil's mind Frankel was always bound for the Sussex Stakes at Glorious Goodwood.

The race was billed as the 'Duel on the Downs' with the Warren Place champion lining up against the excellent four-year-old Canford Cliffs from the powerful Wiltshire stable of Richard Hannon. Canford Cliffs was an outstanding miler. He won the Sussex Stakes in 2010, along with other top races, and beat the French mare Goldikova in the Queen Anne Stakes on the same day that Frankel survived his St James's Palace Stakes scare.

The Hannon-trained horse was ridden by Richard Hughes, who had long thought that Frankel would one day be in opposition to his mount. He had even brought the subject up the previous year with a man who had a foot in both camps, Charles Eddery. He was serving as an apprentice jockey at Hannon's stable but also had strong connections to Warren Place, where his mother Sally Noseda rode out, and Jane Cecil was his auntie. Eddery would sometimes head back to Newmarket and ride work for Cecil. With Frankel emerging as a brilliant two-year-old in 2010 he recalls Hughes tasking him to find out just how good the horse was. Word duly got back to Hughes that the colt was as good a two-year-old as Cecil had ever trained. It was a message that the thoughtful Irishman wouldn't have underestimated. He knew more than most about Cecil from his years as Prince Khalid's retained jockey.

After Royal Ascot the supporters of Canford Cliffs would have believed that the horse could be the first to bring down Frankel's colours. Canford Cliffs was foot perfect in his seasonal reappearance victory; Frankel was far less convincing. Were those trailblazing displays threatening to derail the future prospects of the younger of the two colts? Had his exuberance begun to catch up with him? Would his next race produce a first career defeat? To Cecil and his trusted team, the answer was an emphatic no. Away from the spotlight, Frankel trained perfectly leading into the Sussex Stakes. If he'd had a hint of an infection around the St James's Palace Stakes, there were no signs of it in his Goodwood preparations.

On the Saturday before Wednesday's race, Frankel breezed on the Al Bahathri in a peerless manner. Cecil had his horse exactly where he wanted and only needed to give him a maintenance exercise to have everything in place. Bullet Train led Frankel, who was given a well-judged pre-race piece of exercise by his regular rider, Shane Fetherstonhaugh.

'It was just imperious,' says Stephen Kielt. 'I've seen him do faster gallops; I don't even know if he pulled away that much. But he just floated majestically in the air. You looked at his legs and it was almost like slow motion. Then you looked at Bullet Train who was hard at it. It was just poetry in motion – just unbridled power.

'Of course, he'd come back off the St James's Palace when things hadn't gone right and he'd had a hard race in the Guineas. So for this horse then to be mentally and physically in peak

condition was a sight to behold. There was no danger whatsoever he was going to get beat by Canford Cliffs. You could just
go and enjoy the race.'

On 27 July 2011, the two top milers of their respective
generations met on the Sussex Downs. Canford Cliffs arrived
having won no less than five straight Group 1 races and unbeaten
in almost fifteen months. Frankel came to defend his perfect
100 per cent record: seven wins from seven starts. Something
had to give. The older horse was 7/4 in the betting, while
Frankel – perhaps with a question or two to answer after Royal
Ascot – was the 8/13 favourite. Rio De La Plata and Rajsaman
made up the field as respective 22/1 shots but, as in the build-
up, the Sussex Stakes was only ever about two horses.

In fact, as it turned out, the final stage of the race was only
about one horse – Frankel. The previous weekend Kielt believed
the horse was a certainty and the five-length demolition of
Canford Cliffs confirmed his judgement was spot-on. It was
close to a flawless performance, especially taking into account
that Frankel had to make his own running. Unlike the 2,000
Guineas there was much more control on the front end this
time. Cecil had got him back exactly where he wanted him.
That the feat was achieved was in no small part down to
Fetherstonhaugh's tutoring and patience, an aspect that Cecil
would regularly reference later in Frankel's career.

Tom Queally also deserved credit for his part in the victory.
The pressure was on after Royal Ascot but he couldn't have
offered up a better response than his Sussex Stakes ride. That
afternoon Frankel and Queally were a formidable partnership,
working in complete harmony. The horse found himself in

front from the stalls but there was no early over-racing this time. Queally took him into the business end of the race with measured aplomb, gauging the pace of each furlong before unleashing Frankel's finishing kick at the right time. Hughes had tried to play a stalking game on Canford Cliffs but the combination had no answer when Frankel quickened clear with about a furlong and a half to travel.

'Frankel saw off Canford Cliffs in the twinkling of an eye!' cried race-day commentator Richard Hoiles, the authority in his voice matched only by admiration at what he had just witnessed. 'What a race, what a horse.' Nobody in the 19,000-strong crowd disagreed.

'I'm not surprised at how he won, although it's an awful thing to say,' reflected Cecil, according to Racenews Racecourse Service. 'I was fairly relaxed, my job was done and it was a bit like going to the dentist's beforehand, just waiting for it to be over.' Cecil revealed that he had anticipated the exact winning distance of five lengths. He had contemplated noting the point on paper and producing it from an envelope post race but decided not to tempt fate.

Cecil told the media that Frankel was the best horse he had ever seen. The trainer referenced Blushing Groom, a dazzling two-year-old in France and also winner of the Poule d'Essai des Poulains (the French 2,000 Guineas). He also reflected on the brilliance of Shergar before adding, 'I can't go back to Tudor Minstrel and the days of match races but he's the best in my lifetime. I'm just very lucky to train him.'

As so often with racehorses the discussion soon switched from what had just unfolded to the future. Normally, that just means a horse's next likely engagement. But that afternoon the focus turned to the tantalising prospect of Frankel remaining in training as a four-year-old. For those that own the very best three-year-olds, it's invariably a key question: whether to retire a star at the end of the season for breeding purposes the following spring or race on at four? If the horse is already crowned a champion thanks to Classic glory, there is always a strong argument to capitalise. A Guineas or Derby winner will realise many millions if sold. If they are already in the hands of an owner-breeder such as Juddmonte Farms, Coolmore or Godolphin, then the stud fees from standing such a horse as a stallion are likely to run into significant seven figures, perhaps more, per annum.

So there is no guarantee at all that a top racehorse will be around for long. Only two years earlier Sea The Stars, the outstanding horse of his generation, had been retired to stud after his three-year-old campaign. Cecil outlined at Goodwood that there was a 'possibility' that Frankel would remain in training in 2012. And Prince Khalid Abdullah gave an even stronger indication to the Racenews Racecourse Service that his superstar colt would be raced at four. 'If Henry wants him next season then he can stay with him,' he said.

Frankel may have been the headline act through the summer of 2011 but it wasn't all about him – certainly not at Warren Place. Twice Over and Midday were once again more than paying their way. On the weekends either side of Frankel's Sussex Stakes victory Twice Over won the Group 2 York Stakes and Midday landed a third successive Group 1 Nassau Stakes. Now the two stable stalwarts were on course for a racecourse show-down in the Juddmonte International Stakes at York on 17 August.

Midday was five by that stage and still a force with which to be reckoned. Earlier in the season her groom Shane Fetherstonhaugh wondered if she had begun to have enough of racing. She was 1/3 favourite for a Group 1 in Ireland but had been routed six lengths by a three-year-old filly of Aidan O'Brien's.

'I remember looking at Midday and she had her head down,' says Fetherstonhaugh. 'I was thinking her winning days could be numbered; it was quite upsetting actually. Then the next month she came out and won the Nassau! She was just one of those fillies . . . always came back from defeat.'

Fetherstonhaugh retains a soft spot for the top-class filly that accumulated career earnings of over £2.2 million and was only out of the first four twice in twenty-three starts. He admired her toughness, her iron will to win and genuine attitude. In Fetherstonhaugh's words he 'loved her to bits'. But that didn't mean she was a sweetheart to look after; quite the opposite.

'She was sort of one of those mares where you get in, do what you have to do and leave 'em alone,' he says. 'She didn't actually like company. She wasn't friendly. If other horses came near she put her ears flat back. She just liked her own space.

'One day one of her bandages was outside the door, unrav-elled. So I bent down to roll it back up and as I've come up she has come over the door with her mouth open wide and went to bite the top of my head. It was like one of those cartoon lumps. She nearly knocked me out, knocked me clean off my feet. And I had a lump sticking out the top of my head. It was that sore, but that's what she was like. As she got older she got worse – more moody, grumpy.'

In contrast Twice Over was regarded by all that came into contact with him as the perfect gentleman. The latest addition to his fan club that summer was jockey Ian Mongan. With Tom Queally choosing to ride Midday in the Juddmonte International, Henry Cecil gave Mongan the opportunity to partner Twice Over at York. It was to be the first time the Scot had ridden the horse in a race.

The responsibility confirmed to a wider public what everyone inside Warren Place had long known: that Mongan was an integral member of Cecil's team. His rise to second jockey for the stable was one that nobody in racing could have forecast. Born in Glasgow but raised in Brighton, he had switched from a fledgling career as a jump jockey to riding on the flat. In his early twenties he was runner-up in the apprentices' championship and progressed to become the all-weather champion jockey in 2003.

But if Mongan hoped that his skill on the all-weather circuit would see him ascend to the top tier of jockeys in the weighing room, he was to be disappointed. Access to the best horses and openings within the major yards proved limited. By the middle of 2008, thoughts of giving up had crossed his mind. It certainly seemed his career was in decline. But thanks to an unlikely association with Cecil, the Epsom-based rider was to enjoy a second coming.

Mongan needed a break and he got two that summer. In mid-June, with the eyes of the racing world fixed on Royal

Ascot, Cecil needed a jockey to go to Warwick to partner one of the lowest-rated horses in his yard, Arabian Art. She'd had four starts and failed to win. All the leading players in the weighing room were due to be at Ascot where it was Gold Cup day, leaving Cecil and Claire Markham pondering over who to 'jock-up' for the 68-rated filly. The finger of fate eventually landed on Mongan and he duly partnered Arabian Art to a convincing victory.

The win at Warwick sowed a seed for Cecil. A couple of months later he called on Mongan's services again for another three-year-old filly called Portodora. She was the favourite for a handicap at Folkestone but Mongan was enduring a long losing streak at the time and feared the worst after a stroke of misfortune early in the race.

'My confidence was low anyway and I remember jumping out of the stalls and straight away the girth [the tack used to keep the saddle in place] went right back to the flanks,' he says. 'So I'm looking down and thinking, "How's my luck? I'm either going to fall off this or win." I kept my balance and lucky enough I didn't have to hit the horse or anything as she went and won by a few lengths.'

Cecil was impressed. He saw a high level of horsemanship in Mongan that perhaps others had overlooked. And it was helpful to the rider's future prospects that Portodora was owned by Juddmonte Farms. If required, the trainer could point out that ride to his owners as evidence of Mongan's ability to handle difficult circumstances.

From small acorns an important alliance between Warren Place and Mongan was about to grow. Not that he was expecting any such thing until during the following winter Cecil called and offered him the chance to ride for the yard. Tom Queally was the main man by that stage and Eddie Ahern was also on the team, and Mongan was shocked to be given such an opening.

'I nearly fell off my chair,' recalls Mongan. 'He invited me up to the yard in February and it was all a little bit surreal really. He took me into his study and said he'd like me to be part of the team. That really revived my career.

'I think he was a man that liked to give people chances; he liked the underdog. But he obviously saw something in my riding that he liked. He did say to me that he thought I was very good on fillies and he was a great trainer of fillies. He'd obviously seen millions of jockeys come and go, so he must have seen something in me to invite me up and give me that opportunity.'

The alliance with Warren Place often meant twice-weekly trips to Newmarket from his home in Surrey to ride work. On those mornings, he would receive an ultra-early alarm call before departing at 4 a.m. 'I didn't want to risk the traffic because you can't have a string of fifty waiting around for you, so I used to get up there in plenty of time.'

His commitment was rewarded with Cecil giving him plenty of rides – and winners. By 2011 he was second jockey, resulting in the opening on Twice Over. From their very first piece of work together on Racecourse Side, Mongan felt a huge affection for the big horse.

'If I could say any horse was like Henry it would be Twice Over,' says Mongan. 'He was so laidback and full of class. He was just such a joy to ride and so uncomplicated – such a love-able big giant of a horse.

'As soon as you turned him onto the gallop, away we went. I remember the first time, I sat back behind the lead horse and we were going flat out. I'm thinking. "We've got to go a mile-and-two here and the last two furlongs Henry really wants Twice Over to stride out. There is no way on God's earth we're going to get there; I'm going to be dead on my feet." But once we got round to the three-pole and I asked him to quicken it was just unbelievable. There's not many times I've ridden work going by owners and trainers with a big smile on my face and I think there's pictures of me doing that.

'That summer I started to ride a lot more work on him. I remember Henry used to apologise for dragging me up twice a week and I kept saying to him that it was an absolute joy to come and sit on his horses. I used to love it. It would be the highlight of my week and I'd be praying that I'd be riding Twice Over but all the horses there were pure class.'

Three years after he was contemplating turning his back on the weighing room, Mongan would ride Twice Over in the feature race of York's famous Ebor meeting; the Juddmonte International. Prince Khalid Abdullah had sponsored it since 1989 but never won it. Cecil dearly wanted to change that statistic and in Midday and Twice Over had two contenders with exceptional credentials, though neither was the favourite. Aidan O'Brien trained the odds-on market leader Await The Dawn, while Midday was 5/2 second favourite and Twice Over an 11/2 chance. Mongan saw it differently. He believed that his mount was the one to beat in the select field of five.

'Two nights before, I went running and played the race in my mind,' he says. 'I honestly thought I would win. I know it's easy to say that now but I thought my time had come and I'd win because he was such a class horse. He'd won the time before and, from the feeling I got from him at home, I thought this would be my best ever chance to win a Group 1.'

Await The Dawn's stablemate Windsor Palace served as pacemaker and as they approached the closing quarter of a mile it looked for a few seconds as if the race was going Midday's way. She surged to the front but then edged left towards the inner rail. Looming up behind her was the giant frame of Twice Over.

Engrossed in the spectacle, yards from the finish line, were three of Cecil's staunchest allies: John 'Fletch' Fletcher, Shane Fetherstonhaugh — the respective grooms of Midday and Twice Over — and Michael McGowan. Only a few days earlier Fetherstonhaugh had identified Twice Over as a major threat to Midday's chance. The string was walking down the hill in Newmarket when he nodded across from his filly to Twice Over, who was ridden that day by McGowan. The two men duly shared a short but telling conversation that McGowan recalls.

'I'm worried about him,' said Fetherstonhaugh, glancing at Twice Over.

'What do you mean?' replied McGowan.

'He's the danger.'

'I don't mind as long as one of them wins.'

'No, he looks good.'

Fetherstonhaugh's eye proved spot-on. Midday ran a very creditable race at York but Twice Over had too much for her that afternoon. At the business end of the extended mile and a quarter, Mongan had him rolling and with the winning post in sight the pair thundered to the front. Three or four strides before the line Mongan saw the groove cut into the grass that marked the finishing line. That's when it began to dawn on him that he really was about to fulfil a lifetime ambition and win a Group 1.

'I knew I'd won and it was such a feeling. I've never had a feeling again like it and probably never will have. But it's funny; it was the easiest winner I've probably ever ridden, the easiest race I've ever ridden. Five runners with a big wide open track and it was just so enjoyable. Anyone would have won on him on that day. But I was just fortunate enough to be given the opportunity to ride him.'

Nobody at York was more pleased for Mongan than Cecil, the man who had taken a calculated gamble in bringing the jockey into the Warren Place family. As the winning horse and rider paraded in front of the packed grandstands, Cecil appeared on the rail. Somehow the trainer managed to make himself heard out on the track by his jockey. 'Henry was shouting at me and I heard him through that crowd. He turned and put both thumbs up and said, "Well done," before I got back into the winner's enclosure. I think he was really chuffed for me as much as for the horse.'

The thrill of winning that race has never left Mongan – riding a horse he loved to victory on a major race day in a Group 1. It was also very special on another level. Mongan felt he had repaid Cecil for giving him that chance, the platform, to excel when others hadn't. And that day at York the jockey showed the racing world exactly why the trainer had such faith in him.

Before the close of a memorable year for Henry Cecil he still had two very important appointments in his diary, both marked Queen Elizabeth II. The second of these was to attend the investiture ceremony at Buckingham Palace on Tuesday 15 November when he would receive his knighthood from the Queen. But a month before that he was due to saddle Frankel in the mile-long Group 1 at Ascot that honoured the name of Her Majesty.

It was the fifth and final race of the horse's three-year-old campaign, taking place on the inaugural British Champions Day, coverage of which was shared with seventy-six countries. The organisers simply couldn't have asked for more on their first big day than the draw-card of unbeaten pin-up horse Frankel. They were also granted a stunning autumnal afternoon with a crowd of over 26,000 enjoying warm sunshine as well as a series of valuable races involving top-class horses.

Frankel's two previous engagements at Ascot were contested on the Round course. The Queen Elizabeth II Stakes, however, was being staged over the Straight mile. Another first for Frankel was that he would be joined in the race by his three-parts brother Bullet Train. Cecil outlined beforehand that the four-year-old would be present to ensure a truly run affair. The trainer was keen to avoid a situation where the field only crawled early on, resulting in a desperate sprint through the latter stages. There was never any chance of that unfolding when Bullet Train blasted out of the starting gates. In Ian Mongan's hands he blazed a trail that would eventually see him open up the sort of early lead that Frankel had done all those months earlier in the 2,000 Guineas.

By contrast, Tom Queally sought to hold up Frankel through the opening quarter of a mile or so. But by the halfway point Queally was happy for the 4/11 favourite to use that massive stride and close down Bullet Train. What followed was the sustained surge that was now accepted as the norm with Frankel. Travelling with power and rhythm, the horse delivered yet another emphatic success, this time by four lengths.

Perhaps the best measure of the performance was that the horses in second, third, fifth and sixth were all Group 1 winners at that time in their career. The fourth horse, Dubawi Gold, had finished second in the 2,000 Guineas in both England and Ireland that season. Frankel dismissed them all with ease. 'We need stars and champions – he is a champion,' said Cecil in the immediate aftermath of Frankel's ninth straight victory. 'He is a star to the public and to everyone in the racing fraternity.'

The huge swathe of pleasure surrounding the winner's enclosure was magnified by the knowledge that Frankel would be back for more in 2012. Indeed, Cecil felt the horse was likely to be even better with another winter behind him, a prospect to illuminate the cold and dark months that lay ahead.

Various end-of-season honours were bestowed on Frankel, while Cecil enjoyed recognition of his own feats with that day at the Palace. Allowed to be accompanied by three people he chose his eldest brother, Bow, the eldest of his children, Katie, and his wife, Jane. A wider group of family assembled afterwards for refreshments at the nearby Ritz.

For Henry Cecil, it was the best of times.

Chapter Eleven

'There was just a tiny little blip'

It seems obvious to suggest that winning races with your string is the main aim for any racehorse trainer. Undoubtedly, achieving good results is vital. On a daily basis, however, it's not the proximity or otherwise to the winning post that keeps a trainer's mind occupied; it's the health and soundness of each equine athlete under his or her care. Just like young pupils in a school class, if one horse in the yard gets a snotty nose the likelihood is that several others around it will pick up the same infection. That's why many trainers will gather each lot after exercise and, looking for early warning signs, ask riders if there has been any coughing.

It's inevitable in a town like Newmarket that bugs and viruses will creep from stable to stable. The strings pass each other on the Heath every morning, plus an individual may pick up a virus at the races when stabled overnight. It's likely, too, that a racehorse during its career will suffer an injury setback. Indeed, some will never deliver their potential because they are compromised by structural frailties. Certain problems can be managed by medication and treatment, others are less easy to handle. A racehorse has to be fit to win, so requires a daily exercise programme. But when that animal is prone to injury, it becomes a balancing act for the trainer. To over-extend a horse on the home gallops can trigger potentially damaging consequences.

Frankel was generally a sound and healthy horse when in training, according to his vet Charlie Smith. He was also, by and large, a sound colt and probably the strongest thoroughbred with which Smith can recall dealing. 'He was a joy to look after, really,' is the vet's abiding memory. There was one major scare, however; an injury that had those closest to Frankel concerned about whether his exceptional career would be cut short.

Cecil, as was his method, had begun earlier than some trainers with his string's conditioning exercise in 2012. 'Henry always said, "You don't want to have to rush to catch a train,"' explains Jane Cecil. As he had done through so many years, he eased the horses through that initial stage of freshness experienced in the wake of low-level midwinter trotting in the 'ride' at Warren Place. The next step was to raise the intensity of the canters on Warren Hill before getting going with the first pieces of fast work in late February and early March on the Al Bahathri all-weather surface. Cecil seemed very content with progress when, one morning in early spring, he casually threw his notes onto the table in front of me. 'We have done plenty of conditioning work and I am, on the whole, happy with the older horses,' he had written. His only concern was a lack of rain preventing him from taking the horses onto the turf gallops.

'Although we have the all-weather, there is no substitute for the grass. Three or four times on the natural ground brings them on so much. Unless we have rain in the near future I don't think we will be as forward as I would like going into Newmarket and Newbury where we usually launch quite a few of our nicer horses. If one misses these two spring meetings, one is at a disadvantage.'

Now aged four, Frankel was not due to start his campaign at either of the two April fixtures to which Cecil was referring. His intended seasonal bow wasn't until the Group 1 Lockinge Stakes at Newbury on 19 May, with the possibility of a race-course gallop and an overnight stay at the Berkshire course in the second half of April to ensure against rustiness. I watched the horse in late March during a routine canter on Warren Hill. The power behind the saddle seemed more impressive than ever as he moved effortlessly on a polytrack surface, up the four-furlong incline. His natural exuberance was still evident, while appearing more channelled than a year earlier. He looked like the ultimate racehorse. 'Frankel has done very well, settling and growing up,' wrote the trainer. 'He has grown, strength-ened and, all going well, he could be a better horse this season. Let us pray that things go right for him and no setbacks.'

Cecil's fears materialised on 11 April. Charlie Smith was preparing for his usual morning stud round when he received a call from Mike Marshall, assistant trainer at Warren Place. 'Mike rang and said, "Charlie, you've got to come here now." That was it.' Not that anything obviously dramatic had occurred that Wednesday on the Newmarket training grounds. Just after six o'clock, Frankel had been boxed across to Racecourse Side. It was a gallop morning, which always brought additional excite-ment and focus for those involved, including Frankel. He knew what was ahead of him and was full of himself in the preliminaries. That morning, as was not uncommon, he gave a buck and a kick in preparation. The exercise duly unfolded with no immediate indicator of anything amiss. But back at the stables, it didn't take Shane Fetherstonhaugh long to identify there was an issue with the horse's right front leg, and a potentially serious one at that.

'He'd been over Racecourse Side on the grass, where he'd been loads of times before,' says Fetherstonhaugh. 'Hand on heart, I can't remember him knocking himself or taking a lame step. There were no signs of any problem. It was only when I got back in the box and undid his bandage; I could tell straight away there was a little issue. I was sponging his leg and just ran it down and he flinched. So then I had a look and it just didn't look right. There was a little bit of filling, ever so slight.' Dee Deacon, who was in charge of the barn in which Frankel was housed, and Mike Marshall were quickly on the scene. 'I'm looking at Mike's reaction hoping he was going to say it's nothing serious,' adds Fetherstonhaugh. 'Straight away, by him, I could tell it was.'

The concern was that Frankel had sustained a tendon injury. It's a setback that all trainers dread. One I know in Newmarket believes that you can't bring a horse back from a tendon problem. He told me about a talented colt that had 'blown' a tendon in the spring of his three-year-old career. That was its season over. Everything was done to bring the horse back the following year. He was finally ready to step up to fast work late the following season. In his second gallop, the tendon went again.

'There was just a tiny little blip,' says Deacon, recalling that morning of high anxiety with Frankel. 'Normally his tendons were really straight.' Cecil soon joined them in the box and, responding to Marshall's urgent call, it wasn't long before Smith was assessing the highest rated racehorse in training. Smith found some warmth and pain around the superficial tendon. It was enough to set the alarm bells ringing. 'You were concerned, definitely,' says the vet. 'The question at that stage was, was it an external trauma or was it a strain within? Any significant tendon damage would have been the end of the flat-racing career, or certainly the end of that flat-racing year.' An initial scan was taken at Warren Place and it showed inflammation under the skin and around the tendon. To Smith's partial relief, the scan didn't identify a hole. 'That would have been the end of his four-year-old career before it started,' he says.

This didn't necessarily mean that a hole wouldn't develop in the next few days. A further scan the following week would clarify that, setting into motion an anxious wait. There was also conjecture at that time as to how and when the injury was sustained. To this day, it remains unclear. Cecil's feeling was that the horse had given himself a knock. That was his explanation when he spoke to Lord Grimthorpe later that day.

'Henry was reassuring but he didn't know,' says Prince Khalid's racing manager. 'Henry said it was a bang but he was eternally optimistic. He'd say a broken pelvis was muscle damage, which, by the way, is quite often the case. I knew he was incredibly optimistic so we had to factor that in. That being said, he said, "I've seen enough tendons to know that this isn't a tendon," if you see what I mean! It did not look very pretty, I have to say. But we truly didn't know and, of course, everything he did was news. I said, "We're definitely going to announce it because if it gets out we just won't be able to control it."'

The following morning Juddmonte Farms issued a statement that outlined Frankel's training setback. Cecil was quoted by the *Guardian* on 12 April as saying: 'He is such an extravagant mover that he hit himself. At this stage the injury looks superficial but he will be kept monitored over the next few days.'

It was an unsettling time for all connected to Warren Place, especially for Deacon and Fetherstonhaugh. Deacon jokes now that it 'started turning the hair grey'. But back then it was on her mind that Frankel's injury was down to her application of his bandages prior to the gallop. Indeed, the day after it occurred she even offered to step away from her responsibilities with the horse.

'I had this cloud over me. "Have I put the bandages on too tight?" You can easily, not give a tendon, but make swelling if you put something on too tight. I even approached Henry. I said, "Guv'nor, if you think I've given this a bandage pinch, you can take me away from him." I was so scared that I had done something. He said, "No, it's nothing like that, please don't think that. It will be fine, don't worry." I did get shit off some people about it. It was awful. I even had some nasty phone calls from people outside the yard – "I hear you've broken Frankel." Stuff like that. It was horrendous.'

Deacon's working day would begin around 4.30 a.m. – earlier on work mornings. That week she was getting by on even less sleep than usual due to the stress of Frankel's setback. Not that it stopped her from trying to reduce the swelling on the tendon. The inflammation had to go down significantly before the second scan so it could clarify whether a hole was evident or not. 'The worst bit was the in-between, waiting for the scan,' says Fetherstonhaugh. 'This awful period, it felt like a long time.'

Frankel's training programme was placed on hold but the injury hadn't left him lame. With the Newbury race only just over a month away, Cecil was keen for the horse to maintain a level of fitness through some form of exercise. He decided that Frankel should walk and trot alone in the covered ride at Warren Place, 'just to keep him moving because he was so close to the run,' recalls Fetherstonhaugh. 'Henry wanted it, so that if everything was all right he wouldn't have to start from scratch.' It was during one such solitary stretch that the star horse compounded his problems.

'He was slobbing around the indoor ride and pulled a shoe off on that leg,' says Fetherstonhaugh. 'Then he was lame. I remember walking him into the barn thinking, "This just cannot be happening; this is horrendous."' The problem didn't escalate, though, as the horse suffered no long-term ill-effects from the shoe's brief displacement.

For those at Warren Place there was huge pleasure and pride in working on a daily basis with the world's greatest racehorse. But, as Deacon and Fetherstonhaugh's comments reveal, the stress and strain took its toll on the staff. They lived with the horse's welfare at the forefront of their minds. There was no switching off. 'It was a job that carried a unique set of responsibilities and its fair share of pressure,' says Stephen Kielt.

The flip side was the intimacy that these key personnel were able to enjoy with the horse. For Deacon, it would come shortly

207

before five o'clock each morning as she did her early rounds. As she fed each horse, hers would be the first voice Frankel would hear every day. The only times that wasn't the case were when Cecil beat her in the early-riser stakes. Ahead of evening stables, Deacon would pick up Frankel's groom, Sandeep Gauravaram, and they would be early back to work around 3 p.m. to ensure the horse enjoyed some downtime, picking grass. 'I'd take out Ajaan, his grazing buddy, and Sandy would have Frankel,' says Deacon. 'We'd go and stand out on the paddock for thirty to forty-five minutes. Henry would come out and sit with us on the ground. Lovely.'

Kielt derived great pleasure and satisfaction from the many occasions he would carry out his shoeing duties with 'the big horse'. Frankel was quite a heavy colt when in training and consequently required his front shoes to be changed every twelve to thirteen days. 'When I went into the box every time to shoe him, I was in just such a good place because I was prepared to do him,' says Kielt. 'I went in there as relaxed as could be and enjoyed shoeing him. I didn't find it stressful but found it worrying in between times. Would he partially spread a shoe in the night and stand on a nail? Would he get a corn? Will he get beaten over something that was absolutely nothing to do with me? So there was a lot of worry.'

The one person who seemed most immune to the strain of living with Frankel was Cecil. The fact that he had trained so many great horses over the decades would have helped. Working with champions was second nature to him. He craved it, embraced it, lived for it. Just as importantly, he had a positive mindset when it came to his horses, which he applied to his cancer fight, too. When the occasional setback arose with Frankel, a lifetime of working with horses told him that the injury sustained early in the colt's four-year-old season wouldn't be career-ending. 'I don't think he was nearly as concerned as everyone else,' says Sally Noseda.

Cecil would be proved right, but not before an outbreak of false news on Saturday 14 April. It was Grand National day and a sad one for the sport as the Cheltenham Gold Cup winner Synchronised was put down after a fall at Aintree. As that was being absorbed, speculation that Frankel had been retired was also gaining momentum. 'It supposedly had come from Lambourn – I don't know where,' says Lord Grimthorpe. 'Someone started tweeting that he knew someone and they said Frankel's career was over. It all sort of got into a bit of a snow-ball.' The subject of Frankel possibly not racing again was referenced during the BBC's coverage of Grand National day, triggering a wider media interest. Grimthorpe spoke on the Racing UK television channel to scotch the rumours and outline how a 'definitive scan' would take place the following week.

As all of this unfolded, Cecil was blissfully unaware. In fact, he was at a birthday party in Newmarket that his sister-in-law Sally had organised for her three-year-old twins Richard and James. The following Wednesday, however, Cecil's concerns were evident as Frankel was boxed to Newmarket Equine Hospital for that crucial scan. He drove across town separately and waited impatiently for the outcome. There was an intensity about Cecil at such times; his usual relaxed lightness of touch was replaced by urgency. Despite having around a hundred and fifty horses under his care, only one would have been the subject of his thoughts as he waited for the result. 'He did a lot of box-walking, pacing up and down,' says Charlie Smith, who was among the veterinary team that took the scan of Frankel's leg.

'He came here on the eighteenth and we X-rayed his knee, because it was just below his knee, and we scanned him,' says Smith, who is based at the hospital. 'He came here because you wanted to get the very best quality scan that you could. Our biggest and so-called most sensitive machine is here and it was something that we couldn't afford to make any mistakes with. In the meantime, the leg had straightened up and the heat was beginning to go – it was less painful.'

The scans were duly taken and Frankel was given the all-clear to continue his career. With Newmarket's racing year beginning that afternoon with the Craven meeting, it didn't take long for the good news to circulate. And at Warren Place everyone could breathe much easier again. The 2012 season was underway and they were able to fully look forward to it, once more, knowing that the string would be led by its champion.

Smith says that there was a certain amount of pressure on the vets when it came to that second scan. They knew if they missed anything, however small, it could result in a more serious recurrence of any problem. A searching gallop, for instance, would soon find out any lingering or undetected issue. Cecil, though, had great trust in his vets. Once the assurance came that all was well, he got on and trained Frankel in the same way as if the injury hadn't arisen. With the Lockinge Stakes just a month away there was no chance of easing the horse back with a week or so of trotting followed by gentle cantering exercise. He swiftly made the decision that Newbury remained Frankel's first seasonal objective and went about getting him race-fit for it.

Frankel had missed two pieces of fast work during the lay-off. Some trainers wouldn't have been overly bothered by that as it was a few weeks ahead of a race target. Not Cecil. 'Henry liked to get his hard work in a good deal before and then just sort of breeze up to the race,' explains Fetherstonhaugh. 'Some trainers would gallop them hard on the Wednesday before the Saturday. He wouldn't. I think that put Henry off a little bit because he had to do the hard work later.'

While there was less time than he would normally like to get a horse physically ready for a Group 1 engagement, Cecil made sure Frankel was mentally tuned up by way of a racecourse gallop on 2,000 Guineas day at Newmarket, two weeks before the Lockinge Stakes. It was the racing public's first chance to see him that year and he duly drew a crowd to the parade ring where he was reacquainted with his race-day rider Tom Queally. Frankel was joined by his regular exercise companion Bullet Train, who had three-time champion jockey Ryan Moore aboard, while Fetherstonhaugh partnered Jet Away. The work-out couldn't have gone any better as Frankel initially settled last of the trio before opening up through the closing quarter of a mile. Applause broke out from the grandstands, albeit not quite on the same scale as the rapturous ovation he had received a year earlier when destroying the field in the 2,000 Guineas. They saw enough to convince them that the horse would once again take all the beating in the months ahead.

If race-goers were delighted at the sight of the fit-again Frankel on a racecourse, Cecil was happy too. He watched closely the relaxed manner in which the horse did everything that day on the Rowley Mile. All the hard work teaching Frankel to settle that he and Fetherstonhaugh had put in had seemingly resulted in a more mature individual. That power, that extraordinary talent, was now under full control. It appeared that the mighty engine within him could all but be turned on and off on request.

And to complete a good day's work, Frankel's full brother Noble Mission won his first Stakes race later that afternoon. He was already racing over a mile and a quarter, a distance that Cecil fully believed was also within the older sibling's range, now that he had learned to use himself more efficiently. But that was for the future.

The Newbury build-up continued to go smoothly. As the days count down in a stable ahead of any big race the excitement increases, but so does the pressure for those that are closely involved. Any little issue that might occur at such a late stage can scupper running plans, undermining weeks, often months, of work. As a consequence, vigilant grooms are on an even higher level of alert around a horse. Even so, problems beyond a staff's control can still crop up. So it proved little more than twenty-four hours before the Lockinge Stakes.

Cecil's travelling team were busy making their preparations before setting off for Newbury and the increased level of activity stimulated Frankel. Always a highly intelligent horse, he recognised the signs. 'He would start to wind himself up, start to get in the mood for racing,' recalls Kielt. 'That was always a worry because you had this massive powerhouse of a horse that's suddenly thinking he's ready to run.' On that day, Kielt had just set off for Newbury when he received a call from Marshall, who conveyed some alarming news about Frankel. 'He was being a bit fractious in the box, kicked a wall and moved one of his racing plates, behind,' says Kielt. 'The shoe didn't come completely off so there's a risk and a danger at that stage that he would stand on a nail, in which case he wouldn't be running in the Lockinge. So it was a very fraught time.'

Kielt turned his car round and swiftly returned to Warren Place. In the minutes it took him to get back, another farrier had been urgently recruited to remove the shoe and prevent that worst-case scenario of Frankel damaging his hind hoof on a nail. Even so, Kielt recalls the stress in the yard. 'I came back to a situation of anxiety; the horse is tense and the lads are tense.' Kielt needed a quieter environment to work. So, with Marshall's authoritative assistance, the box was cleared and within it a becalmed Frankel was soon re-shod. He was ready, at last, to travel to Newbury.

Cecil wanted decent ground for the race and he got it. The going description was 'good' at Newbury, where Frankel would face a five-strong opposition, including his three-parts brother Bullet Train, who would serve as pacemaker. It was the second race in which Ian Mongan would be aboard Bullet Train and he was determined that there would be no repeat of his British Champions Day tactics seven months earlier when he had shot off like the proverbial scalded cat, offering little support to his stable companion. Queally, Cecil and Mongan had subsequently spoken about how Bullet Train should best be deployed and it was decided the horse should be ridden as if he was in fast exercise on the home gallops where Frankel routinely travelled in behind him. If nothing else, the familiarity could only be a positive. 'I think it brought the best out of Frankel because he used to follow Bullet Train all the time,' says Mongan, assessing the riding plan. 'So I would jump out, make sure he was there behind me – which he always was – and we'd treat it like a bit of work. Just keep extending and extending rather than me tearing off.'

Mongan's determination to do everything right for Frankel was clear that day at Newbury. He popped Bullet Train out of the stalls to establish an early lead and the pair had barely gone half a furlong before the jockey glanced behind him to establish Frankel's whereabouts. He looked again just beyond the opening furlong-marker and then once more with just under three-quarters of a mile to go. Content that Frankel was in position, Mongan started to lift the tempo, bit by bit. It was an impeccable piece of race-riding in its own right.

Frankel, sent off in the market at 2/7, was travelling strongly enough in second place with main market rival, Excelebration, sitting in his slipstream. Excelebration had finished four lengths behind him in the Queen Elizabeth II Stakes at Ascot the previous October but came to Newbury with the benefit of an early season run under his belt. A month earlier the colt, under new ownership and now trained by Aidan O'Brien, had easily won a Group 3 at the Curragh. So he was race-fit and duly well positioned by O'Brien's son Joseph as the small field approached two furlongs out with the Lockinge Stakes up for grabs.

Not for the first time, though, Frankel was to prove a different class. He joined and passed Bullet Train in a matter of strides either side of the two-furlong marker before pulling clear in the unique style to which racing followers had grown accustomed. With five lengths in hand at the line from the runner-up Excelebration, it was Frankel's tenth victory in succession and his sixth in a Group 1. For Cecil, watching from the stands with his sister-in-law Sally, it was vindication of the decision to stick with the schedule in the wake of the vet's all-clear the previous month. 'I was really nervous the day of the race, but he didn't seem to be at all,' says Sally. 'He was just adamant Frankel was going to win.'

Back home watching on television, Fetherstonhaugh also confessed he was somewhat anxious and not solely because of the interruption to the horse's training regime. 'There was a question mark in my head – had he trained on?' says the groom. 'Had he improved or gone back? You don't know. His work was always exceptional, he looked fantastic and you're getting the vibe. They were saying beforehand how well he looked; he'd filled out and matured. But yes, there was a little bit of trepidation.'

An insight into how challenging it often was for Fetherstonhaugh to live his life alongside Frankel is provided by Claire Markham, now Mrs Fetherstonhaugh. She recalls the moment when Frankel was having his first scan during his tendon scare. 'Everyone was sat in the yard waiting to see what the results were,' she says. 'The only person who wasn't was Shane. He just removes himself from situations. The build-up to the Lockinge, then, was very tense.'

The mental and physical energy expended by all of Cecil's team during that rollercoaster spring was worth it for that minute and thirty-eight seconds that it took Frankel to sweep to success at Newbury. Everyone connected to the horse could breathe easy, at least until the next morning. The Lockinge Stakes won't be remembered as one of Frankel's career-defining performances. But for Shane Fetherstonhaugh it would, according to Claire, be on the shortlist of his favourite races for 'the relief of winning after that injury'.

Chapter Twelve

'We have got to do something about this now'

For centuries, trainers have sat on horseback to watch their string at exercise. Henry Cecil was no different for most of his career, though in his final years he would drive out to the gallops. There he would stroll the last hundred metres or so to a spot that was approximately three-quarters of the way up Warren Hill where others from his profession would also be waiting for their horses. One or two could be relied upon to have a phone seemingly constantly attached to their ear. Cecil still hardly ever carried one – he never really learned how to use it – and certainly not onto the Heath. Other trainers, perhaps on the back of their hacks, may have huddled to discuss handicap marks recently handed out by the official assessor, or which horses might be running where in the coming days. In among the hustle and bustle, Cecil cut an altogether more relaxed figure. He would often sit back on the grass as his final lot of the morning made their way up Warren Hill. Not exactly common practice among the training fraternity, but as his good friend Ed Vaughan says, 'He never really conformed, did he?' If somebody such as Vaughan or David Lanigan was around, Cecil would sometimes stay to shoot the breeze after his horses had cantered.

But he was rarely ever more at ease than on a summer's afternoon, surrounded by his string as they enjoyed a pick of grass in the paddock at Warren Place. Staff almost laugh in disbelief when recalling Cecil sat in among horses' hooves. 'He'd come up to you, lie down literally next to your feet and have a smoke, not a care in the world,' says Shane Fetherstonhaugh, shaking his head at the memory. 'You would never just lie down next to a horse; it only takes one to spook and they'd be all over the place. I used to be paranoid a horse was going to jump on him – they never did. I always found that was when he was at his best. If he was on really good form, he'd lie or sit there for twenty minutes, half an hour, just talking about the horses.'

That laidback demeanour is caught in a photograph that Jane Cecil sent to me for use on Cecil's website, and was taken by her son James McKeown on 16 June 2012, the Saturday before Royal Ascot. The couple had been invited by trainer Peter Moody to see the Australian super-mare Black Caviar, who had journeyed across the world for a race on the final day of the Royal meeting a week later. She was temporarily stabled in Newmarket. Moody had been across to meet Frankel and duly offered a return visit.

It was just three days before Cecil would saddle Frankel at Ascot in the Queen Anne Stakes. He had spent the previous four months or so doing everything in his power to ensure the horse was in peak condition for the race, but that weekend afternoon it was another racing superstar that was the sole focus of his attention.

In the photo Cecil, in jeans, light blue shirt and horizontal-striped jumper, is appraising Black Caviar while brushing his left hand over her formidable hind quarters – the chief power source. Meanwhile, the fingers of his right hand rest casually in a back pocket of his jeans, the thumb splayed out. He has natural poise and looks content. What the image doesn't show, however, is that Cecil's illness had returned.

He had been in remission for three years, receiving rituximab maintenance therapy during that time to help target and kill any lymphoma cells remaining after chemotherapy. 'He was basically well,' is consultant haematologist Dr Crawley's assessment of that period. But a check-up showed that the situation had changed in the early part of the 2012 season. Cecil needed treatment but his commitment to his horses, especially Frankel's training and race programme, meant that finding time in the schedule was problematic.

'We were discussing starting further treatment; I think it might have been April time,' says Crawley. 'As soon as we raised that question, the diary came out and "Well, I can't have treatment because of this, this, this and this." I do remember being worried because Henry had his schedule. I was wondering, "How are we going to actually have you well for this schedule?" It just seemed to me like this was heading for a potential problem.'

The Queen Anne Stakes was without doubt one of the most visually spectacular performances that Frankel ever produced. The official margin was eleven lengths but, as the television footage shows, it was Frankel first, daylight second. Such was his superiority at the line you almost needed to turn your neck to find the runner-up – his old adversary Excelebration, who just held off Side Glance.

The cameras caught a moment unfolding in slow motion on Tom Queally's face upon passing the winning post. A smile starts to appear and it grows and grows before he pulls his right hand back and gives his mount an affectionate pat down the neck. The coverage also shows the Queen and the Duchess of Cornwall, through a set of binoculars, watching closely from the Royal Box as Queally turns back to trot the champion in front of the packed grandstand.

Frankel pulled off a shoe during that victory parade. It was the only false step he took all day in a display of equine perfection. The words of Clare Balding and former top jockey Willie Carson, hosting the BBC broadcast, reveal their awe at what they had just witnessed. 'The visual impression this horse gives is unlike anything I have ever seen before,' said Balding. 'It is staggering to watch.' Carson offered a response that was even more vigorous in its appreciation of Frankel's brilliance. 'This is the best racehorse that you have ever seen, I have ever seen, that anybody will ever see.'

Respected form assessors Timeform agreed. The then sixty-four-year-old operation reacted by giving Frankel the highest evaluation figure – 147 – it had ever awarded to a flat racehorse. Cecil, in a cream patterned tie with matching carnation in his morning-suit buttonhole, wasn't being drawn into weighing up Frankel's achievements with those of other champions. 'He is a great, great horse and you needn't ask me about him,' the Racenews Racecourse Service recorded him as saying. 'I don't understand the comparisons between different countries, generations and distances and how people say one horse is 1lb better than another. It's double-Dutch to me. People have seen him and can judge for themselves.'

The vast majority present that day were left in no doubt as to who was the greatest. The quality of the victory is well illustrated by the fact that the runner-up Excelebration would comfortably win his next two races, both Group 1s, in August and October, but Frankel had simply annihilated him in the Queen Anne. 'That was pretty special,' recalls Bullet Train's rider Ian Mongan. 'I led Frankel that day and he just took off. He was gone.'

Mongan had jumped to the fore from the stalls and was soon checking over his left shoulder for the pink cap carried by Queally. As in previous races, they hadn't gone many more strides before Mongan took a second peek, then a further one with about three-quarters of a mile left to travel. This wasn't a reflection of any concern he may have had; he was simply gauging the race tempo by observing Queally's body language. 'My job was to make sure Frankel wasn't keen,' Mongan says.

If he felt Queally, in his slipstream, was anything other than relaxed, the pacemaking rider would ask Bullet Train to 'just go a little stride quicker'. If he assessed that Queally and Frankel were at ease, Mongan knew that he was setting the right pace in the early parts of the race. Once the field was within the closing half a mile, Bullet Train would up the ante. The plan was to make sure the gallop was an unrelenting one that only a supreme horse such as Frankel could thrive on.

'I would always, in my mind, ride my race to the two-pole. That was my winning post,' says Mongan, explaining the tactics that he would deploy in Frankel's four-year-old campaign (apart from the Juddmonte International Stakes in which he rode

Twice Over). 'So I would pick Bullet Train up and start to extend him just before the three. Then I'm going for glory.'

That afternoon, Frankel was at his peak. His aggression and dominance were apparent as he muscled his way past the Joseph O'Brien-ridden Excelebration with just over three furlongs left to race. It was the alpha male asserting himself. The conviction with which Frankel moved to the front signalled what was to come through the closing 400 metres or so. That giant ground-grabbing stride pattern was a sight to behold, mesmerising on the most prestigious racing stage of them all. 'He ticked all the boxes,' remarked Queally in the Racenews Racecourse Service report.

Cecil felt the horse had strengthened up again in the early part of that summer and was racing properly from the starting gate to the finish line. At no stage early on did Frankel tug for his head or give a hint that he wanted to launch his unstoppable run on his own terms, rather than at the request of his rider.

'You have to unleash Frankel in good time and then gallop the others into the ground,' said Cecil in the same report. 'He's got that long stride and I wanted him produced between two and two and a half furlongs because he takes some catching. He keeps going when other horses don't. He did exactly what I thought he would.'

Watching in front of the grandstand was Shane Fetherstonhaugh. Although officially off-duty, there was no such thing for Fetherstonhaugh when it came to that horse. 'I was probably better watching at home; I got quite nervous being there,' he says. 'You never know if something is going to go wrong. But I'm glad I went, glad I can say I was there when he did that, arguably his greatest performance. It was just amazing.

'Do you know what I looked at? How well he settled. He was asleep and he was in and around horses. He didn't get lit up. He literally had to bump himself out, give a little nudge to Joseph O'Brien on his right-hand side. It was just game over.'

The fact that Frankel was so relaxed will have given Fetherstonhaugh an enormous sense of satisfaction. The Queen Anne Stakes victory had been months, years in the making for everyone connected to the horse, not least Fetherstonhaugh. Or Fetherstone-Hall as Cecil once referred to him in a set of notes that season.

Cecil was very aware that his groom's input had been telling. Frankel had been blessed with all the physical attributes required to be a magnificent racehorse but he needed the trainer and a gifted rider to manage his mindset. Cecil knew that it was imperative that his star charge switched off and travelled early in his exercise and wasn't minded to over-race too soon. He had therefore needed an intuitive rider to interpret his wishes on a daily basis so that the hours of required tutelage could be undertaken on the home gallops. Fetherstonhaugh had proved to be the right man for the job, building on the good work that Dan de Haan had done on the two-year-old Frankel in 2010. The Irishman had thrown himself into the role. 'You don't come into work, then finish and go home. He was a horse that's your life,' recalls Fetherstonhaugh. 'He just took up everything. Before you went to bed, he's the last thing you think of. You wake and he is the first thing you think about, especially in the build-up to his races.'

Warren Place colleague Stephen Kielt feels the groom's contribution was 'priceless'. Frankel may well have been all-consuming for Fetherstonhaugh, but he was able to remain unflustered around the horse. His natural empathy with animals was also in his favour. Not that he would allow himself to be a pushover for any horse. Like teenagers, they will seek to push the boundaries on occasion. Fetherstonhaugh, for all of his quiet demeanour, would not let the horses he worked with get away with things they shouldn't. Frankel knew where he stood with his day-to-day rider. Those who observed them felt there was a mutual respect between the two, just as there was between trainer and groom.

'I think Shane is the type of guy to ride a big colt like that,' says Kielt. 'He's a tremendous horseman; calm, instinctive, an authoritative figure. He's not going to be intimidated, yet he's gentle. You have to be confident but you have to be kind. Shane had a lot of confidence, rightly, in his ability. He is a tremendously gifted rider.'

Kielt, who saw so much of Frankel's conditioning on Newmarket Heath, was also privy to how Cecil and Fetherstonhaugh always seemed to be on the same wavelength. It's not uncommon in racing yards for a lad or lass to think they know best in certain circumstances. 'More graft, less grass,' is a phrase I've heard from stable staff keen to get horses fit and racing. The frustration could be equally audible if they felt a trainer was overworking a horse; 'Why is he galloping the shit out of it?' Yet there was never any chance of Fetherstonhaugh ignoring orders from his employer when it came to Frankel.

'Henry was training the horse and Shane was carrying out his instructions to the T on the back of the horse,' says Kielt. 'I think a lot of lads couldn't do it and I think a lot of lads choose not to do it. Shane was able to take Henry's wishes and carry them out confidently, correctly. And I think he would be able to relay clearly what was happening underneath him. Shane's contribution shouldn't be underestimated.'

That early evening Fetherstonhaugh, a pal of his and I drove back to Newmarket, high on the exhilaration of Frankel's show of strength in the Queen Anne Stakes. We didn't need to say too much, there was just a glow that accompanied the trip home. At one point on the M25 motorway, not far from the landmark site that is Wembley Stadium, we ground to a halt in the rush-hour traffic. We inched forward until drawing level with a horsebox travelling in the left-hand lane. It carried the name of H. R. A. Cecil and the address, Warren Place Stables. All around us commuters were journeying, camped in their own bubble. The chances are that none of them realised that at that moment they were in the presence of greatness. We knew though. We knew that in that horsebox was a passenger whose value was nigh-on priceless.

It was just a week or so later that I started to realise all wasn't well with Cecil. I had been commissioned by Sky Sports News to do a day-in-the-life piece with Fetherstonhaugh. Cecil had given the feature his blessing but was unable to contribute as his voice had completely gone. Instead, Lord Grimthorpe agreed to talk about the key role Shane was fulfilling when it came to maximising Frankel's talent. Cecil was on Warren Hill as usual that morning and came up to explain in a strained whisper that he was unable to speak.

His farrier, returned from a short post-Ascot holiday in Crete, was quick to pick up on the decline in health. On Kielt's first day back, after flying in only hours earlier, he was weary and in need of his caffeine fix when he walked into the lads' coffee room at the end of first lot. That was when he would invariably bump into Cecil, who would be grabbing half a cup before he walked across to the top end of his stables and met the returning string. The two men would be alone. The time was often treasured by Kielt as he listened intently to Cecil's insights about the horses. That July morning was different.

'He could hardly get the words out about how he wanted me to look at a lame horse. Nothing of great importance, it was just something that wasn't quite right,' says Kielt. 'You were almost startled at how ill he looked; a real eye opener. I'd walked in and here was this extremely ill-looking frail guy that just seemed a different guy to [the one] I'd seen a week or so before. I found it quite hard to just be talking to him. It was a bit of a shock. There's a man that's obviously very unwell and there's me griping about being a bit tired.'

That early July morning, I wasn't really aware how sick Cecil was becoming. Shortly after 7 a.m., as Frankel and the string made their way down the Long Hill walking grounds, Cecil was in among his horses as alert as ever. On the surface, it appeared to be business as usual. But this wasn't just a throat infection or a cold. The lost voice was an obvious indicator of the problems that Dr Crawley had already discussed with Cecil.

'To be clear, Henry had the same illness all along,' says Crawley. 'Specifically, the disease was a follicular lymphoma, which is probably the commonest of the low-grade lymphomas. Lymphomas are cancers of white blood cells, lymphocytes, and they typically result in large lymph glands. But they're diseases which are systemic from the very beginning, almost always, because they're blood cancers. Blood moves around. This is a disease that you can't cure. All the chemotherapy that you give suppresses the disease. You can suppress it for long periods of time sometimes – many, many years – but at some stage if you wait long enough it reappears.

'Sometimes it reappears in the same place and sometimes it reappears in another place. So Henry had a disease that was originally in the abdomen. There was that big lump and we treated that. Then, when it reappeared in 2012, it was lymph glands in the chest and at the top of the neck, which was then affecting the voice. So it was the same thing, come back in a slightly different place.'

The ongoing conversation about when Cecil's working schedule could best accommodate treatment now assumed a greater urgency. The consultant haematologist recalls, 'I think the voice going was the thing that triggered, "Actually, we really can't wait any longer; we have got to do something about this now. This is no longer a when-shall-we-do-something."'

Yet Cecil was just about to mastermind a crucial phase of his star horse's career. Frankel was ready for the next step; the training cycle that would lead, via a race at Glorious Goodwood, to the Juddmonte International Stakes at York in the last part of August. It would be a very new test for Frankel as the distance of a mile and a quarter would be further than he had ever been asked to tackle before. A champion miler, now he would need to take on a different bracket of horses, several of whom were already proven at middle distances.

Adding extra interest, and perhaps a little extra pressure, was the fact that Frankel's owner sponsored York's flagship Group 1 race. Also, the horse was now public property. His victory at Royal Ascot had further heightened media interest in him. He was no longer a horse that captivated just racing fans; he now had folk from all over the world interested in his every move.

This was the intense environment in which Cecil had to train Prince Khalid's colt. It was an all-encompassing situation that a person in full health would find energy sapping. The Warren Place trainer was becoming increasingly unwell. Treatment was now imperative. Not that there was any chance of him ever stopping work. He would never have dreamed of stepping away from his responsibilities with the string, especially this horse of a lifetime with which he had been engrossed for the previous two-and-a-half years.

There was only ever going to be one path to follow at this stage. Yes, he knew that he had to receive treatment, but it was not going to be at the expense of his passion. The horses must come first. It meant that the months ahead were set to stretch him to the limit. Indeed, he would be presented with his greatest ever challenge.

Chapter Thirteen

'I want to be there for Frankel'

'How long have you got?' laughs Lord Grimthorpe when the subject of Frankel's day at York arises. For, of all Frankel's races, the Juddmonte International Stakes is arguably the most memorable.

There was a highly charged atmosphere around the race-course due to a combination of factors. Frankel's trainer was going racing for the first time since Royal Ascot, two months earlier. The public were shocked by his frailty. Cancer and intensive chemotherapy had severely debilitated him, and he had a walking stick and a trilby hat, worn to cover the fact that his hair had been ravaged by treatment. Henry Cecil's determination in adversity was etched all over his face as he watched every step of Frankel's preliminaries.

The horse had become as used to the spotlight as his trainer but he was under more scrutiny than ever before that day – 22 August 2012. No longer was he within the comfort zone of the mile races he had contested since May of the previous year. His thirteenth career appearance would see him compete over an extended ten furlongs, just over a mile and a quarter, on the Knavesmire in York. This is a historically marshy area of the

Roman city that for hundreds of years was the site of public hangings. It was where Dick Turpin, probably Britain's most famous highwayman, went to the gallows in 1739, eight years after it had first staged horseracing.

That August afternoon there was a bumper attendance of 30,163, up by over 50 per cent from 19,457 a year earlier. Frankel had transcended racing and captured the imagination of sports fans and beyond. The organisers of the British Champions Series realised his stock was still in the ascendancy. He even starred in his own advert, aired the weekend before the Juddmonte International across the ITV network in Yorkshire. In a neat piece of digital marketing, British Champions Series proclaimed him as the first racehorse to have his own TV commercial. The advert and the accompanying PR campaigns contributed to the tens of thousands that flocked to the Knavesmire.

'When you have a big crowd at York, usually it's buses that they have come in,' says Lord Grimthorpe, who was serving in his first year as the racecourse's chairman. 'This time it wasn't; it was cars. People got into their cars, from all parts of Britain, and they just came in their droves. They suddenly said, "We're going to go and see this horse."'

As he walked from the pre-parade ring to the saddling boxes, Frankel drew a succession of admiring gasps. Strong, toned and alert, he had never looked better. But no race is ever won in the preliminaries. The proving ground is always the track. On paper this appeared to be Frankel's stiffest assignment. Not only was he encountering a new distance but he also had to take on different rivals. If there were any chinks in Frankel's armour, top-class middle-distance performers such as St Nicholas Abbey and Warren Place stablemate Twice Over had the ability to expose them. Even so, no Frankel fan – nor bookmaker – envisaged defeat.

Three weeks earlier Frankel had won the Sussex Stakes at Glorious Goodwood for the second successive year. For the first time in the horse's career his trainer had not been present to saddle him. In the second half of July, Cecil had begun an intensive chemotherapy regimen.

On Tuesday, the seventeenth of that month, it was confirmed that there had been a 'progression' of his lymphoma. The disease was evident in the lymph glands in Cecil's chest and at the top of the neck, which was duly affecting his voice. The following day he received the first of three EPOCH regimens (intensive chemotherapy intended for treatment of aggressive non-Hodgkin lymphoma) that would be administered to him in the space of seven weeks. During that time his illness could no longer be treated in the day unit at the Nuffield Hospital in Cambridge; he now had to stay for several nights as an inpatient. 'It was getting increasingly intensive chemotherapy,' says Dr Crawley. 'He was getting increasingly toxic – hair loss, issues like that.'

Crawley makes the point that such treatment would result in 'the vast majority of people' taking considerable time off work. That was never going to be the case with Cecil. The trainer's focus remained on his horses. It probably needed to. He concentrated on the health of his string to distract himself from his own worsening condition. It was how he had responded to his initial cancer diagnosis.

But he was older now, almost seventy. Also, the toxicity of the treatment and how it subsequently made him feel meant he could no longer try to ignore the illness. He could no longer call on his own willpower to drive him through to the other side.

There were dark hours, normally a couple of days or so after Cecil returned from a short stay in the Nuffield Hospital. Sickness would force him to stop, and he hated those times. On his better days he would tell those close to him that he was going to 'beat this thing'. If he was doing something at the time, he would stop to look you in the eye as he spoke. But during that summer, despite his survival instincts telling him to get up and work, there were occasions when he simply had to rest.

'He did tolerate chemotherapy extremely well,' recalls Crawley. 'He had this complete mindset that it was not going to stop him — and it didn't on the whole. During that summer things changed. Previously Henry had been pretty bombproof in terms of dealing with things. He really did shrug off side effects and coped extraordinarily well. Over the course of that summer he started to look really quite frail. I guess that's the point; his absolute determination to overcome things didn't work any longer. There were times when he just couldn't do things. And he never really picked up his strength after that.'

There were now two all-important schedules: Frankel's training programme and Cecil's treatment times. Both were focused around the Juddmonte International Stakes. The trainer had known for a long time that the York race was the right one to ask the horse to compete over a longer distance. For work-rider Shane Fetherstonhaugh, it's not inconceivable that his boss had

Bullet Train (Danny Dunnachie) leads second-from-left Frankel (Shane Fetherstonhaugh) as the Warren Place string step out onto the Newmarket Gallops. *(Chris Bourchier)*

The moment jockey Ian Mongan realises he's about to win a first Group 1 as Twice Over lands the 2011 Juddmonte International Stakes at York. 'It was such a feeling,' says Mongan. 'I've never had a feeling again like it and probably never will have.' *(Steve Cargill)*

Cecil receives the trainer's prize from the Queen after Frankel's Queen Elizabeth II Stakes win at Ascot. Less than a month later he was knighted at Buckingham Palace. *(Steve Cargill)*

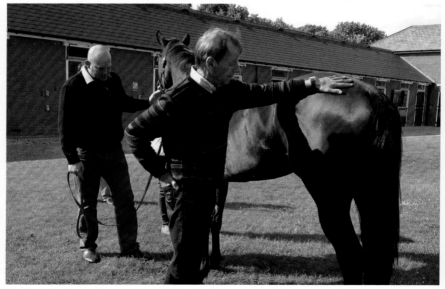

The Saturday before Royal Ascot in 2012: Cecil runs a respectful hand over champion race-mare Black Caviar. Her trainer Peter Moody (pictured) had earlier visited Warren Place to see Frankel. *(James McKeown.)*

Frankel gives one of his most exhilarating displays in winning the 2012 Queen Anne Stakes at Royal Ascot by eleven lengths. *(Steve Cargill)*

'People got into their cars, from all parts of Britain, and they just came in their droves,' says Lord Grimthorpe, recalling how Frankel played to a full house at York for the 2012 Juddmonte International Stakes. *(Steve Cargill)*

'I want to be there for Frankel' – the progression of his cancer failed to stop a frail Cecil attending the Juddmonte International at York. *(John Walton/EMPICS Sport/PA Images)*

Shane Fetherstonhaugh puts Frankel through his paces in the shadow of Newmarket's grandstand before the 2012 Champion Stakes. *(Chris Bourchier)*

Prince Khalid Abdullah's racing manager Lord Grimthorpe walks the course at Ascot ahead of Frankel's last race. *(Alan Crowhurst/Getty Images)*

Jockey Tom Queally celebrates as he returns to the Ascot winner's enclosure after the Champion Stakes, Frankel's final race. *(David Hartley/Rupert Hartley/REX/Shutterstock)*

The effects of Cecil's illness and many hours of treatment are evident as he and Tom Queally accept the 2012 Champion Stakes spoils. *(Steve Cargill)*

Travelling head groom Michael McGowan leads Frankel on a second lap of honour after his final race. 'It was a nice moment; the pressure's off and you can just relax,' remembers the Liverpudlian. *(Steve Cargill)*

8 November 2012 – Frankel's final morning at Warren Place. Cecil watches on as groom Sandeep Gauravaram leads the colt towards an awaiting Juddmonte horsebox. *(Tony Rushmer)*

Jane Cecil and her daughters Carina (left) and Anne-Marie stand alongside Frankel's brother Noble Mission, winner of the 2014 Champion Stakes. *(Tony Rushmer)*

A young Henry Cecil fishes the Kashentroch 'pool' on the Crathes Castle estate.

been sitting on such a finely honed idea for a couple of years. 'Henry had that planned out from very early on, probably as a two-year-old,' he says. 'That was the day he was going to step him up.'

Cecil was not nearly so engaged about when his chemotherapy was to be administered. As well as being unpleasant and unsettling, it was an unwelcome distraction. All Cecil really wanted to be occupied by was Frankel's upcoming races and the requisite preparations. The horse was always to the front of his thoughts; in particular, the prospect of taking him to the Juddmonte International Stakes. 'I remember we had the discussions about York,' says Crawley. ' "How are we going to get there; when are you going to come and have chemotherapy? And no, we can't wait another six weeks before you treat again." '

Cecil's treatment regimen resulted in his absence at Glorious Goodwood on Wednesday 1 August. For travelling head groom Michael McGowan, who had driven down with Frankel and Bullet Train the previous day, it was a slightly uncomfortable experience. 'There was probably a bit more pressure. If something did go wrong . . .' says McGowan, his words trailing off.

In his mid-forties by that time, McGowan was known within racing to be one of the best at his job. He also had Frankel's groom Sandeep Gauravaram with him for the Goodwood trip and they were joined ahead of the race by Cecil's respected assistant Mike Marshall. But they were missing the extra reassurance that Cecil's presence provided on the big days. 'Everything seemed to go like clockwork when Henry was there,' says McGowan.

As it transpired, Cecil's meticulous planning helped ensure that the Sussex Stakes went without a hitch. Unlike a year earlier in the same Group 1 race, there was no Canford Cliffs in the field to suggest that Frankel's unbeaten record might come under threat. Indeed, only four went to post and Warren Place's champion was sent off a 1/20 shot – the skinniest odds for a race that he would ever be. The bookmakers were right with their prohibitive price. Frankel was never extended as he cruised into contention behind Bullet Train before stretching clear to win by six lengths while eased down. The horse was now twelve from twelve.

Cecil greeted the horsebox home that night. Jane sent a picture for the website of her husband, in jeans and beige jumper, speaking to Sandeep, who was standing alongside the horse moments after walking off the lorry. A couple of days later, I collected Henry's post-race notes, which conveyed his evident satisfaction at events on the South Downs and looked ahead to the last part of Frankel's career.

'I was delighted with Frankel in the Sussex Stakes,' he wrote. 'He has grown up a lot mentally and took it all like a true professional. The idea was to be as easy as we could with him as it was a warm-up for the Juddmonte International at York. He seems to have come out of his race really well and is on course for the Knavesmire. He will finish off, hopefully, his racing career at Ascot in the Champion Stakes or Queen Elizabeth. Whether, with the gap between York and Ascot, he contests the Prix du Moulin in France is questionable. Maybe it will be beneficial leading up to Ascot but we will see. Frankel will tell me what course I should take.'

His voice, while occasionally improved, was still causing difficulties so he was increasingly using the website to provide bulletins on Frankel. The website was gaining an ever-increasing amount of traffic through the 2012 season. In the previous six years, Cecil's written thoughts had been almost exclusively about the horses but that summer his cancer battle had resulted in much conversation among racing folk and coverage in the media, and he started to address the subject of his health in his website notes. 'Although I have had some medical treatment lately and have not been able to go racing, I have been able to work at home,' he wrote a couple of days before the Juddmonte International. 'I am very hopeful that I will be able to travel to York for the Wednesday to saddle my horses. I just cannot miss that day and want to be there for Frankel.'

Cecil walked into the breakfast room when I was collecting his notes that Monday. It was upsetting to see how sick he looked. The first thing I noticed was his skin colour. It had yellowed as a result of the rigorous chemotherapy regimen, the latest course administered only the previous week. He was so thin too. 'A lot of that was chemotherapy,' says Dr Crawley of Cecil's appearance at that point. 'He had this thing in his chest, causing some swallowing problems and eating was not easy – loss of appetite. He lost loads of weight around that time. I think that was a combination of the fact that the disease had progressed quite significantly and we were giving him fairly intensive chemotherapy.'

I had not seen him for a few weeks and his appearance took a few seconds to process. Before he had come in, I had read that line he had written about wanting to 'be there for Frankel'

– and now I realised just how much the horse meant to him. To be as weak and unwell as he clearly was and yet still to be thinking about Frankel astonished me. How could anyone be that driven, that motivated when their own health was failing them to such a level?

That morning, I looked at Cecil in a different light. I had long known of his skills as a trainer and his charisma. The talent, the insights and even the comedy were all still there, but it was the indomitable spirit that I noticed now.

Lord Grimthorpe witnessed the same iron will when he went to see Cecil at Warren Place shortly before the race. The visit reaffirmed in Grimthorpe's mind just how tough a time the horseman was enduring. At one point in the conversation, he shared his concern about him travelling to saddle Frankel at York. 'I said, "Henry, you've done what you needed to do to get this horse there, you don't have to go." He said, "I'm coming." He was as determined as anything to go to the races that day.'

Henry Cecil's eye never lost sight of the ball in the weeks leading up to the Juddmonte International Stakes. Only once was there a hint of a hiccup and that was circumstances beyond the trainer's control. With Ian Mongan due to renew acquaintances with Twice Over in the York feature race, Eddie Ahern was tasked for the first time with pacemaking duties on Bullet Train. Cecil was keen to ensure that no stone was left unturned in the preparations, so one morning he set up a gallop in which Ahern was due to get a feel of the role by leading Frankel on the Limekilns gallops. Cecil always enjoyed the amiable Ahern's company – apart from that morning. The horses duly arrived, only there was no sign of Ahern. It didn't go down well with Cecil. 'He got his cigarettes and threw them across the heath,' recalls secretary Claire Markham.

Cecil decided Dermot Sullivan, the groom tasked with walking to and from the training grounds on Bullet Train, would now have to ride him in the exercise. Sullivan (known in racing as 'Fada') barely had a moment to absorb the change of plan before he trotted down on Bullet Train alongside Frankel, ridden as usual by Shane Fetherstonhaugh. 'I'm trying to fill Fada with confidence – "just let him bowl, just drop your hands, he'll be grand",' recalls Fetherstonhaugh.

At the Norwich Road crossing point, yards from where the horses were due to start off, Ahern arrived in the nick of time. Even then, the gallop didn't start off smoothly as he and Bullet Train almost went without Frankel. 'I was still getting led on,' says Fetherstonhaugh. 'We're roaring at him to wait, so he has pulled up.' Fetherstonhaugh cantered to catch up before the gallop began in earnest.

Eventually it played out in satisfactory fashion with Frankel exhibiting his wellbeing once again on the Limekilns. That training ground is probably Newmarket's most hallowed and since racing began in the town has only been used for the purpose of exercising horses. The depth of the moss around the base of the grass stems gives it a good underfoot quality. Horses always seem to give of their best on it, trusting themselves to let down fully. Frankel particularly used to relish the Round Gallop, traditionally the strip where trainers prepare their Derby prospects. It has an elbow where riders ease their mounts to the right before it rolls through a series of small dips next to a hedge.

'The horse always galloped great anyway but he loved it round there,' says Fetherstonhaugh. 'Before you turn into the straight over by the hedge he wouldn't pull, he'd be relaxed. Then the minute you turned into the straight and changed legs he was just fantastic to ride. That's a hard gallop, a testing gallop, that just climbs all the way up and you'd be struggling to pull him up. He'd be running off with you down the hill. Henry used to tell us to pull up early because he didn't want him to run down the hill but you still couldn't stop him once he got into his stride. I remember some mornings there, just thinking, "God, this thing is unbeatable."'

Fetherstonhaugh recalls a pre-York workout on the other side of town, on the Cambridge Road polytrack. The rider says it was 'probably his last gallop before the Juddmonte'. Frankel was once again to be led by Bullet Train, this time ridden by his usual partner Danny Dunnachie. The Racecourse Side training ground, which rises at the outset and then turns to the left, was one that Frankel always seemed to appreciate. But that mid-August day Fetherstonhaugh wasn't initially sure how well the gallop had gone as he barely finished a head in front of his sibling.

'He didn't go flying by, he just got upsides,' says the Irishman. 'Henry was waiting down by the bottom gate and I remember saying to Danny, "Jeez, did that not work well or did your lad work great?" Danny was adamant, "No, no, no. My lad, that's the best he has ever worked." I wasn't sure myself and was playing it back through my mind. Then Henry came up and I could tell before I even got close to him that he was happy. I said, "Well, he's happy, it must have been better than I thought."'

Cecil approached Fetherstonhaugh with one key question on his mind: will Frankel stay? His eyes had already told him the answer at Royal Ascot; likewise, the horse's homework since Glorious Goodwood had indicated the same. Cecil almost always relied on his own instincts in such situations rather than the feedback from lads. This was different, though. This was Frankel and this was Shane Fetherstonhaugh, the man he had entrusted to ride his star pupil for the previous twenty months. 'He's relaxed now, he'll definitely stay,' was the reassuring response Cecil heard that morning. 'It was just the perfect time for the horse to step up in trip,' says Fetherstonhaugh. 'Henry had him just where he wanted him.'

It was mid-evening when Dee Deacon got the expected call from the lads on the horsebox to say that Frankel was five minutes from home after his facile success in the Sussex Stakes. As usual in that situation, she dropped what was she doing and made haste back to the stables. She had already carried out her duties as head groom at morning and evening stables, overseeing the thirty or so boxes that were under her care. For Deacon, it was no problem to travel a mile or so from her home to the yard for a third time in a day. Her commitment to her employer and his horses meant she needed to ensure everything was fine with Frankel. She checked his legs and prepared his feed, among the other tasks that had to be done. Cecil was there too. 'You're coming with me to the Juddmonte,' he told her. Deacon expressed her gratitude and happily thought to herself about the outing to come but nothing could have prepared her for the emotions and excitement of that day.

It started in routine fashion; in at 4.30 a.m. for the feeds before preparing horses for first lot. It was a Wednesday and that meant gallopers. There were also workers at second lot before she zipped home to get ready. Cecil was as good as his word – he was taking Deacon to the races. Or rather she was taking Henry and Jane Cecil, for the groom was charged with driving the Mercedes 170 miles from Warren Place to York Racecourse. At 10.30 a.m., the powerful saloon car pulled out. Henry Cecil sat behind Deacon. A glance in the rear-view mirror re-emphasised that her passenger wasn't well. 'He'd just had a load of treatment and did look really poorly,' she says. 'I thought, "Let's get this over and get Henry back home. I'm not going to enjoy today."' Cecil slept for some of the journey, but every now and then would crack a joke or two, lifting Deacon's spirits. The nearer they got to the racecourse, the slower they went. The Frankel factor had caused virtual gridlock. There was even a concern about whether they would reach the course in time for Cecil to saddle Noble Mission and Thomas Chippendale in the Great Voltigeur Stakes, thirty-five minutes ahead of the big race.

'We came off the A1 onto the A64 and hit so much traffic and thought we're pushing this now,' says Deacon. 'We were just queuing and queuing. But the final bit of the journey you realised what a special day it was. There were these signs on the side of the road leading into York saying, "Frankel's coming!" People, the general public, had put these boards up. When we finally got to the racecourse, the crowd was just astonishing.'

By the time they had crawled through the last stretch of the trip, there was barely a car-parking spot left – even in the spacious area reserved for officials, owners and trainers. 'This is all your fault,' joked Deacon. She received a little smile in return but could tell at that stage Cecil was 'really pensive'. On arrival at York, he put on a black felt hat and grasped his walking stick. It was the first time he had ever taken one racing. Before they went in, Jane Cecil handed Deacon a piece of paper. Written on it was a doctor's name and the location of the on-site medical team.

York Racecourse has always been a magnificent setting for a major race day. It has stature and yet each race-goer feels comfortable. Everyone is welcome. There is style matched by substance, plus a unique charm that not only draws racing diehards but many others who love a sense of occasion and fun. That afternoon York excelled itself. Flowers seemed to be everywhere, adding to the colour of the day. The sun shone with vigour too. There was a very definite feelgood factor to accompany the Frankel factor at the racecourse.

York's team was carrying out final preparations. The anticipation was probably greatest for one man in particular, Lord Grimthorpe. The racecourse is almost in his blood. Raised half an hour or so away in the Ryedale village of Westow, he had raced there just about all of his life. One of his friends was Nicholas Wrigley, who he ended up succeeding as York's chairman in 2012. Grimthorpe and Wrigley used to go to the track together as teenagers. One summer's day in the early 1970s, they followed around a most flamboyant character in lime green trousers. 'He must have had white Gucci shoes, I suppose,' recalls Grimthorpe. 'We had no idea who he was and found out.' Their pied piper that day was, of course, Henry Cecil.

Cecil, though, wasn't the reason why Grimthorpe was at the entrance of the County Stand on 2012 Juddmonte International Stakes day. He was in position for the arrival of his employer, Prince Khalid Abdullah, sponsor of the big race since 1989 – and owner of Frankel. It was Grimthorpe's fourteenth year as his racing manager and he had enjoyed many special occasions along the way. Nothing quite compared to York that afternoon.

'The place was buzzing,' he says. 'I stood outside the County Stand entrance waiting for Prince Khalid to come and it felt like I shook a thousand hands. "Thank you for bringing him. How's Henry?" One chap had a green waistcoat with a pink sash [Prince Khalid's racing colours]. The level of expectation was just enormous. The paddock, from the first race onwards, they sat, stood; no one moved.'

William Derby, chief executive and clerk of the course, was overseeing his many race-day responsibilities. He and his team were determined to ensure the day went smoothly and a huge amount of thought had gone into the logistics. There had been a stack of operational issues to address, not least Frankel's security while on site. For the first time, the horse had his own police escort. Derby had engaged two uniformed officers to be with him and Cecil's staff from the moment he exited the stabling block until he returned. There was a ten-minute or so walk across the Knavesmire to negotiate and the racecourse management was leaving no stone unturned. 'The policemen's job was to walk twenty metres ahead of and behind the horse

just to make sure no one got too close,' says Derby. 'Not from
a threat. Just making sure people didn't forget he was a fully
primed racehorse.'

Derby had spoken to Cecil in the build-up but only about
factors connected to the horse and the race. Cecil's condition
wasn't discussed but the York boss was very aware of it and his
medical team were briefed accordingly. A PR plan was in place
too. Derby and I had spoken at length before the meeting
regarding the in-race and post-race media situation. In truth,
that was always something that Cecil would determine but it
was decided that I should be in the proximity of the trainer
around the Juddmonte International, before bringing him to
the County Stand afterwards so he could join the Prince and his
family in their private box.

There was one area that Derby couldn't influence, however
– the race. Forty years earlier, Brigadier Gerard suffered the
only defeat in his eighteen-race career when Roberto beat him
in the International at York. This had been seized upon by the
media in the days before the renewal involving Frankel. Derby
couldn't help but notice the 'Knavesmire Graveyard' coverage.
For nine years he had been in charge at the racecourse and, in
his words, had always been 'fairly impartial' as to who won and
lost. Not that day. 'I can't tell you how anxious I was that the
bubble would burst,' he says. 'I've never wanted a horse before
or since to win so much at York . . . this was different.'

Derby makes the point that Frankel wasn't being presented
with a nigh walkover opportunity or a celebration race. He was
going to have to prove himself against several Group 1 stars.
One horse in particular triggered a flash or two of doubt in

Shane Fetherstonhaugh's mind. That rival was St Nicholas
Abbey, whom Cecil's employee had seen up close and personal
at Churchill Downs the previous November in the Breeders'
Cup Turf. Fetherstonhaugh was in Kentucky for his beloved, if
sometimes grouchy, Midday. It was the mare's final race. Well
beaten into sixth place on that occasion, the winner was none
other than St Nicholas Abbey. Fetherstonhaugh was profoundly
impressed by the style of the victory.

'I'll never forget it, I stood on the rail by the winning line and
St Nicholas Abbey came by us,' says Shane. 'He was absolutely
winging. I thought, "He is a proper horse." He looked like he'd
just jumped in with a furlong to go; Joseph O'Brien was struggling to pull him up. That always stuck in my mind and I knew
they [Frankel and St Nicholas Abbey] were going to clash
somewhere during the next season. I thought if there's one
horse that could beat him, if our lad got boxed in or something
happened, this would be the one. I kept it to myself.'

Not long after arriving at the racecourse, Cecil met up with his
daughter Katie and her family. That lifted the trainer's spirits. As
he saddled Frankel's brother Noble Mission and stablemate
Thomas Chippendale for the Great Voltigeur Stakes, it seemed
every eye was on him. A wider audience, via the television
cameras, was seeing the trainer for the first time since June. The
television pictures highlighted the transformation from the man
who had commanded the winner's circle after the Queen Anne
Stakes at Royal Ascot. Even Fetherstonhaugh found himself
stunned by the pictures as he prepared to watch the races at
home with Claire Markham. It brought it home just how sick

the boss was. 'I remember thinking, "He looks so ill." I had seen him the day before and it hadn't crossed my mind. When you are around someone that's ill, you don't notice as much.'

Ian Mongan, at York to ride Twice Over, knew that Cecil was severely weakened. There was something else that struck him – courage. 'He was pretty bad,' says the jockey. 'A lot of men in his situation would have been in bed giving up the ghost. It just shows what a man he was.'

The Great Voltigeur Stakes did not pan out as well as Cecil had hoped. There was no early tempo to the race and the crawl did not suit either Noble Mission or Thomas Chippendale, who finished fourth and fifth respectively behind Thought Worthy, who was given a good tactical ride from the front by William Buick. As she watched the race and Cecil's subsequent dismay, Deacon wondered if the afternoon could get any more fraught. She followed him, in her words, 'like a puppy' as he went to put on Frankel's saddle. By this point, the bars and food areas were completely empty. It seemed as if just about all the 30,000-plus crowd were squeezed into every nook and cranny around the parade ring. 'Everyone sought a vantage point,' says Derby.

As the horses stepped onto the track, Grimthorpe was offered reassuring words from an unlikely source: Coolmore supremo John Magnier. Magnier and his associates had three rivals, including St Nicholas Abbey, from the Ballydoyle stable of Aidan O'Brien in opposition. Magnier told the racing manager that their horses would be running fair and square, jumping out and ensuring there was a good pace set. 'I said, "Thank you, that's very kind,"' recalls Grimthorpe. 'I think the idea for the Ballydoyle horses was to set a good gallop because they knew St

Nicholas Abbey stayed well and they weren't sure about Frankel. Nor was anyone. I say that; if you win the Queen Anne by eleven lengths on the straight mile at Ascot you'd be pretty confident he would win the Juddmonte, ten and a half furlongs. But it's a four-furlong straight at York . . .'

The bookmakers were convinced as to what the outcome would be. Frankel was the 1/10 favourite, St Nicholas Abbey was next best at 5/1, while Twice Over was 16/1 to win the race for the second successive year. Not that Cecil would have given the odds a second glance from his vantage point relatively close to all the bookies' boards. Deacon and I followed him, Jane Cecil, her sister Sally and Henry's daughter Katie into a packed standing area in front of the County Stand. Owners and trainers would often watch from the steps in front of the media suite at York. But it was the spot that TV cameras would usually scan first around the big races as they sought the reactions of connections. That day, we were deep among the throng and there was no cameraman in sight. The trainer was almost invisible. 'He was just so on edge,' is Deacon's opinion. 'Henry was almost like, "I want to be in my own space, it's my time now – leave me alone." I think it meant so much to him.'

Deacon felt that a silence enveloped the Knavesmire as the minutes ticked down before the starting stalls opened. Cecil had moved five yards ahead of the rest of us. He smoked nervously, looking at the concrete and, occasionally, turning a small circle as he did so. In those moments and the two minutes, six seconds of the race that followed he was as alive as he had ever been. Frankel gave what was for many experts the most complete and spine-tingling performance of his life.

He was, in truth, slightly slow to break from the gates. Race-day commentator Stewart Machin referenced it immediately in his call: 'Frankel just missed half a beat, perhaps by design.' Bullet Train was sent to the front but couldn't hold that position as Robin Hood and Windsor Palace hustled their way through to assert. Frankel was settled with a trio of horses at the back. At home in Suffolk, Fetherstonhaugh was living every stride, giving himself a running commentary in his mind. 'Fuck me, he's a long way back . . . these horses are going a right good clip . . . and, you know, they don't stop . . . he has to stay!'

Not long after the nine runners turned for home Tom Queally made his move, close to the stands rail. With three furlongs to run, St Nicholas Abbey was just ahead of Frankel and on his immediate inner. At that point both horses remained held together by their respective riders and poised for battle. It seemed sure that the last quarter of a mile or so would give us a protracted head-to-head with no quarter asked or given. Two great horses locked in combat.

How wrong we were. Approaching the two-furlong pole, Joseph O'Brien started to get animated in the saddle; Queally on the other hand sat quiet, a perfect study of balance and concentration. Then, in a couple of monstrous yet effortless strides the race was all over. Frankel assumed full control in a split-second move that triggered an extraordinary roar of approval that all but shook the ground under our feet.

Watching the race from arguably the best vantage point was Channel 4 reporter Derek Thompson. He was travelling furlong-by-furlong in the camera car and witnessed Frankel from almost touching distance. 'I followed him and couldn't believe what I was seeing,' says Thompson, with the sort of awe usually reserved for someone catching their first sight of a tiger hunting down prey in the wild. 'I was right close up, next to the cameraman, and there was Tom cruising, sitting with a triple handful.'

Fetherstonhaugh marvelled from afar at the scenes shot from the camera car, his early race concerns blitzed. In their place was something akin to shock. He, along with Queally, knew best of all what it felt like to be aboard such equine excellence but to see Frankel in full cry that afternoon was something else altogether. 'You can't believe what you are watching,' says Fetherstonhaugh. 'There was a side-on view and it's like something you see in a film – you think it doesn't work like that. He's coming up the rail and one by one they're just dropping out and he's just going by them like that; just cantering up . . . unbelievable. It was just beautiful.'

The race was to become the proverbial procession. Queally still didn't relax. With almost a furlong to go his elbows started to move back and forth with the reins. It was almost the opposite of an urgent call to action. If anything it was a reminder to Frankel: don't drop your guard now, fella. Not that there was any chance. Frankel was in the zone. He lowered and lengthened, seemingly oblivious to the crowd who were going wild just yards to his right. He smashed the line with a full seven lengths back to Farhh. A fraction behind him was St Nicholas Abbey, swept aside and vanquished on the day. It had been the ultimate show of strength from Frankel.

'I rate York as his best performance,' says Stephen Kielt, who watched from the County Stand steps. 'The power, ease and command he had in the race. The way he quickened . . . he just cruised.'

The first congratulatory voice that Henry Cecil heard after Frankel passed the winning post wasn't that of his wife Jane or daughter Katie. It was a hale and hearty Yorkshireman's. He hadn't so much as given the trainer a second glance before or during Frankel's bravura display. None of the folk around him did. It was as if they granted him a respectful space for his thoughts. That changed immediately as the post-race clamour kicked in. 'Well done Henry, lad!' Variations of the theme were offered as Cecil took the few steps towards his wife, daughter and sister-in-law. There was just a moment or two for elation and relief with his family before Cecil led the small group to the front where Queally was parading the champion racehorse.

My abiding memory of the whole day was not Frankel's power move just over two furlongs from home. It was nothing to do with the horse at all. Just as we walked towards the corner of the County Stand approaching the parade ring and winner's enclosure, Cecil and wife were four or five yards in front of us. As they strolled Cecil, with languid style, threw an arm around Jane. He smiled down at her as she drew in closer. Gone was any sign of the illness and treatment. Likewise, there was no hint of any tension. In fact, I never saw him as happy as he looked in that moment. His greatest horse had passed his stiffest test with flying colours and the woman with whom he was in love was at his side to share the experience. 'The whole thing was just like an American film,' says Deacon. She's right, but the race and the surrounding scenes were fact not fiction.

There was unreserved joy around the parade ring. The winning horse was greeted by the enthusiastic race-goers. The same outpouring, if not greater, was accorded to the winning trainer. 'Three cheers for Henry,' they cried. 'York really welcomed Frankel,' says British Champions Series boss Rod Street. 'The Yorkshire racing community know what a great racehorse is and they welcomed him. The reception to Sir Henry was special and it was another "I-was-there" moment.'

There had been a question mark over whether Cecil could carry out the customary post-race debrief in the winner's circle with the media. The Channel 4 team was desperate to get the interview. By a stroke of luck their reporter was the man who, earlier that summer, had sat down on Warren Hill in Newmarket with Cecil and received encouragement in connection with his own cancer battle: Derek Thompson.

'Andrew Franklin, the producer, said in my ear, "Tommo, you've got to get Henry." That was the story, obviously. I told Andrew that there was five hundred million people around him, everyone trying to get an interview.' In typically determined style, Thompson wasn't going to be put off. He edged through his media colleagues and offered his congratulations before asking for a few words.

'It was, I'm certain, my most emotional ever moment on Channel 4, talking to the great man. Every few months I'll think of that interview and think of him. That, to me, was a very special moment; that he trusted me – we helped each other. He could hardly speak, but he wanted to express what it was like. It was wonderful. Remember the pressure that was on him. Although he had the best horse in the world he had to train it, he had to win races. That was his job and he didn't mess about. But he trained this horse in such a thoughtful way – different class. The way he reacted and talked to me that day was spellbinding, moving, very, very emotional. When I'd said "Thank you for that" and turned away, I just went "wow" to myself.'

Cecil told Thompson that Frankel's victory left him feeling 'twenty years better'. It showed too when the call came for him to accept his trainer's prize. Gone was the walking stick. He strode up to receive his trophy. With the presentation completed, Cecil headed from the winner's circle in the direction of the County Stand entrance where he would relive the race with Prince Khalid. It was less than a hundred yards, but the walk took around twenty minutes. Cecil signed autograph after auto-graph. One man explained that he had driven up from Suffolk with his young child to cheer on Frankel and Cecil. The trainer listened, no hint of impatience on his face. He then signed the man's race-card and there was a smile on that face. He didn't stop smiling.

Upstairs in the private box, Cecil would enjoy the glow of success with the Prince. The two men shared a deep and endur-ing friendship and this was a day to savour. Cecil's appetite returned too, as he allowed himself to relax fully for the first time in a long while. 'That was the fun thing, that he came to the box and ate a grouse and a lobster,' says Grimthorpe. 'I always said he was like a boa constrictor, he could just swallow a grouse like that!'

For Grimthorpe that was the Frankel race day, above all others, that he would bottle up and take to the desert island.

'No question,' he says. 'The crowd, the track, the horse, the trainer; all those things. We ran the gamut of emotions because nobody could believe that Henry would live another six minutes, let alone another ten months. From that point of view, the contrast of the strength and virility of Frankel against the frailty of Henry was just part of the whole dynamic of the day.'

For Dee Deacon the most exhausting of days still had a final act to play out. A deepset migraine had been partially alleviated by a cup of tea and a couple of painkillers in the office of William Derby. But she was on standby for a call from Jane Cecil regarding the return journey down south. There were stable runners at York the following day, plus a prominent Yorkshire-based owner of Cecil's was staging a dinner during the Ebor meeting at which Jane would represent her husband. So Deacon was to drive her employer home. It remains one of her fondest memories from fifteen years of working for Cecil.

As the two of them set off, Cecil was in ebullient spirits, a complete contrast to the feeble figure she had transported seven or so hours earlier. 'What a different person; sat in the front, shoes off, feet on the dashboard – yap, yap, yap,' says Deacon, smiling at the memory. 'You couldn't shut him up. He was just like a giddy school kid. He was on a huge high talking about the horse, the day: "wasn't it wonderful, sorry we had such a bad journey up".'

As they made their way back down the A1, Cecil decided he wanted a break. 'I'd like a cup of tea. Would you like a cup of tea, Dee?' They stopped at a Little Chef and drank their tea on picnic benches outside. The conversation changed. It took on a more wistful note. 'I'd love to buy a holiday home for Jane in Devon,' said Cecil, his imagination roaming. 'We chatted there about anything but racing. It was lovely,' says Deacon. It was a very special journey home. It flew by. I've been in racing over thirty years and that was the best day I've had. I'd give my right arm to do it all over again.'

For Cecil, too, it was a day that he treasured. His pride in Frankel's performance was immense. There was relief, too. No more could anyone question the horse's ability to win beyond a mile. 'Frankel did everything right,' he wrote in a set of notes for publication on his website. 'His win was, to me, very impressive and he seemed to get the trip really well. The outcome was a tremendous relief and, those who doubted him in any way, their thoughts surely were put to rest. Hopefully, we will see him at Ascot for his final racecourse appearance in the Champion Stakes. There is a chance he may have a run in the Prix du Moulin at Longchamp before, but it is far from certain. Frankel will tell me the best thing to do.'

At times Cecil's emotions on a racecourse could be detected, especially when his lip wobbled after Light Shift won the 2007 renewal of the Oaks. It was his written correspondence, however, that conveyed just what that afternoon in York meant to him. 'Wednesday was one we at Warren Place will never forget. The Yorkshire racing crowd gave him [Frankel] a wonderful reception and I was so pleased we managed to get to the Knavesmire as the North really appreciates seeing good horses. I would like to thank so many people for helping make it such a wonderful occasion and one I will cherish and remember for the rest of my life.'

Chapter Fourteen

'All comers, all grounds, all beaten!'

It was the day of the Champion Stakes at Ascot and, towards the end of morning stables, Charles Eddery walked into the breakfast room at Warren Place. The house was like a second home to the young jockey, whose father Paul was a mainstay of the stable from the 1980s into the early years of the twenty-first century and rode many winners. Born in 1991, Charles was never far from the yard in his schooldays. Henry Cecil used to take the youngster onto the Heath to watch his dad ride work. In his early teenage years, Charles would jump on one of the Warren Place hacks called Bug, a coloured quarter horse, and accompany the trainer as the string exercised. It was only ever going to be a career in racing for the lad whose uncle was the legendary jockey Pat Eddery.

Charles spent the whole of his 2005 summer holidays staying at Warren Place. He and Henry Cecil were almost inseparable through those weeks. 'We watched the Ashes after morning stables,' says Eddery, recalling the series that gripped the nation as England's cricketers finally beat their Australian rivals for the first time since 1986–7. Cecil wasn't a huge cricket fan but enjoyed exceptional sport played by the best. That summer he may have had more time than in the past to absorb himself in the action. While Pietersen, Vaughan, Flintoff and company were busy wresting back the Urn from the Baggy Greens, there were barely forty horses at Warren Place and only a handful possessed above-average talent. Even some of Henry's diehard followers feared he would be pulling up the stumps on his career in the not-too-distant future.

In a low moment, a year or so before, such a thought may have crossed Cecil's mind. Indeed, it may have even lingered. Not any longer. English cricket was enjoying a long overdue revival and Cecil believed he could stage his own too. One night he shared his positivity with his houseguest. 'I'll come back,' was the short and simple message he confided in the fourteen-year-old.

'I was only young and didn't know him when he was good,' says Eddery. 'So I just said, "Yeah, we'll come back."' It was to be seven years before Eddery gave the brief exchange a second thought again. In the interim he joined the powerful stable of Richard Hannon as an apprentice jockey, returning to Newmarket to ride work at Warren Place during the Frankel era. Indeed, in July 2011, he would boot home a winner for the yard as the Jane Cecil-owned Celestyna triumphed at Folkestone. At the start of the following year he started working full time for Cecil. So it was that Eddery and a man who was much more to him than just his employer were together on the very last morning of Frankel's remarkable career.

'They were going racing and I just popped in,' recalls Eddery. 'Henry said, "I just want to have two minutes with Charles before we go." I was still in my riding-out gear. He asked me if

I was coming and I told him no, I was going to watch the race at home. He got everyone out from the breakfast table and went through the race with me – how he wanted it to unfold. Then he said, "I don't forget . . . I told you we'd come back." '

If ever a day confirmed that Cecil had returned to the very pinnacle of his profession it was Saturday 20 October, 2012. The second British Champions Day had been sold out for weeks. Ascot was the hottest ticket in town with the public desperate to see the ailing trainer bring the best horse he had ever trained for one last showdown race.

In the days leading up to the Champion Stakes the public inter-est was as great as I can recall for a flat race in Britain. Although not finalised at that point, it was almost guaranteed that the horse would be retired to Prince Khalid Abdullah's stud after Ascot. Frankel fever seemed to be everywhere. One morning even the Household Cavalry Mounted Regiment paid their respects to the horse. The guards swapped their uniform for the famous green and pink silks of Prince Khalid as they undertook their morning exercise.

That week there was a huge amount of race-day preview coverage, and not just in the sports pages. The *Sunday Times* magazine sent the renowned David Walsh to interview Henry Cecil for a feature that ran over four double-page spreads. The Frankel story continued to intrigue and charm ever more people.

But there was concern at Warren Place. Not with the horse's welfare. Frankel seemed to be holding his form very well despite having been in full training for the whole season, bar those few days early on when the injury scare forced a temporary curtailment. The worry within the yard was the seemingly endless rain that was tipping down at Ascot through the week. On one day alone almost 16 millimetres fell.

The condition of the ground has always been a key determinant of horse races. Consequently the majority of the trainers are on constant weather watch through the eight months of the flat season. Many horses will have a specific ground preference. There are those who want the traditional summer 'going' – rattling, fast conditions. Others are better suited when there is some 'give' underfoot. There is a very small minority of horses who thrive in ultra-testing soft or heavy conditions.

Some believe that a horse's action will dictate what type of ground the individual requires. They say the low skimming action is made for good-to-firm conditions allowing a horse to bounce off the turf with ease and speed. The theory expands that a thoroughbred with a high-climbing knee action will be much less at home when they hit such a surface. It's argued that those animals would benefit from some cushion that soft ground is more likely to offer. Yet I have also heard trainers and jockeys dismiss the 'action' argument when it comes to ground suitability for a horse.

Trainers, especially if they have trained members from the same family, will assess a horse's pedigree as a potential indicator. If the brother performed in the soft then there's an increased likelihood that its sibling will. Similarly, a sire and dam's suitability for a ground can be passed down through the genes. Certainly the progeny of some stallions are renowned for coping better with ground extremes, whether it's as firm as a tarmac road or bottomless as a bog.

The soundness of an individual is always going to play a major part. If the front legs of a half-ton horse hurt every time they hit fast ground then the horse is not going to fully let down, however low and fluid is its action.

Attitude is all-important on soft ground. There is no doubt that such conditions are more exacting for a horse. They have to work harder and thus become tired more easily. Only those horses with a certain type of determination will power through the pain barrier. Others will take the easier option.

As the rain continued to fall ahead of British Champions Day, the media focused on the ground challenge that Frankel would have to overcome at Ascot. He had only ever raced once before on a soft surface. That was on his debut at Newmarket in August 2010 and he handled it well enough to defeat fellow newcomer Nathaniel, who went on to be a Group 1 star in his own right.

That said, the nature of summer soft ground on the chalk-based July Course was not the same as the more exacting autumn underfoot conditions that Ascot would present. Also, set to be in opposition was Cirrus Des Aigles, winner of the Champion Stakes a year earlier and renowned for relishing bottomless ground. That year the French-trained gelding had already won a Group 1 race in 'the heavy' and warmed up for Ascot with a nine-length success in similarly tough conditions in a Group 2 a month earlier. Despite his reputation as a mudlark, Cirrus Des Aigles was a very fine horse on good ground too. Early in 2012 he had defeated St Nicholas Abbey in a Group 1 in Dubai, earning almost £2 million for his victory.

Stephen Kielt was considering all the implications of the heavy rainfall ahead of the keenly anticipated mile-and-a-quarter contest at Ascot. As per usual, he was waiting for Cecil to drive into the yard after first lot. When the dark blue Mercedes saloon pulled up, Kielt followed his routine. He joined the trainer by the coffee machine where he would listen and learn on a daily basis. After five years at Warren Place, Kielt could pretty much instantly recognise his boss's frame of mind. 'He was a man of many emotions,' says Kielt. 'When he was in the mood, you could talk to him about all types of things. There were other times you'd know you'd be wasting your words.'

That morning Kielt sensed a pensive undercurrent. With the racing pages of the daily papers full of conjecture about Frankel's ability to cope on the ground at Ascot, the farrier was interested to see what Henry's take on the subject was.

'Frigging rain – there's more forecast,' the Northern Irishman said, venturing his thoughts on the depressing weather picture. A flicker of concern appeared on Cecil's face. 'I'd instinctively have picked up on it but you would have to have really been tuned to see it,' says Kielt. 'I remember the look in his eyes, as clear as day. He looked worried, but it was a fleeting second of a look. Then he said, "Well, the mother handled soft . . . it's no problem to him. He might even be better on soft." But his eyes didn't lie.'

I also recall Cecil's anxiety about the ground. Having dropped into Warren Place early one morning, we spoke briefly about the effects of the weather. Cecil wasn't worried if Ascot rode soft but if it became heavy he had a phrase that he used more than once that week: 'We are in no-man's-land.' The notes he had prepared for me expanded on his comment.

'He has never encountered it,' he wrote about the prospect of heavy ground. 'With his action and turn of foot, one cannot be sure that he would appreciate it. I always think that really good horses have a great turn of foot. Heavy ground just turns things into an endurance test.'

There was reference too to Cirrus Des Aigles. Cecil was all too aware how the French challenger would relish such a test. Nathaniel was another in the field who Cecil felt was capable of making the race a stiff assignment for Frankel. The John Gosden-trained horse shone at Ascot in winning that summer's King George VI and Queen Elizabeth Stakes.

'It will be far from an easy race with Cirrus Des Aigles and Nathaniel in the line-up,' was Cecil's assessment. 'They are two good horses who will go in the ground and get the trip really well. They have to be really respected.'

So many elements around a horse race are beyond a trainer's control. The opposition and the ground are just two. But that week, perhaps more than any other before in his training career, Cecil made sure he was on top of everything that he could influence. For example, he knew of just about every oat Frankel consumed in the days before the race. 'He eats everything put in front of him and would eat more, although I dare not overdo him,' wrote Cecil in a lengthy note.

He also spoke to Kielt about shoeing Frankel. This was unusual. In general, Cecil just let his farrier get on with the job. A couple of years earlier, just before the Dewhurst Stakes, Kielt tried to raise the subject with his boss. Cecil cut him off with a raised hand. 'You know what you're doing,' he told Kielt.

The approach brought out the best in Kielt. It allowed him to work with a quiet confidence in his own ability. Cecil's style of delegation-with-trust helped take away much of the pressure. It therefore surprised him that the trainer chose to talk to him early in the week, ahead of the Champion Stakes.

'I want you to be careful,' stressed Cecil.

'I will be.'

'No, I've no other options with this horse.'

'I'll shoe him like my life depended on it.'

The conversation underlined the tremendous importance of the race for Cecil and, for all his famously laidback appearance, he wasn't immune to the pressure.

A week earlier a large throng of media and members of the public turned out first thing in the morning to watch Frankel gallop at Newmarket Racecourse. Tom Queally had the unusual experience of watching Frankel's quarters power clear of him. The jockey was on the lead horse Midsummer Sun, while Shane Fetherstonhaugh was aboard Frankel. The exercise couldn't have gone better.

That morning Cecil wore branded clothing from the Frankel range, recently launched by Juddmonte. The horse now had his own logo, a flashy white signature alongside a blended green 'F'. Cecil's black padded jacket carried the logo, high on the left side of his chest. The trainer also had a black cap on that he had taken to wearing that autumn. Across the front a message read 'How's Life?'

Cecil looked sturdier on his feet than he had done at York but his face remained gaunt and drawn. He had brought Frankel to gallop on Cambridgeshire Day a week and a half earlier. There was still more than an hour to go before racing started but the horse's appearance put a sizeable increase on the gate and his devotees soaked up every minute, watching him walk beforehand in the parade ring. The exercise with Bullet Train and Specific Gravity pleased connections and public alike. As he moved effortlessly clear in the shadow of the Rowley Mile grandstand a burst of loud applause accompanied him through the final furlong.

In the interim between the two workouts, Cecil received further chemotherapy. While the after-effects of the treatment increasingly took their toll on him, he knew only one way to deal with his cancer: single-minded positivity. It rubbed off on those around him and many of us believed that he would stave off the disease, despite how ill he would often look. After all, he had beaten it once before; why not again? There were stages too when he definitely picked up and, on occasion, the voice would sound stronger. According to Dr Crawley, however, these were 'transient responses' to the rounds of chemotherapy. He adds that Cecil was 'a bit better at times, but never really back to how he had been'.

Through 2012 he went in again and again for treatment. Sometimes it would be given in the day unit. On those occasions he generally chose to go alone with the minimum of fuss. He would drive himself to the Nuffield Hospital and regularly sit in solitude as a bag of chemotherapy was intravenously administered into an arm. It would take four or five hours to give some of the drugs. Occasionally he would just receive a ten-minute injection. In the latter stages of his illness he would go in for three or four days at a time as the chemotherapy was given continuously. Cecil would ask the nurses if the treatment could be speeded up. Not because it was uncomfortable, but because he wanted to be back working at Warren Place as soon as possible.

After a session, when the worst effects had passed, his desire to fight was very apparent to those around him. He would tell me, in typically upbeat manner, just how much chemotherapy he had been able to stand over the previous weeks and months. How he had swiftly recovered from a previous cycle to enable a further one to take place in the coming days. There was no complaint about the hand he had been dealt, nor was there any self-pity.

It was the horses that occupied his mind – even when he went for important consultations with Dr Crawley. Sometimes, as the haematologist spoke, he would notice Cecil busy with pen and paper. The trainer would be doodling horses. 'My notes are littered with sketches,' Crawley says, laughing.

The string's minute-to-minute wellbeing was a very real distraction for Cecil, but it was more than that. It went much deeper. It stimulated him, challenged him, drove him on. No horse did that more than Frankel. The sense of responsibility to the horse meant that he would be at Ascot, just as he was at York. 'There was absolutely no way that he was not going to be at those events,' says Crawley. 'He'd have gone dragging a bag of chemotherapy and a nurse with him.'

The last time I saw Frankel on the Newmarket gallops was Thursday 18 October – two days before the Champion Stakes. It was also the last day I reported for Sky Sports News. Until early spring in 2012 I had never worked in television. But

Frankel had become a big story during the previous year and I called the television channel on the chance that there might be some work connected to it. Timing is everything in journalism and I happened to be the right man in the right place with the right connections. Hence I did my first package for Sky Sports News about Frankel, including exclusive interview material of Cecil and footage of the horse cantering on Warren Hill. From there I ended up doing a series of racing packages and a bit of football work for the broadcaster.

It was far from the first time that my working relationship with Warren Place had proved invaluable. As Newmarket's retained racing PR manager for a number of years from 2008, on more than one occasion I went to Cecil asking him to host a big-race meeting preview morning. Occasionally, he would roll his eyes as it could be inconvenient but, in general, he helped as he felt it was important for Warren Place, 'to do our bit'.

The benefits from having an association with the stable and its trainer were many, but they weren't why I had forged the working relationship at the outset. That was simply down to my curiosity and an undoubted sense that I had never met anyone like Henry Cecil.

Walking into the breakfast room of his house first thing in the morning never lost its draw. Sometimes he would be else-where, so I would make a coffee and scan his copy of the *Racing Post* or *Daily Mail*. It wouldn't be long before he would walk in. 'All right?' he would ask, in a manner that usually suggested he was busy and I needed to look lively. On other occasions, he would be at the table surrounded by paperwork, including his notes for the website. 'It's all there . . . everything you need. Just check with Jane before you put it on . . .'

That morning, two days before the Champion Stakes, the Sky Sports News cameras rolled and presenter Alex Hammond came 'live' to me on Warren Hill. She spoke down the line about how Frankel had transcended racing. It was undoubtedly true. He had become a sporting superstar. 'Team Cecil' was getting recognition everywhere. That autumn *ZOO*, a so-called 'lads' mag', bestowed one of its annual awards upon the team. And the fact that Sky Sports News, a station that majored on football, was dedicating considerable airtime to Frankel underlined his stature.

As we spoke, Hammond referenced the rain-drenched ground. It was the question that just wouldn't go away. The pictures from that morning showed Frankel as a study in cantering composure. Surely underfoot conditions couldn't get this perfect racehorse beaten, could they?

I drove down to Ascot on the Saturday morning with David Walsh of the *Sunday Times*. David will be remembered as the key journalist in bringing to light the doping programme of cyclist Lance Armstrong, who was stripped of all seven of his Tour de France crowns, but he has a great understanding of many other sports. He and I have occasionally shared a press box reporting from football grounds, but most of our conversations have been about racing. As we travelled to Ascot, his excitement at the prospect of Frankel's final race matched my own. David was set to write the cover story for the *Sunday Times* sports section plus a further article inside and I also had a Frankel piece to write for a Sunday paper, so we were bound for the Ascot media suite, superbly positioned opposite the finishing line, on the second floor of the towering grandstand.

As we made our way around the M25 shortly after eleven o'clock, Lord Grimthorpe was at Ascot undertaking an altogether shorter journey. He was walking the course, which was officially described as 'soft, heavy in places'. Those more testing places were on the far side of the course. One area is called Swinley Bottom. After a further six millimetres of rain had fallen on Friday to top up the significant amount the course had already taken, some wags were referring to it as Swinley Bottomless. 'We'd had nearly an inch and a half of rain that week,' says Ascot's clerk of the course, Chris Stickels.

Stickels walked the course just before Grimthorpe's elevenses exercise. The two men had spoken in the build-up and the racing manager had been suitably reassuring. 'I remember Teddy Grimthorpe being fairly confident of running,' says Stickels. 'In the conversations he had with us he was saying, "I am going to come and walk the course but if the ground is as you say it is, I'm pretty sure we're going to run."' In such situations Henry Cecil would invariably want to let his horse take its chance. Indeed, seasoned Cecil watchers knew that he rarely pulled one out on the day of the race due to ground unsuitability. His inclination was always to run unless the ground had become unsafe. In high summer, if a surface was seriously fast and one of his horses might not let down on it, then he may consider withdrawing at a late stage. That was never going to be the issue that day at Ascot.

Even so, there were a few very anxious faces as Grimthorpe, clutching a stick and wearing wellingtons, made his way around the track. A group of media assembled not far past the finishing line, eager to hear the news. But Grimthorpe spoke to Stickels first to confirm Frankel's participation. It was a green light and the 32,000 sell-out crowd would get to see racing's star attraction.

Despite the high quality of the preceding action, everybody's attention seemed to be locked into the 4.05 p.m. race – the fifth and penultimate one on the card. 'It was one of the most remarkable occasions,' says Rod Street, a key driving force behind the British Champions Day innovation. 'What was really interesting was, like any Champions Day, there was some very, very high quality fare on offer leading up to the Champion Stakes. But it was as if nothing mattered and that people were simply waiting for that race. It was palpable, that anticipation in the air.'

Just as at York two months earlier, folk were intent on finding their spot to gaze on Frankel. This was the era in which the smartphone came to prominence and everyone wanted to photograph the horse, their souvenir of the day they paid homage to racing's greatest horse. When Frankel followed his brother Bullet Train into the parade ring, a respectful round of applause broke out. There were people looking on from every surrounding vantage point – the bridge, the back of the grandstand – and there was no spare standing room around the parade ring where many waved the green and pink flags that had become a feature of Frankel's race days.

The flight instinct is never far away from a thoroughbred and even the experienced Bullet Train had his head up, mindful of the activity and noise that was around him. But, a few steps behind, Frankel seemed oblivious to all the animation and vibrancy. He had his head down, strolling around in a manner that suggested he was totally unruffled by events.

Cecil, in navy jacket and grey trousers, stood in the paddock with Prince Khalid and Lord Grimthorpe. It was a momentous day for the trainer, not least because so many members of his family had come from all parts, hoping to witness a Frankel victory. His brothers Bow, Jamie and Arthur were at Ascot; so too were his three children Katie, Noel and Jake.

Earlier, Cecil had spoken to his two jockeys in the weighing room. All that remained was for him to give Tom Queally a leg-up on Frankel while his assistant Mike Marshall did likewise for Ian Mongan, who was renewing his acquaintance with Bullet Train after riding Twice Over at York. There were four other runners to go to post. Bar those with connections to his competitors, everyone else at the racecourse seemed to be rooting for Frankel. The expectation was immense. But racing is a sport where bubbles are pricked for fun. Nobody at Ascot was more aware of that than Shane Fetherstonhaugh. Standing with his partner Claire, it crossed his mind just how cruel a sport racing can be. 'Please don't do this to the horse, don't do it to Henry,' thought Fetherstonhaugh.

Michael McGowan, Cecil's travelling head man who had been there every step of the way of the Frankel journey, also felt a pang of anxiety after sending the horse on his way to the start. His fears were focused on the fact that Frankel, as always an overwhelming favourite with the bookies, had been on the go since early spring and was encountering a very worthy opponent in Cirrus Des Aigles. 'Frankel was taking on a mud lover; a tough, tough horse,' says McGowan. 'I thought to myself, "If there's a kink in this fella now with this ground – and at the end of a long season as well – he's something that could turn him over." That's probably the only time I was worried.'

Cecil was surrounded by his family on the steps in the area reserved for owners and trainers. High above him, in isolation on the top floor of the grandstand, was Richard Hoiles. Twenty years after making his first racecourse call at Bath, Hoiles was poised for arguably the biggest commentary of his career. With his binoculars and a television monitor to help him through the next two minutes or so, Hoiles was ready, having done his usual pre-race homework.

'He was 2/11 so the chances of defeat, in theory, were relatively slim,' says Hoiles. 'You could be pretty happy that it was highly likely that he would win, given what had gone before. So you're trying to make sure you can do him justice. But at the same time there's nothing worse, I think, than something that sounds really pre-prepared. As it happened, what went on at the start completely threw everything on its head.'

Frankel had been slowly away in his previous race at York. But at Ascot, such was his laidback demeanour when the gates sprang back, he dwelt and lost a handful of lengths. The surprise in Hoiles's voice is evident as he announces Frankel's sluggish break. He then explains how Frankel has to be pushed into the bridle to close the gap. The crowd was hushed, concerned at what would happen next. Hoiles, too, was no longer so sure. Would the early use of energy cost the horse at the finish?

'All of a sudden you are beginning to think, a) he might not win . . . b) he might not be very successful in winning now, because he has had to do a lot,' says Hoiles. 'Ian Mongan on Bullet Train is just looking for him – where the hell is he? – trying to get him on his back, trying to help him.'

With the combination of the mile-and-a-quarter distance, the demanding conditions and the stiff track, Cecil had issued firm instructions to Mongan about riding tactics. 'Henry wanted me to make the running but to try and make it like a mile race. So pop out, really steady them up to the mile and then go and make my race.' With Frankel missing the kick, Mongan faced an unexpected dilemma. Should he continue in front or opt to take a pull and wait for Queally? Mongan chose the latter route, allowing Cirrus Des Aigles to move to the fore.

The split-second judgement call from the jockey, in what was surely the most important race of his life, proved spot-on. Mongan knew that if he had joined battle with the French horse, it could have compromised Cecil's plan. 'I didn't want to sit upsides Cirrus Des Aigles, go too quick and turn it into a mile-and-a-quarter race,' he says. Had the tempo increased too much too soon it may have drawn valuable resources from Frankel, on the back of recovering from that slow start.

Queally duly settled his mount in fourth place, shadowing Nathaniel. Aware that Frankel was in position, Mongan's next move was to push up on the inner of Cirrus Des Aigles. Hoiles noted this development in his commentary and said, 'So, Cirrus

Des Aigles leads . . . Bullet Train just trying to make himself a nuisance up the inside, once more.' The pair engaged through the middle part of the race in an interesting sideshow before the main duel.

As the field turned for home, the hollering from the crowd grew wilder. The volume seemed to grow with every giant stride that Frankel took. 'There's thousands and thousands of people all cheering for one horse and you don't ever have that,' says Mongan. 'The roar was just unbelievable.'

His mount Bullet Train was beginning to weaken when Cirrus Des Aigles was smoothly angled into the closing straight by his charismatic rider Olivier Peslier. On the immediate outside of the French horse was Nathaniel, who was about to be hard ridden from the two-furlong marker by jockey William Buick. Wider still but travelling with full purpose and without duress at that point was Frankel. The anticipated head-to-head with Cirrus Des Aigles was on.

Standing just a couple of steps back from Cecil was Kielt. All week the farrier had suffered bouts of nerves about the moments that were set to play out in front of his eyes. His very worst fears centred on Frankel suffering defeat after a shoe had flown off right in front of the packed Ascot grandstand. 'Generally if a horse pulls a shoe it's because they maybe don't stay the distance or they go lame or they get really tired. So I was thinking, "If this horse gets tired, if he really doesn't like this ground, he's going to flail all around and probably whip a shoe off after he's beat. Then I'll be hung, drawn and quartered – the man who got Frankel beaten."'

For Kielt, the closing stages of the Champion Stakes would

present Frankel with a greater challenge than he had faced in any of his thirteen other races. Cecil had previously told him that he could bring a top-class horse to peak for a couple of races each year. The Queen Anne Stakes and the Juddmonte Stakes had been two such occasions for Frankel in 2012. It was always going to be a test after York to keep the horse right and produce him for one last effort on strength-sapping ground. But Kielt knew there was one crucial factor that could tip the balance in Frankel's favour: the training of Henry Cecil.

'Henry didn't like sloppiness in horses or humans,' he says. 'He'd be sympathetic but you'd be expected to get on and do the job. A lot of his horses, I'd have said, were tough. They would know how to battle. I think he trained them so that when they had to dig deep and go through the pain barrier for him, they probably did. But he wasn't really having to ask them all the time because he was such a sympathetic trainer.'

Kielt saw Frankel dig deep against a backdrop of the most cacophonous noise. The colt joined Cirrus Des Aigles, under the whip, with over a furlong to run. Having assumed control, Queally had to ride with urgency through the closing stages as his chief rival refused to wilt. Up in the commentary box, Hoiles was mindful of what had gone on at the beginning of the race and didn't want to hail the champion too soon.

'When he went to the front I was thinking, just be careful, there's no guarantee he'll see this right out. It could be a hard-fought length or even the other horse rallying if he's going to get tired. He'd done the running to get there; he'd given them three or four lengths start.'

Sure enough, Cirrus Des Aigles' challenge was unrelenting. But as the line drew ever closer it became clear to Hoiles that Frankel had everything covered. The horse was going to remain unbeaten; there was going to be a fairy-tale finish to his career.

Ascot was at fever pitch and Hoiles matched their animation. As Frankel brought down the curtain on his career with an ultimately comfortable length and three-quarters victory, the commentator cried, 'All comers, all grounds, all beaten! Frankel won the Champion Stakes and lives up to the title.'

Those fitting words came to Hoiles as he saw it. All too often he had heard commentaries where a potential outcome is prematurely presented as a fait accompli. In such instances a call can sound contrived. 'People don't understand this – they always say you must have prepared. But you have to trust yourself to find the right words. They've got to fit the moment,' Hoiles says.

Even so, he knew that this was a story not just about Frankel proving unbeatable, but also combating the toughest conditions and top-class opposition. The killer line had to contextualise as well as describe.

'I definitely wanted to get in something to do with the ground,' confirms Hoiles. 'That was the different dynamic. The ground had been a massive issue. When I started that sentence I honestly didn't really quite know what the end of it was going to be. I would love to say it flashed in, in its entirety – it didn't. It sort of staggered out . . . it wasn't prepared in any sense or form. I was happier with the bit afterwards about the Champion Stakes living up to the title. Thank God I knew what I was saying for the last sentence, because halfway through the early bit I really didn't have a clue!'

Hoiles's words at the climax of the race have stood the test of time: 'All comers, all grounds, all beaten!'

Eleven months later they would be recalled. The words sat at the foot of a page in the Order of Service card as Sir Henry Cecil's life was celebrated at Ely Cathedral.

Chapter Fifteen

'Half of the horse is keeping him alive, the other half is killing him'

The post-race scenes, on the track and off it, were among the most euphoric witnessed in Ascot's history. After handshakes from a couple of other jockeys, Tom Queally was joined by Ian Mongan. As the two men trotted back on Frankel and Bullet Train, they briefly linked arms for the army of assembled photographers. Moments earlier, Mongan had been shouting encouragement to Frankel and Queally in the closing stages of the race. The sense of occasion was almost overwhelming for Mongan.

'I was just screaming, getting a little bit teary,' he says. 'I think it was the roar of the crowd that got me the most; just everyone cheering for that one horse. The way he came past me, I knew he would win.'

The huge ovation given to Frankel continued as Queally took him in front of race-goers for one final victory parade. He stood up in his saddle, raising a triumphant arm. Next, he pointed at Frankel as if to say, this is all about him, I'm just the lucky lad who rides him.

Emotions continued to ride high as Frankel was led off the track. Queally leaned forward and draped both arms around the horse in a display of gratitude and affection. Michael McGowan and Sandeep Gauravaram brought him onto the horse walk that tunnels underneath the grandstand. Assistant Mike Marshall joined them, congratulating Gauravaram and Queally. A job well done, fourteen wins from fourteen starts.

And as Frankel made his way out towards the back of the grandstand, a slim, smartly dressed man in a grey three-piece suit advanced to offer Queally his hand. The jockey stooped down to return the gesture with a hug. For it was Shane Fetherstonhaugh. Queally knew that without the groom's enormous input, the horse on which he sat would not have maximised his potential. It was a brief shared moment. True to form, as swiftly as he appeared, the self-effacing Fetherstonhaugh retreated from the limelight to walk with his partner Claire.

At the same time a very short but intriguing conversation was taking place. Prince Khalid Abdullah, who had watched the race from his private box, was making his way down towards the winner's enclosure. Alongside him was Lord Grimthorpe, who said: 'You know what you're going to be asked now. They're going to ask, "Are you going to retire the horse?"'

It had commonly been accepted in the weeks leading up to the Champion Stakes that it was going to be Frankel's final race but there had been no official word on the subject prior to Ascot from the horse's owner, neither publicly nor even within Juddmonte. 'We'd discussed it fairly extensively, to say the very least,' says Lord Grimthorpe. 'We talked about it but the Prince never said anything in terms of "I'm going to retire him," or "I'm going to keep him in training." Henry, not even secretly, would like to have carried on. He always said to me, "Don't let my illness stop you from training him next year." '

As he descended the long escalator within the Ascot grand-stand Prince Khalid still kept his own counsel on Frankel's future. In response to Lord Grimthorpe's comment about the inevitable upcoming question from the media he had simply nodded to indicate his awareness of the situation. 'But again, still he never said anything to me,' recalls Juddmonte's racing manager.

Prince Khalid made his way into the winner's enclosure where celebrations of Frankel's brilliance and bravery showed no signs of dying down. Folk punched the air in sheer pleasure. A fanfare sounded. The PA system carried Clare Balding's tele-vision broadcast on the BBC in which she heralded the 'world champion'.

Henry Cecil had earlier walked into the paddock and thou-sands of race-goers demonstrated their enduring affection for him with a rousing 'Three cheers for Sir Henry!' The now familiar cry drew a stronger-than-ever response. Cecil spotted fellow trainer and staunch ally Ed Vaughan close to the winner's circle and wandered over.

It seemed fitting that Vaughan was present to witness such an historic moment. After all, on the morning of Frankel's debut it had been Vaughan in whom Cecil had confided, declaring that the horse might just be the best he had ever trained. The ensu-ing twenty-six months had shown the master trainer to be spec-tacularly correct in his assessment. 'I am so thrilled for you,' Vaughan told his great friend. 'You have done an amazing job with him.'

As Queally gave his debrief to Cecil the two men were joined by Prince Khalid, who listened attentively with a serene smile on his face. Still, everyone waited on clarification of whether Frankel would set foot on a racecourse again.

The BBC's reporter Rishi Persad was sent in search of the all-important post-race reaction. But before he spoke to the horse's owner, there was a poignant interview with Cecil. The strength of the trainer's barely audible voice gave one indication as to the wretched hold his illness had on him. Another was how drawn and lined his face had become, while wisps of thinning hair were evident below the back of his brown felt hat.

Even so, the spirit of the man came through as he explained how much he had enjoyed training the horse before offering a quote that will be referenced as long as Frankel is remembered. 'He's the best I've ever had, he's the best I've ever seen; I'd be very surprised if there's ever been better.'

Cecil and Persad talked on air for barely thirty seconds but sometimes it's quality not quantity that's key at such telling moments.

'Sometimes when you do an interview you know it's going to be emotional beforehand,' says Persad. 'You feel something in your throat and in your stomach. That's how I felt all the way through that interview with Henry. He couldn't speak properly at the time and just said, "Please don't ask me too many questions." You could go on and on and on in an interview like that but I was trying to be respectful of his wishes.'

It was an emotional day for Persad and his colleagues as it marked the end of more than sixty years' coverage of flat racing by the BBC – Channel 4 had secured the rights to cover all of racing's showcase meetings from the following year. But Persad got the answer to the question that was on many people's lips.

'It was the last four minutes, I believe, of the BBC's coverage of horseracing and the producer kept saying to me you need to find out about Frankel so that we can give that news,' says Persad. 'I was still down in the winner's enclosure – I could see the Prince there – and I think I said to Teddy [Grimthorpe], "Has there been an announcement?" He pointed me in the direction of the Prince. So I just said, "Sir, do you know is he going to carry on or is he going to retire?" He just said, "That's it." I remember him putting his hands up, making that gesture like, "That's the end."' Persad duly reported back to his producer and twenty seconds later he was on air telling millions of viewers that Frankel had run his last race.

At the same time, the final scenes of the horse's public life were playing out in the parade ring where he was granted not one but two laps of honour – a rare privilege. It seemed apt that the groom leading him round was Michael McGowan. The Liverpudlian had been unconvinced by the colt when riding him shortly after he had come into Warren Place in January 2010. Now, in front of thousands at one of world racing's most iconic venues, McGowan was side by side with a horse hailed as a champion for the ages. It was a scene he couldn't have imagined in his wildest dreams as the tightly packed crowd's applause for Frankel kept coming. 'They were just clapping him all the way, twice round,' says McGowan. 'It was a nice moment; the pressure's off and you can just relax.'

Watching on from a corner of the parade ring was Rod Street. A few years earlier he and his colleagues had craved a flag-bearer when they ventured into uncharted territory and set about constructing the British Champions Series. The marketeers had a bold vision for the future of horseracing but even they wouldn't have dared draft a script outlining the feats that Frankel delivered. From lighting up their launch day with that explosive 2,000 Guineas success at Newmarket, he had gone on to win another eight races staged under the BCS banner.

Street and his team couldn't have wished for more, but they got it. The horse also happened to be trained by one of the most charismatic men to set foot on a racecourse. Not just that, but he masterminded the latter stages of Frankel's career while battling against debilitating health challenges. It was a story that captivated so many people and extended far beyond horseracing's boundaries. Through Frankel and Cecil's achievements, the sport engaged and won over a whole new audience. Consumer research conducted by Street's team showed that, when it came to racehorses, people knew who Red Rum, Desert Orchid and Shergar (not entirely for racing reasons) were. They now also recognised Frankel.

'He was one of the first breakthrough horses of the modern generation that the public could name,' says Street. 'That really shows the impact he had. Once he got to double figures – once he was undefeated in ten races – he really started to resonate with the wider public, which was one of the aspirations of the Series.

'His performance at York – that day was the real breakthrough moment when he went from being a very well-known horse in racing circles to a horse the public were talking about. Coupled with Sir Henry, for whom the racing world had great affection, you had this remarkable story of a kind, gentle man fighting a terrible illness nurturing a not entirely straightforward superstar horse.'

The extent to which the story had captured the imagination could be gauged by the following day's *Sunday Times*. Across the cover of the broadsheet newspaper's sport supplement stretched an action shot of Frankel that conveyed his physical attributes above a neat headline that simply said, THE GREATEST. For once, horseracing had relegated football's Premier League into second place in the Sunday papers.

Of course, many column inches were dedicated to Frankel's future. He would be heading home to Banstead Manor for a new career at stud. Not exactly a bookend, rather a seamless transition from racing in Prince Khalid's colours to joining his outstanding band of stallions and potentially shaping the breed for generations to come. It was an exciting prospect and again helped horseracing reach beyond its own parish.

It was the eye-popping economics that had people talking. A *Sunday Times* article by the racing writer Andrew Longmore gave a hypothetical equation based on Frankel annually covering 100 mares at £100,000 each for a duration of ten years (his initial stud fee, announced the following month, was actually set at £125,000). The real value of Frankel's racing career was suddenly being absorbed and understood by many who had never given the breeding business much of a thought. If – and it was a mighty if – he proved anywhere near as outstanding a stallion as he had been a racehorse, his worth would be £100 million according to Longmore's hypothesis.

The colt's lucrative stud potential brought into sharp focus exactly how much pressure there was on Cecil, Queally,

Fetherstonhaugh and all of Team Frankel during the final months of his racing career. It was not just that he had to prove himself at a new distance beyond a mile, nor even that he remain unbeaten. It was the fact that all of those who came into daily contact with the horse lived with the stress of knowing that it was their responsibility to ensure he stayed sound and healthy when so much was at stake. Even Cecil, with all his experience and know-how, wasn't completely immune to the strain. In Lord Grimthorpe's mind, the trainer's all-consuming concentration on the horse's welfare resulted in a dichotomous situation.

'He was utterly driven and a lot of people would say, "Isn't it wonderful that Frankel is keeping Henry alive?" I said, "Yes he is but half of the horse is keeping him alive, the other half is killing him." I always remember him saying to me, "You don't know what it's like from when that horse steps out of his box to when he steps back in it." Pressure is self-inflicted but equally Henry had that susceptibility, I think. That's not a flaw; that was part of his make-up.'

The fact that Cecil was keen to keep Frankel in training at five indicates that the pleasure the horse gave him considerably outweighed any pressure he felt from the responsibility. But there was no doubting that the physical demands of overseeing Frankel's career combined with his own intensive chemotherapy treatment took their toll on the trainer. Cecil hinted at this when I caught up with him late that afternoon at Ascot. We spoke for a minute or two in a reception room, adjoining the weighing room, where winning connections can enjoy a glass of something while watching a re-run of their race. As well as offering my congratulations, I was seeking a quote for the report on Cecil's website. 'I have enjoyed every moment of training him, though at times it has been quite strenuous,' he said. As I understood it, the latter part of that sentence indicated just how hard the previous three or four months had been on him.

I visited Cecil at Warren Place one afternoon the following week. My wife and two sons, aged seven and five, came too. I wanted them to see Frankel before he left the yard. Cecil had been in hospital for treatment and Jane mentioned to me before we arrived that he wasn't feeling great. Aside from his weakened voice, however, it was hard to tell he was so unwell such was his enthusiasm. We started off in Frankel's box where Cecil took each of my boys by hand to feed the horse a carrot. After that, he insisted we visited a greenhouse in which he had grown a bumper haul of pumpkins, giving us one to take away for the upcoming Halloween.

He was in full Warren Place tour mode and next stop was the fish pond in the rose garden. Jane explained that they had already been fed that day but Cecil wanted the lads to have the pleasure of seeing the fish come to the surface for additional grub. Lastly we ventured into his study where, with an actor-like flourish, he produced an ancient sword. We were also shown the fossilised dinosaur egg and the shark's tooth that were among a treasure trove of unusual possessions.

Cecil had probably given that tour to hundreds, maybe even thousands, of people over the thirty-five-plus years he had lived at Warren Place, but he conducted it as if it was the first time despite the ravages of his illness. Once again, I inwardly acknowledged that Henry Cecil was a one-off.

Just under a fortnight later, on 8 November, I was back at Warren Place for a landmark day: Frankel's last under the care of Cecil and his team. The Juddmonte team were due to collect the horse that morning and there was a wistful mood around the yard. Sorrow and relief were the two strongest emotions. On the one hand, the whole team was saddened by the departure of the horse. After all, they couldn't expect another like him to come along any time soon. Yet those that worked daily with the horse for the previous seasons could breathe a little easier. They might even get a significant chunk of their life back.

Under blue skies and the watchful eye of Cecil, Sandeep Gauravaram led Frankel onto a horsebox for a final time. It turned out to be a very quiet, low-key send-off. The team gathered round and took a deep breath as Frankel left Warren Place, brilliant and unbeaten after a fourteen-race career that ended up gripping millions of people worldwide.

'People were sad to see him go, I was delighted,' says Shane Fetherstonhaugh. 'I knew that his career was over and was delighted to see him go back to where he came from looking a million dollars. We'd done our job. We all stood there watching him get on the horsebox and I thought to myself how well he looks. "What are they going to think at the stud now? This is a horse they handed to us and now we're handing it back." That was a real happy day for me when I saw him heading off. To see him go off to stud, sound, healthy and well, that was a great achievement from everyone involved with the horse.'

The part that Fetherstonhaugh played for the previous two years had been acknowledged in writing by Cecil just before Frankel's final race, and the words meant everything to Fetherstonhaugh.

'This season Shane has ridden him entirely at home,' penned Cecil. 'What Frankel has done during the year is outstanding. I would not like to take all the praise for his preparation. I have arranged his training schedule and preparation but Shane has carried out my orders to perfection. It would be nice to say we, Shane and I, have trained Frankel together.'

If there was self-doubt in Fetherstonhaugh's early days partnering the colt, by the end of their alliance it had been replaced by much more positive feelings. Both horse and rider had gained a great deal from one another. Frankel had developed so much but so too had the groom. There was now a deep-rooted self-belief within Fetherstonhaugh.

Brian Fetherstonhaugh, who passed away in the mid-1990s, would have been thrilled by his son's integral involvement in the making of the racehorse.

'I wish he could have just seen it,' says Fetherstonhaugh. 'I remember him taking me to the stables for the first time when I was ten, or whatever it was, and dropping me off. And to see how it turned out, riding the best horse in the world, oh he would have been so proud. He loved the horses; they were his life.'

In the moments after Frankel left the yard, Cecil might have walked back into his house for a late-morning coffee or perhaps taken a contemplative stroll down into his garden. He did neither. Instead, he jumped into his car and followed the horse to Banstead Manor Stud. He was going to see the handover right the way through until Frankel was installed in his new box at Juddmonte. There was to be no switching off until the move was complete.

That morning, his notes for the website were longer than usual, almost two sides of A4 written in his small and not always easy to decipher handwriting. I worked for Cecil for seven years, but that lengthy note, written early on 8 November 2012, is the one upon which I reflect the most:

Thursday morning Frankel leaves Warren Place for Banstead Manor to start his stud career. It is a sad day in many ways as he has given us so much pleasure over the last three years. There is no doubt about him being a brilliant racehorse. In fact I am pretty certain that there has never been a better or more talented thoroughbred in the history of racing.

Frankel had the speed to be a champion sprinter, although I feel if he had been trained for that he would mentally have not survived very long. Once he grew up and settled he got a distance with the turn of foot that makes champions.

He has continued to develop and improve and if he had stayed in training another year [I] feel that races like the King George and Queen Elizabeth and Breeders' Cup mile and a half would have been at his mercy. However it was very sporting of the Prince to keep him in training as a four year old and the risks of another season were really not worth taking.

Yes there will be a big gap at Warren Place to fill without him and I will be very lucky to ever get another horse of that extraordinary quality and ability. Still one has to look forward and hope that there are some stars of the future within the occupants in the yard.

There are so many people who have enjoyed his presence on the racecourse and [I] feel he has done a great deal to gather interest in our sport; through people who before his arrival on the scene have never followed racing.

It was a great day at Ascot on Champions Day although the ground was far from his liking. In fact he was bound to struggle in it. I knew he would win but that it would be a real test of courage. With people coming from all over the world to see him in his final appearance it would have, I feel, ruined the day if I had withdrawn him.

He has given me so much strength this season with my personal health problems, feeling that I had to be there for him at home and the racecourse. Although only missing the Sussex Stakes because of treatment, [I] had made sure that I was there for him on the Heath and to saddle him on the racecourse.

I have been training my horses quietly at home and trying to pace myself. Being very vain [I] have not been racing otherwise for two main reasons. Firstly I have temporarily lost my voice and secondly after 600 hours of chemo in three months, [it] looks as if I would not be alive the next day.

I want to thank Frankel for so much and [I have] enjoyed the challenge. Also I want to thank so many people for their support and kindness. And I know if it had not been for my wife Jane helping me through what I have to admit has been a difficult year in more ways than one – without her by my side – [I] am certain that I would not have been able to do it and Frankel too might have suffered.

Jane and I are very fortunate that Banstead Manor is only ten minutes away so we can continue our friendship with Frankel and make sure he is behaving himself.

Thank you Frankel for a very special part in my training career.

Henry Cecil without Frankel was an odd thought. He had made the point himself that the champion's departure left a sizeable gap in the yard, but what about the Frankel-sized absence from his own day-to-day life? Training the horse had most definitely given him a reason to get up long before dawn on many a morning. He had relished that opportunity. It called upon all of his experience, all of his talent, all of his genius. How could he not have felt incredibly alive while that process unfolded?

The horse was his masterpiece, so they said. Cecil now had nothing left to prove, perhaps even to himself. That autumn he had already scotched rumours that he was set to retire ('the only retiring I intend to do is to a good holiday in Dubai to build up my strength for next season'). But could the desire to work, the intensity, really remain at the same high level in the face of an illness that increasingly refused to cede any ground?

Chapter Sixteen

'When you hit a critical point then everything tumbles out of control quite quickly'

Frankel wasn't the only significant departure from Warren Place as winter approached in 2012. His three-parts brother Bullet Train shipped to America to stand at stud. Henry Cecil knew what a help Bullet Train had been in the training of Frankel. For two seasons the horse had led his sibling on the gallops and served in many races as a trusty pacemaker. 'He never faltered on any occasion,' wrote Cecil.

Twice Over also left Newmarket behind. After six seasons in training he headed off to South Africa for a stallion's berth. Cecil had an enduring fondness for the horse and was very sorry to see him go after all the triumphs they had shared together. 'Having had him for a number of years he became a really good friend,' explained Cecil in his notes.

As well as delivering fitting tributes to stable stalwarts, Cecil also found himself writing acceptances for end-of-season awards that were coming his way. The reason why the trainer was writing the words rather than offering them in person was that he was going through extensive treatment. For several months he had been receiving R-DHAP. This is a cancer drug combination (that includes chemotherapy) for a high-grade non-Hodgkin lymphoma that has come back. Cecil also completed a course of high-dose radiotherapy to his chest in the weeks before Christmas.

Inevitably, such a major treatment programme had a debilitating effect. One afternoon that December, I dropped in at Warren Place and found Cecil dozing in the breakfast room. He was leaning forward, resting his head on the table. He soon stirred but didn't raise his head. I'd never seen anyone look so utterly exhausted before. I felt I ought to go but he insisted on fetching a couple of Christmas presents that he and Jane had bought me. He was equally adamant that I should open them right there and then. There was a tie, a piece of knitwear and some socks, which triggered a conversation about a clothing range he was planning with a London tailoring friend. Suddenly he was transformed, going off to find a couple of items that had already been made up for him: a fine sports jacket in a herringbone pattern and a navy cashmere coat.

He was enthused and energised by the clothes and the design project. Therefore, as I drove home that night, the lasting impression was one of a man preparing for years to come. I had not forgotten how tired and thin Cecil had seemed on my arrival at Warren Place that afternoon but I allowed myself to put it to the back of my mind. My eyes were telling me one thing but his strength of will had convinced me of another. That he would carry on. That, in his words, he would 'beat it'. His belief was infectious.

The following month, during which Frankel was rated as the best horse of all time when the World Thoroughbred Rankings were revealed, he and Jane went to Dubai on holiday. They usually had a fortnight or less on vacation but this time they felt the benefits of a full three weeks away. The warm days, good food and rest helped restore Cecil. Even so, the impact of the recent radiotherapy was still very evident. Cecil's back was sore and red, requiring a cream to soothe it.

While away, Cecil enjoyed a bit of shopping as per usual. On one trip out, he ordered eighteen new shirts in his two favourite colours – blue and yellow. It was another indication of how the trainer was planning for the season ahead, but the size of the order reflected the effects of his illness on his existing wardrobe. 'He had an excuse because all his shirts were too big around the collar,' says Jane, who had long been accustomed to her husband's passion for clothes. 'He found this almost gold-yellow colour and hadn't seen it since he was in his twenties and he absolutely loved it. He was so excited about the colour.'

Cecil had always greatly enjoyed browsing ties. Over the years he had built up a huge collection: Hermès, Lacroix, Valentino, etc. But there was always room for another. So it was that in Dubai he spotted one he liked in a hotel close to where he was staying. Jane pointed out that it had skulls on, to which Cecil drily replied, 'It's very appropriate, isn't it?' They left the tie behind, or so Jane thought. Not long after the couple returned to Warren Place, Jane spotted it. Somehow, Cecil had found a way to add yet another tie to his collection.

The holiday boosted his health and spirits. 'It was incredible how much he regenerated. He really picked up,' says Jane. 'He definitely regained some strength and off he went again.'

I saw Cecil not long after he had got back to Newmarket. Aside from a suntanned face, what was most noticeable was that his hair had thickened out. He certainly appeared a lot better than during my pre-Christmas visit. And, of course, he was full of optimism.

'No Frankel but I am quietly confident that we have a promising team to go into 2013,' read the opening line of the notes he gave me one early spring morning. His words went on to pinpoint some of his nicer prospects, including a well-bred unraced filly called Riposte. But what was most striking were the final few lines of Cecil's seasonal preview.

'I have cut down the string by around 40-something horses as I want to just pace myself after a difficult season with my health being a nuisance. But after a good holiday in Dubai I expect to be firing on all cylinders and [I am] looking forward to the challenge of next year.'

Having seen him and read his positive bulletin, not for the first time I felt Cecil was a rare type of man who could call on reserves that enabled him to fight an extended battle against cancer. It looked as if he might have pulled through the trying times of midwinter when the flat-racing world reconvened at Newmarket's Craven meeting in mid-April 2013 – so often the starting point for Cecil's string over the years.

On the first day of the fixture Hot Snap powered into the 1,000 Guineas picture with an impressive win in the Group 3 Nell Gwyn Stakes. The chestnut filly, running in the distinctive silks of Prince Khalid Abdullah and partnered by jockey Tom Queally, scored with more than two lengths in hand. It was Cecil's eighth success in the race. With Shane Fetherstonhaugh leading her into the winner's enclosure that spring afternoon, it seemed that the Warren Place bandwagon was rolling on in time-honoured fashion. The following day Cecil toasted another Group 3 victory with a filly. This time it was the sprinter Tickled Pink who was successful, landing the Abernant Stakes.

To Henry Cecil's many followers in Newmarket and beyond it looked as if the new season held huge promise. In Hot Snap he had the favourite for the 1,000 Guineas, scheduled for just over a fortnight's time back at the Rowley Mile. He also had a string of well over a hundred to train and the horses had started the season with a bang. Behind the scenes, however, Cecil's health had deteriorated rapidly through the early spring. On 20 March his consultant haematologist Dr Charles Crawley confirmed that there had been disease progression. Cecil began further chemotherapy – R–Bendamustine – but his body was no longer in a position to deal with what was an increasingly dangerous situation, despite his mind remaining up for the fight. The truth was, as Cecil plotted Hot Snap's training programme ahead of the 1,000 Guineas, he had barely six weeks left to live.

The last time I sat down and spoke with Henry Cecil was at the start of May 2013, just before the 1,000 Guineas. We were in the Pantry, the restaurant and delicatessen owned by Jane's eldest daughter Anne-Marie and husband Vince. Cecil could barely speak but was still very much himself as he showed while talking to Emma Spencer, the Channel 4 racing presenter. Spencer was busy developing a piece about notable Newmarket locations and Cecil was keen to tell her to visit the Devil's Dyke where the ghost of legendary nineteenth-century jockey Fred Archer is said to ride a light grey horse. With the restaurant buzzing with people and Cecil's voice so weak his words were inaudible, he took the time to write them down and show Spencer. It was typical Henry Cecil.

That day also saw him hand over the final set of notes he wrote for his website. He had collated a few thoughts on Hot Snap, outlining possible future plans. His sign-off words were, 'She will tell us which way to go.' Once again, trademark Cecil.

The 1,000 Guineas was a race the trainer knew all about, having previously won it five times. Many who attended the Rowley Mile racecourse on Sunday 5 May were expecting him to land a sixth victory in the first fillies' Classic of the year. Hot Snap was duly sent off as the 5/2 favourite but proved to be a long way off her best that afternoon. She could only finish ninth of fifteen. A firm hint that it was a sub-standard effort was the fact that the winner Sky Lantern, whom Hot Snap easily beat in the Nell Gwyn Stakes, finished almost six lengths ahead of her in the Guineas.

Shortly before 5 p.m. that afternoon Cecil saddled Magic Of Reality ahead of a Listed race. It was a task he had carried out countless times, only this was to prove significant. Not that Cecil knew it at the time, but the filly was the last he would ever saddle on a racecourse. She would finish fourth of eight.

Neither Hot Snap nor Magic Of Reality had given the trainer's followers anything to cheer about. But those that looked closely at the trainer will have been more far more concerned by his appearance that day than any modest performances on the track. It wasn't so much Cecil's frailty, as it had been at

York eight months or so earlier, it was more how alarmingly thin he looked. Even in the two-and-a-half weeks since the Nell Gwyn Stakes the weight seemed to have just fallen off him. It was a clear sign that he was increasingly unwell. And this time the treatment options had just about run out.

'We were dealing with progressive lymphoma,' says Charles Crawley. 'There was nothing we could do which was going to control it. You see this with people who are otherwise pretty fit and well – and I think Henry was in that sort of category, despite his age; their bodies tolerate an awful lot for a while and they compensate and they cope and actually it doesn't cause too much problem. But when you hit a critical point then everything tumbles out of control quite quickly. You get to the point where it's stopping you eating, so you start breaking down muscle very rapidly. You run into pain; you end up with painkillers which make you feel a bit sleepy, dopey, and it all just snowballs on top of each other.

'Again, it was predominantly in the chest the disease that we were dealing with, rather than in the abdomen. But there was disease elsewhere and it would have been in the abdomen to a lesser extent. There's a high likelihood there was disease in the bone marrow as well. You've got this cancer which is just dividing and growing and using up a huge amount of resources. It takes a huge amount of fuel, food, to maintain it and it behaves a bit like a parasite.'

As well as the weight loss and exhaustion, Cecil had started to experience a worrying shortness of breath, but he refused to let his health issues stop him from training. The horses were running well and Royal Ascot was only a few weeks away. His instincts were telling him that this was a time of year he needed to be fully switched on and working. So he would be up first thing each day, doing what he knew best. The horses had always been a welcome distraction from his illness, a great motive for him to get up and keep going. After all, as he told me the very first time we spoke, training was a way of life. But it was becoming harder by the day for him.

One morning in early summer Ed Vaughan saw Cecil out on the Limekilns as their respective third lots were cantering. Vaughan was shaken by his friend's appearance. 'He had a tube in his nose and was so frail,' says the Irish trainer. 'I was just so shocked.' But despite the extent of his illness, Cecil was his usual positive self as he chatted away to Vaughan. There was no self-pity, no moans or groans.

'He was unbelievable,' says Vaughan, reflecting on his friend's courage in adversity. 'He never whined about it. He just got on with it and wouldn't give in. He'd look thin and gaunt but he'd still be up there [on the Heath]; he was tough as old boots.'

That late morning Vaughan needed little persuasion from Cecil to head to nearby Moulton where they sat outside the village Post Office. The two men shot the breeze, just as they had done hundreds of times. Cecil didn't eat but insisted that his companion opt for a sausage roll. 'That was the last time I saw him,' says Vaughan.

Quietly, and perhaps not even consciously, the great trainer was saying a few farewells. Well into the second half of May, Stephen Kielt was walking into town one afternoon after parking up at the bottom of Warren Hill opposite Curtis's forge. He had just set off when he noticed a familiar car . . . his boss's aubergine-coloured Jaguar.

'I'd have passed Henry a thousand times on that road there and not once would he have ever waved,' says Kielt. 'He'd drive along and you'd never know if he'd seen you or not. He'd probably be in his own little world. That day he was driving alone, heading towards Warren Place and he beeped the horn and gave a wave. I always think that was his way of just saying goodbye.'

The light-hearted fun that was central to his personality was still evident. Late on the morning of Saturday 25 May, his secretary Claire Markham accompanied him out onto the Heath to watch third lot on Long Hill from the car. Cecil had asked if she minded coming along as he kept feeling faint and light-headed. But as they sat there in the layby next to Long Hill, she found Cecil to be 'on good form' as he cracked a series of jokes. She enjoyed laughing along with her employer that morning, but it's a bittersweet memory for Markham. Close up she saw just how poorly he really was.

Early the next week Michael McGowan was coming back from exercise on the talented four-year-old Thomas Chippendale when he saw Cecil, who had driven into the yard to watch the horses return. McGowan gave the thumbs–up to indicate that the colt he was riding was in good form. Cecil's response came as a surprise. 'He looked at me and just waved,' recalls McGowan, who felt the gesture was so out of character for the trainer. The travelling head groom was still thinking about it as he rode the horse back to its box. 'He'd never wave; he was too proud to do something like that.' The thought crossed his mind that perhaps he should have gone over. Not long afterwards McGowan ventured across to the house but Cecil wasn't there. He had gone to hospital for the final time.

Before the master of Warren Place departed he sat in his beloved garden where he was joined by Charles Eddery. Cecil was struggling to speak but what conversation there was revolved around the horses, naturally. The young jockey was asked how the Galileo filly he rode out was progressing. After a couple more minutes or so chatting about the horses, the conversation came to a poignant conclusion. 'He said something like, "I'm going to go to hospital; look after them for me,"' remembers Eddery. 'I said, "OK," and walked away. I knew and he knew but I didn't want to say my final goodbyes. He didn't want that. It was tough and then he went. He used to go in hospital quite a bit and come out. But he was looking so frail that time, you just thought, "I don't think he has got too much more to give. He has given it all."'

As he left Warren Place that day Cecil must have wondered if it would be for the last time. He was brave in confronting his cancer but the odd remark and gesture from that time hint at his own awareness of how ill he had become. He wasn't prepared to give up: that in itself was abhorrent to him. But he was making preparations for a situation of which he might no longer be part. His message to Eddery to look after the horses may just have referred to an intended interim absence, but only days earlier, when he had come back from a hospital appointment, out of the blue Cecil mentioned to Jane that the horses would have to run under her name at Royal Ascot. It was a standalone statement that wasn't further commented on, but it indicated how Cecil was inwardly aware that he was probably addressing the final stages of his illness. Not that he was accepting it. When he went into hospital he made that clear. Jane recalls, 'He just said, "You have to do something; I have to get better."'

Cecil duly began a different line of treatment and he hoped for a turn in his favour. After all, personally and professionally Cecil had conjured more than one comeback in the previous few years.

He had barely been in hospital for twenty-four hours when Frankel's half-sister Joyeuse made a winning debut at Lingfield. Cecil was using the race as a stepping stone to Royal Ascot. His favourite meeting was three weeks away and it wasn't something he could simply walk away from. From his room in the Nuffield Hospital he carried on working. Jane would see him every day and worklists would be drawn up, while entries and declarations were conveyed.

That all helped maintain the business-as-usual feeling within the yard. And despite the days ticking by in his absence, belief remained within the staff that the captain of the ship would soon be returning to the helm. There wasn't any heightened sense of distress or panic in the yard. Dee Deacon says, 'We just carried on as normal. That's exactly how he would have wanted it and that's how we dealt with it.'

June opened with the Derby. There was no Warren Place representative that year but Cecil watched the race with interest. Aidan O'Brien ran five at Epsom and beforehand Cecil told Jane that he felt that Ruler Of The World was the pick of them. The horse duly won by a length and a half at odds of 7/1.

Two days later Warren Place took the wraps off a couple of well-bred debutantes. Archive, from one of the fine Juddmonte families, was narrowly beaten at Leicester in the afternoon. Tom Queally, showing just how hard jockeys have to work, travelled on to Windsor for an evening card and partnered Court Pastoral in a median auction maiden race. She was a three-year-old filly out of Teggiano, the 1999 winner of the Group 1 Fillies' Mile, and was sent off as the 5/2 second favourite behind the Sir Michael Stoute-trained market leader Omnipresent.

Countless times the two powerhouse stables had taken one another on over five decades, often with much more at stake than there was that evening at the Berkshire track. But what was, on the face of it, a comparatively small contest (first prize was £2,587) would later hold greater significance. For Court Pastoral's narrow success would be the last of Sir Henry Cecil's career. In the style of so many of the stable's runners, she raced to the fore. Into the final stages the filly displayed battling qualities to take Cecil's worldwide tally of winners to 3431; 418 of those victories came at the very highest level.

There were further Warren Place runners that week, including on the following Saturday, but no more winners. The final horse to represent Cecil was Ghost Runner at Newmarket. Victorious on his previous run, the three-year-old colt was too keen early in his race and never threatened to feature in the closing exchanges on the July Course. That weekend Cecil may have been too unwell to give the result more than just a fleeting thought. For the first time in all his years of living with a dreadful disease, he no longer had the physical resources to fight it.

Mentally too, the will to carry on was rapidly ebbing away. That Sunday afternoon Jane offered to go outside into the hospital garden with him. He shrugged to indicate he wasn't bothered. A long-term smoker, he didn't even want a cigarette.

Cecil was someone who was always thinking about the next race, the next work morning, the next day. It's why he never wanted to spend any length of time reflecting on past feats. He was always fully focused on the future. Except now he knew his might not extend beyond a few hours. Did he, on that Sunday evening or the following day, allow himself to reflect on all the races that he masterminded, the horses who would not have scaled the heights without his touch? We'll never know. His family, friends and team would hope that his thoughts turned back to the good times as he reached the final furlong.

On Tuesday 11 June, Sir Henry Cecil died. He was seventy years old. His passing was met with disbelief by many connected to the stable. We were all aware how poorly he was, of course we were, but over the seasons, and in particular through the second half of 2012, we had become accustomed to him fighting back against his illness. Through those early June days, many still couldn't bring themselves to think about the prospect of Cecil dying any time soon.

'When Jane rang me, I was shocked to the core,' says Lord Grimthorpe. 'Those of us that were around him didn't believe he was going to die. He didn't believe he was going to die and therefore we believed with him.'

We found out the worst in late morning. Jane was at the hospital in Cambridge and wanted to make sure that the Warren

Place team were told as quickly as possible. Mike Marshall gathered everyone close to the archway at the back of the Main Yard and I passed on the sad news.

'OK, a lot of people could say, "You must have been expecting it." Well, actually, no,' says Dee Deacon. 'It was still a huge blow, like it was something that we didn't expect. I went out to the front and sat under one of the trees and I sobbed and I sobbed. "Shit, it has finally happened."'

That sentiment was probably how most of the team felt.

There was blanket coverage of Cecil's death. In Britain, it was broadcast on national television and radio. The print media coverage was extensive, especially in the *Racing Post*. The 12 June edition carried a full-page picture of Cecil and the headline, GENTLEMAN, GENIUS, LEGEND. Tributes followed across the next six pages of the paper, while there was a powerful image of the jockeys observing a minute's silence at Salisbury and an inset of the Horn of Leys symbol on that famous flag, so often the signal of Group 1 glory, flying at half-mast at Warren Place. In the middle of the *Racing Post* was a sixteen-page supplement. The front cover of the supplement showed Cecil enjoying the scent of a bloom from one of his many rose bushes.

The response, in the media, in Newmarket and in racing, reinforced a few thoughts in my mind. It reminded me how brilliant a trainer he had been and for how long he had been such a dominant force. Over the years I had become used to walking in the back door at Warren Place and making myself a coffee unprompted. On such occasions, the master of the house would be quick to remind me that I only had time for half a cup as first lot was just about to pull out. He kept me on my toes and I never felt as if I was fully at home.

Racing industry professionals, racecourses and institutions all paid their respects and showed their affection in the days following Cecil's death. But equally, it was the response from the general public that left the profound impression that the sport had lost its best-loved figure. Among all the letters and notes of condolence was an anonymous card and roses 'from our garden' tied to the main gates of Warren Place, which Jane noticed first thing in the morning after the trainer's death. The card read:

The Late Sir Henry
So sorry to hear you have lost the battle with illness.
Peace is with you now as you rest with God.
Thank you for always speaking to us,
no matter how busy you were.
A true gentleman

Many people thought of Cecil as a gentleman. He was also 'a sensitive soul', as Lord Grimthorpe points out. Nobody from the Warren Place team of 2007 will forget that wobbling lip as Cecil fought back his emotions after Light Shift landed the Oaks. Yes, there was that hint of vulnerability about him at times and indeed he was a gentle man as well as a gentleman – but he was also a hugely strong individual.

The well-known American sports broadcaster Stuart Scott was diagnosed with appendiceal cancer in 2007, and his fight against the illness ran across a similar timeframe to that of Cecil's. Scott continued to live a very full life right up to his death in

January 2015. In the previous summer, he accepted an award with the words: 'When you die, it does not mean that you lose to cancer, you beat cancer by how you live, why you live and in the manner in which you live.'

That sums up Cecil's stance. Yes, he died in June 2013 as a result of cancer, but for several years people drew inspiration from his resolve. As much as circumstances allowed, the disease was ignored, not given the time of day.

The challenge became ever more difficult, of course. People saw just how seriously debilitated he had become when he saddled Frankel that summer's day for the Juddmonte International Stakes in August 2012. But admiration of Cecil was increased by his bravery that afternoon. 'I want to be there for Frankel,' he wrote in his pre-race notes for the website.

The substantial impact of his cancer couldn't be missed at York but transcending that was his management of a champion horse. In nurturing a two-year-old Frankel from a raw and exciting talent through to the polished equine perfection that he became aged four, the master of Warren Place delivered an exemplary body of work.

When that achievement is assessed alongside Scott's words, you find compelling proof of how a man produced his very best, despite the extreme adversity he was confronting. Is that not beating cancer? For me it was and always will be.

That is why I will think of those times as nothing other than the triumph of Henry Cecil.

Epilogue

It's September 2018 and there has barely been a week in the five years–plus since Henry Cecil died that thoughts of him haven't crossed my mind for one reason or another. It may just be something as simple as catching a replay on television of one of his horses winning a big race. Alternatively I might see a face from the Warren Place days riding out for another string on the Heath. The main reason for Cecil remaining an influence on my life, however, is as a result of professional ties.

For two and a half years after his death I retained a strong link with the stables and Jane Cecil. She took out a training licence and carried the baton, overseeing a series of big-race winners including Noble Mission, the full brother of Frankel. Noble Mission ended up winning the 2014 Champion Stakes, the same Group 1 race that Frankel finished his career in two years earlier.

On that occasion and other big days it almost seemed like Cecil was still around us – his influence certainly seemed present at the heart of his stables. It was only in 2015, after it had been announced that Warren Place was to be sold and when the final horses had left the yard in November of that year, that his absence really hit home. It dawned on me that a unique era had come to an end.

One of my final visits to what was then an empty Warren Place was shortly before Christmas 2015 when I noticed just how quiet the place had become. Over the years I had grown used to hearing the sounds that accompany day-to-day life in any racing stable; the resonance of latches on the stable boxes being pulled back and forth or the clicking heels of the lads pacing up and down the yard. And it was a place where I would invariably hear laughter. Late in 2015, apart from the harsh calls of the jackdaws in the surrounding trees, Warren Place had fallen silent.

Missing was the vibrant and colourful atmosphere, created by Cecil. He had nurtured it with his presence on a daily basis, building a community whose foundation stones were trust, diligence and enjoyment. As well as the horses, people had grown and flourished. 'It was like a family,' says Michael McGowan, recalling what it felt like when he started working for Cecil. 'He wasn't just the boss – he looked after staff as well.'

My association with the yard may have come to a natural conclusion but I have been lucky enough to have kept a connection with the best horse Cecil ever trained – Frankel. Each summer since 2013, I have helped Juddmonte Farms with its organised tours in which the public get to see Frankel parade at close quarters at Banstead Manor Stud.

Since their inception, every tour has been a sell-out and I have loved being involved. Not just because it has given me the chance to see close-up how Frankel has developed into a majestic-looking stallion, but also because of the opportunities to meet with like-minded Frankel-ophiles. There have been many healthy discussions about which race represented his greatest performance. For the record, the three that get his ardent fans most excited are the Juddmonte International, the Queen Anne and the 2,000 Guineas. Usually the conversations extend into reflections on the horse's trainer, serving as a reminder that affection for him continues to run deep.

Frankel's first foal was born on the day Cecil would have been seventy-one: 11 January 2014. The foal, eventually given the name of Cunco, became the first of Frankel's progeny to race two years later. Naturally he made a winning debut and it's no surprise that the father has gone from strength to strength at the stud where he was born back in 2008.

On occasion I have wondered about the prospect of one of his sons being called Cecil to honour the trainer's memory. After all, the expert team at Juddmonte did a wonderful job in identifying a standout colt to be named after Bobby Frankel, the American trainer whom Prince Khalid held in such esteem.

Of course, that was a brave call and not without risk in a sport in which there can never be any guarantees. Perhaps to roll the dice again and bestow the title of Cecil on a promising young horse might just be asking a little too much of the racing gods.

'I'm not saying it couldn't happen,' says Lord Grimthorpe, to whom I spoke on the subject. 'Everyone loves the idea of it and it has been talked about endlessly but it's not as straightforward as it might sound.'

★   ★   ★

Of course, my latest link to Henry Cecil over the last year or so has been this book. I had often thought about such a project, but for a long time put off committing to it for a string of different reasons. The access I had been granted at Warren Place, however, along with Cecil's notes for the website, persuaded me that I ought to write down an account of those years. His comeback was surely one of racing's greatest ever stories, and I had the good fortune to see it from around the time that the shoots of recovery were becoming evident in 2006.

As the seasons went by, I wanted to reconnect with that era of resurgence. I wanted to speak to the people that were there, to hear their perceptions of it. Many of them knew Cecil far better than I did and many saw him every day. They have enriched my understanding of the man and allowed me to return to those momentous times. And what I have grown fully to appreciate is the lasting impact that he has had on people's lives. They do not think of Cecil as simply a great trainer; he was admired by so many for reasons beyond horses.

It was apparent from the conversations just how much Cecil moved people. Indeed, one person admitted to missing him more than their beloved late father, saying: 'What was so special about Henry [was] that he made me and lots of other people feel incredibly good about themselves, good about life. He was exceptionally giving and that is very, very rare.'

Three-time champion jockey Richard Hughes remembers Cecil as just being very different. When Hughes was retained by Prince Khalid he would occasionally ride out at Warren Place, where he was given the full tour: flower beds and toy soldiers *et al*. At breakfast the Irish rider was asked by Cecil if he wanted soldiers with his boiled egg. 'Those little things were very important to him,' says Hughes. 'I'll go a lifetime and never ever have an experience like it. In its own little way, it was lovely.'

Jockeys, owners, racing managers and staff all had the greatest respect for him. It became clear to me that, for some, it extended beyond that. He was like a mentor, even to those who had considerable experience. 'Henry always took time to explain something,' says Alan Cooper. 'He would say "Come here, Alan." And we would look at a horse and he'd explain what was either right or wrong. It wasn't only about horses that we would talk. We'd go for nice walks around the garden and talk about the roses or the fruit. And we'd go tasting – see whether the figs were ripe or not. It was a pleasure and a privilege to be able to do that in a very relaxed way.'

When Cecil turned his attention on someone, it could feel like there was nobody else to whom he would rather be talking. So it was not surprising that many of his staff were staunchly loyal as well as very fond of him. He would encourage and educate, especially those whom he recognised were keen to learn. Consequently many of his employees thrived and developed in their time at Warren Place. 'He made me pride myself more in what I did and how I represented myself,' says Dee Deacon.

Just as he knew when a horse wasn't quite right, he would also pick up if an employee was down. 'He would recognise when people were low, perhaps with personal problems,' says Stephen Kielt. 'He had time to try and help them or offer words of encouragement.'

One such person was George Bell, who was going through a divorce from trainer Michael Bell at the time that she became part of the Warren Place team, during the Frankel era. She had previously noticed how Cecil's string always seemed to be the happiest on the Heath and so decided to write to him, enquiring about the possibility of riding out. Cecil duly rang her, saying of course she would be welcome.

'He was so sensitive to the whole situation and was very understanding,' recalls George. 'My confidence at the time was at rock bottom and so to be trusted to ride work on his good fillies was hugely uplifting. I will never forget when he once commented that I had "good hands". Coming from Henry, this was an enormous boost and gave me the courage to carry on.'

I learned, beyond my own recollections, that Cecil was a very good employer and friend to many at Warren Place. I also learned that he was a devoted husband to Jane. She remembers that early one summer morning she saw him padding out into the rose garden in his socks again. As she looked out through the drawing room window she wondered why he couldn't just put on some shoes – after all, he possessed countless pairs. But any such thoughts vanished the moment Cecil came back inside the house and, from behind his back, presented Jane with a single yellow rose. It was Warren Place's first rose of the year and he couldn't wait to give it to her.

I was surprised by the level of emotion many expressed during the research interviews. There were tears, but mainly there was laughter and I can't help but think that Cecil would have wanted it that way. He would certainly have rolled his eyes if he had heard Ed Vaughan talking about the supper that his friend once attempted to cook him. Cecil filled the kitchen and breakfast room full of smoke as he fried some chillies. Vaughan says the smoke was so thick it burned their eyes, but Cecil remained unflustered, cooking away with a cigarette in his spare hand.

Claire Markham enjoyed watching Cecil prepare the exercise board ahead of the following morning. Cecil would amuse them both by hinting at unlikely rider–horse combinations. As he roared with laughter, she would glimpse the gold tooth in his upper jaw. On such occasions, she would know that he was in full belly-laugh mode. He would tease her too about her Derbyshire accent, once prompting her to say that she would put on a posh accent for the next visitor to the yard. 'Don't you dare,' she was told in no uncertain terms.

Michael McGowan has several good yarns from those days, including one when Cecil had signs put up about it being unacceptable for staff to come into evening stables under the influence of alcohol. Anyone who did would be instantly dismissed. Shortly after that, McGowan was with his boss having a coffee in the lads' canteen early one morning when a stalwart yardman bumped into three cars as he arrived for work. The pair watched on as the yardman staggered about before Cecil's exasperation came to the surface. 'Do you want to know something about him?' The trainer paused and McGowan feared for his colleague's future employment. Instead a resigned Cecil added, 'If he stopped drinking he'd probably die.' Not a word more was said on the matter.

I have wondered what Cecil would have said if I told him I was writing a book about him. I have even imagined the location and timing for asking his opinion. It would be early morning outside the back door of Warren Place and we would be exchanging small talk while Cecil puffed on a cigarette. If I was confident that he was in good form, I would mention it . . .

'I'm more for it than against it,' he might answer, his words initially reassuring. But after another gulp and exhalation of smoke, he would probably follow up with a pay-off line that might or might not be issued in jest: 'Of course I won't ever read it . . . I'm too busy, you know.' With that he would turn on his heels and languidly stroll off through the black gates into the yard, his head full of plans for the occupants of the 140 or so boxes.

All human beings are complex and it's an impossible task trying to sum up any individual's personality. My interpretation of Henry Cecil, based on the seven years in which I regularly saw him, is that he had a unique aura, in which old-fashioned values combined with patrician benevolence and a remarkable strength of character.

If that evaluation sounds slightly abstract, one strand of his personality that couldn't be missed was his thoughtfulness. He took an interest in those around him and it wasn't just for show. He could be considerate in unusual ways, and I have met many people with stories to illustrate this. One of mine stems from when I told him that I was planning to buy a new suit and shoes, having started doing some work for Newmarket Racecourses. Not long afterwards he gave me a catalogue that he had received in the post – 'New Shoes from Shipton & Heneage'. On several pages he had ticked a shoe and, in red pen, written 'Tony'. Next to the black Winchester he had added an extra word, 'smart Tony', and in the case of the tasselled Barnwell loafer, 'very smart Tony'. There were eight pairs of shoes that he had flagged up for me, most costing over £200. I was very touched, although I'm not too sure he was quite aware of an average sports journalist's wages.

For many, Cecil possessed a rare charm. A photograph in the drawing room at Warren Place captured it in full effect. Aged in his late sixties, Cecil was snapped attending a black-tie function. The picture showed him in conversation with an older lady and her face is a study in delight. There is a smile both on her lips and in her eyes. The lady in the photograph is the Queen.

Cecil did not just extend that charm to royalty or his owners. One day I was sitting in the breakfast room at Warren Place and two men walked in, one of whom Cecil excitedly introduced as Mr Kipper. The man had brought some fish, and was treated by the trainer with the sort of hospitality reserved for a best friend.

Another time we were stood together at Doncaster races when some Yorkshire race-goers engaged him in conversation. One of them brought up a chat that his father had held with the trainer on those very steps a couple of decades or so earlier. Cecil replied that yes, he recalled that very chat. The man looked as if not merely his day had been made, but his week and month. Not long after, he and his group shuffled off. It was only then that Cecil admitted he had no such recollection of the conversation, but he didn't want to disappoint the race-goer.

These anecdotes are wistful, but they should not obscure the fact that there was a colder and more remote side to Cecil.

Once I saw him taking to task a journalist over an article that he felt wasn't helpful towards a fellow trainer. Cecil never swore and barely raised his voice, and yet I don't recall witnessing a sterner admonishment.

He was a complex man and, among the charm and humour, he would push his staff hard to perform better and he could be stern, exasperated and exasperating in equal measure. It's quite informative that Teddy Grimthorpe's professional assessment of him and the more personal one offered by Jane Cecil are strikingly similar. In evaluating the fourteen years spent working with the trainer, Grimthorpe's first reaction was to say, 'Henry was everything.' When I asked Jane to define what her husband was like she replied, 'He was all things.'

I visited Jane towards the completion of this book. She now lives in the middle of Newmarket and, unsurprisingly, her home contains many reminders of Cecil. The study is full of the books that he owned, some of which are about racing, but there are others that reflect his wider interests. For instance, there is one written by fashion designer Paul Smith and there are also a few on gardening and roses. Outside her back door is an exquisite light pink and white Pierre de Ronsard bloom – one of Cecil's favourites. 'It's hard not for me to think about him all the time, which is lovely,' says Jane. 'He is everywhere in the house.'

He is still everywhere in the world of racing, too. Memories of him, his charm and his winners, still abide. It is unlikely that anyone who met Henry Cecil has ever forgotten him.

Acknowledgements

As a general rule, I would seriously caution against incurring a ruptured Achilles tendon. For those who have avoided this injury, take it from me that it's rather painful in the short term and then a major inconvenience for many months. For example, sleeping in a boot vaguely resembling those worn by the Cybermen in *Doctor Who* is not something I'm eager to repeat any time in the future.

However, I did find there was one very definite advantage to being laid up with an Achilles injury in January 2017 – it allowed me finally to write a book that I had been talking a good game about for a number of years. Barely capable of moving from the kitchen table (clutch foot propped up on a nearby chair), let alone leave the house, I had time on my hands and a laptop in front of me. The tendon rupture was just what I needed to encourage me to really get down to work.

The injury was the final nudge I needed to go through with writing about an extraordinary time in Henry Cecil's career, but by that stage I'd already received meaningful encouragement and support from a lot of people, including Graham Sharpe, John Carter and Alyson Rudd – the latter whom I met at a lunch. She listened to my idea about a possible book concerning Cecil's comeback and messaged the literary agent David Luxton between our main course and dessert. The following day David and I were in touch, and a month or two after that Little, Brown imprint Constable had made us an offer.

David has been nothing other than most helpful since our first conversation. His deep love of sport is only matched by his knowledge of the publishing industry. It has been a joy to work with him, as it has also been with my editor Andreas Campomar and his colleague Claire Chesser at Little, Brown.

Over the last couple of years I have been lucky enough to interview more than thirty people, who are all connected in one way or another to Henry Cecil's resurgence. I am grateful to everyone who gave up their time to share memories and perspectives.

I spoke to a lot of former Cecil employees, among whom I would especially like to thank Dee Deacon, Claire and Shane Fetherstonhaugh, Stephen Kielt, Michael McGowan and Joan Plant. In particular, Warren Place farrier Kielt's insights and recollections have been priceless. While Henry once wrote that he and Shane Fetherstonhaugh trained Frankel together ('I arranged his schedule and preparation, Shane carried out my orders to perfection'), I would like to think that Stephen has helped in a similarly influential manner with this book. What a great friend he has been these last eighteen months or so.

John Gosden was very generous with his time and his foreword is full of insight, honesty and warmth.

One of the first things I did after agreeing with Little, Brown to write the book was to call on Matthew Ramsay to become my right-hand man. Matt read and reread every chapter, not only picking up on more grammar and spelling mistakes than I'd care to admit to, but also offering astute thoughts on structure and overall planning. Matt, let me apologise for those 'clunky' turns of phrase! There was the odd occasion, too, when he served to raise the spirits of a temporarily disconsolate writer. My dad, Christopher, also deserves a mention at this point for similar input. I really hope there is no sentence in this book that includes a split infinitive, Dad.

I would like to thank Racenews, who have long been just about every UK racing journalist's friend. Ben Cox was so kind early in this project, going through Racenews's extensive archives of their race day reports and sending across reams of relevant information regarding Cecil's revival successes.

Racing photographers Steve Cargill and Chris Bourchier have given up considerable time to source their libraries and provide images for this book. Similarly, I am grateful to Trevor and Gill Jones.

A few years ago, there would have been a time that I'd simply not have been able to write a book. Many thanks to Nicola Patterson from the Cambridgeshire and Peterborough chronic fatigue syndrome/ME team for helping me to get back up and running – literally. Well, at least until that small setback with the Achilles.

Talking of which, I can't thank my wife, Julie, enough and daren't tally up just how many mugs of tea I owe her for all the time that I sat around injured. The fact is I owe Julie a lot more than for just brewing up. She lived through every chapter; not just checking over first drafts, but patiently listening while I outlined the challenges and problems that arose as I wrote.

All these years she has had to live with my sports obsession – there's always one more race to watch, one last hole to play, a final minute to go – that has swayed my attention from far more important matters. Her loyalty and love have been unstinting.

Last but not least, I would like to thank Henry and Jane. If they had not invited me into Warren Place back in 2006, my life would have been so much the poorer.

Tony Rushmer
January 2019

Index